Interest around the world has been growing regarding the Brazil 2014 World Cup, not only because of the performances in arts and sports – we are accustomed to watching these types of events – but the riots raging in the streets against the Government. Because in many senses this event was unique, Tzanelli´s book deserves our attention and recognition. After McLuhan's legacy, this is one of the smartest arguments that explores the connection of arts, globalization and cross national identities.

Maximiliano E. Korstanje, *University of Palermo, Argentina.*

In her spectacular deconstruction of the Football World Cup in Brazil, Tzanelli demonstrates the designs and disconnections behind the scenes in terms of moving systems of power, culture and chrono-spatiality. Socio-Cultural Mobility and Mega-Events is the first full length, mobilities informed theoretical analysis of a significant mega-event and Tzanelli offers us a subtle and sophisticated account of the ethics and aesthetics of the life-worlds of football.

Kevin Hannam, *Leeds Beckett University, UK.*

Socio-Cultural Mobility and Mega-Events

In June 2014, Brazil opened the 20th FIFA World Cup with a spectacular ceremony. Hosting the World Cup was a strategic developmental priority for Brazil: mega-events such as these allow the country to be ranked amongst the world's political and economic leaders, and are supposed to propel the country to its own unique modernity. However, alongside the increased media attention and publicity came accusations of governmental 'corruption' and overspending.

In *Socio-Cultural Mobility and Mega-Events*, Tzanelli uses Brazil's 2014 World Cup to explore how mega-events articulate socio-cultural problems. Critically examining the aesthetics and ethics of mobilities in the mega-event, this book explores these socio-cultural issues and controversies:

- the background of staging mega-events, including the bidding process and the host's expectations for returns;
- ceremonial staging and communications between artistic representations and national symbolism;
- the clear reaction mega-events almost always generate in national, regional and global activist circles, including accusations of overspending and human rights violations.

This interdisciplinary study will appeal to scholars and students of the sociology of mobility, sociology of globalisation, cultural sociology, social and anthropological theory, as well as the sociology of sport, human and cultural geography, and leisure and tourism studies.

Rodanthi Tzanelli is Associate Professor of Cultural Sociology at the University of Leeds, UK.

Routledge Advances in Sociology

1. **Virtual Globalization**
   Virtual Spaces / Tourist Spaces
   Edited by David Holmes

2. **The Criminal Spectre in Law, Literature and Aesthetics**
   Peter Hutchings

3. **Immigrants and National Identity in Europe**
   Anna Triandafyllidou

4. **Constructing Risk and Safety in Technological Practice**
   Edited by Jane Summerton and Boel Berner

5. **Europeanisation, National Identities and Migration**
   Changes in Boundary Constructions Between Western and Eastern Europe
   Willfried Spohn and Anna Triandafyllidou

6. **Language, Identity and Conflict**
   A Comparative Study of Language in Ethnic Conflict in Europe and Eurasia
   Diarmait Mac Giolla Chríost

7. **Immigrant Life in the U.S.**
   Multi-disciplinary Perspectives
   Edited by Donna R. Gabaccia and Colin Wayne Leach

8. **Rave Culture and Religion**
   Edited by Graham St. John

9. **Creation and Returns of Social Capital**
   A New Research Program
   Edited by Henk Flap and Beate Völker

10. **Self-Care**
    Embodiment, Personal Autonomy and the Shaping of Health Consciousness
    Christopher Ziguras

11 **Mechanisms of Cooperation**
    Werner Raub and Jeroen Weesie

12. **After the Bell**
    Educational Success, Public Policy and Family Background
    Edited by Dalton Conley and Karen Albright

13. **Youth Crime and Youth Culture in the Inner City**
    Bill Sanders

14. **Emotions and Social Movements**
    Edited by Helena Flam and Debra King

15. **Globalization, Uncertainty and Youth in Society**
Edited by Hans-Peter Blossfeld, Erik Klijzing, Melinda Mills and Karin Kurz

16. **Love, Heterosexuality and Society**
Paul Johnson

17. **Agricultural Governance**
Globalization and the New Politics of Regulation
Edited by Vaughan Higgins and Geoffrey Lawrence

18. **Challenging Hegemonic Masculinity**
Richard Howson

19. **Social Isolation in Modern Society**
Roelof Hortulanus, Anja Machielse and Ludwien Meeuwesen

20. **Weber and the Persistence of Religion**
Social Theory, Capitalism and the Sublime
Joseph W. H. Lough

21. **Globalization, Uncertainty and Late Careers in Society**
Edited by Hans-Peter Blossfeld, Sandra Buchholz and Dirk Hofäcker

22. **Bourdieu's Politics**
Problems and Possibilities
Jeremy F. Lane

23. **Media Bias in Reporting Social Research?**
The Case of Reviewing Ethnic Inequalities in Education
Martyn Hammersley

24. **A General Theory of Emotions and Social Life**
Warren D. TenHouten

25. **Sociology, Religion and Grace**
Arpad Szakolczai

26. **Youth Cultures**
Scenes, Subcultures and Tribes
Edited by Paul Hodkinson and Wolfgang Deicke

27. **The Obituary as Collective Memory**
Bridget Fowler

28. **Tocqueville's Virus**
Utopia and Dystopia in Western Social and Political Thought
Mark Featherstone

29. **Jewish Eating and Identity Through the Ages**
David Kraemer

30. **The Institutionalization of Social Welfare**
A Study of Medicalizing Management
Mikael Holmqvist

31. **The Role of Religion in Modern Societies**
Edited by Detlef Pollack and Daniel V. A. Olson

32. **Sex Research and Sex Therapy**
A Sociological Analysis of Masters and Johnson
Ross Morrow

33. **A Crisis of Waste?**
Understanding the Rubbish Society
Martin O'Brien

34. **Globalization and Transformations of Local Socioeconomic Practices**
Edited by Ulrike Schuerkens

35. **The Culture of Welfare Markets**
The International Recasting of Pension and Care Systems
Ingo Bode

36. **Cohabitation, Family and Society**
Tiziana Nazio

37. **Latin America and Contemporary Modernity**
A Sociological Interpretation
José Maurízio Domingues

38. **Exploring the Networked Worlds of Popular Music**
Milieu Cultures
Peter Webb

39. **The Cultural Significance of the Child Star**
Jane O'Connor

40. **European Integration as an Elite Process**
The Failure of a Dream?
Max Haller

41. **Queer Political Performance and Protest**
Benjamin Shepard

42. **Cosmopolitan Spaces**
Europe, Globalization, Theory
Chris Rumford

43. **Contexts of Social Capital**
Social Networks in Communities, Markets and Organizations
Edited by Ray-May Hsung, Nan Lin, and Ronald Breiger

44. **Feminism, Domesticity and Popular Culture**
Edited by Stacy Gillis and Joanne Hollows

45. **Changing Relationships**
Edited by Malcolm Brynin and John Ermisch

46. **Formal and Informal Work**
The Hidden Work Regime in Europe
Edited by Birgit Pfau-Effinger, Lluis Flaquer, and Per H. Jensen

47. **Interpreting Human Rights**
Social Science Perspectives
Edited by Rhiannon Morgan and Bryan S. Turner

48. **Club Cultures**
Boundaries, Identities and Otherness
Silvia Rief

49. **Eastern European Immigrant Families**
Mihaela Robila

50. **People and Societies**
Rom Harré and Designing the Social Sciences
Luk van Langenhove

51. **Legislating Creativity**
The Intersections of Art and Politics
Dustin Kidd

52. **Youth in Contemporary Europe**
Edited by Jeremy Leaman and Martha Wörsching

53. **Globalization and Transformations of Social Inequality**
Edited by Ulrike Schuerkens

54. **Twentieth Century Music and the Question of Modernity**
Eduardo De La Fuente

55. **The American Surfer**
Radical Culture and Capitalism
Kristin Lawler

56. **Religion and Social Problems**
Edited by Titus Hjelm

57. **Play, Creativity, and Social Movements**
If I Can't Dance, It's Not My Revolution
Benjamin Shepard

58. **Undocumented Workers' Transitions**
Legal Status, Migration, and Work in Europe
Sonia McKay, Eugenia Markova and Anna Paraskevopoulou

59. **The Marketing of War in the Age of Neo-Militarism**
Edited by Kostas Gouliamos and Christos Kassimeris

60. **Neoliberalism and the Global Restructuring of Knowledge and Education**
Steven C. Ward

61. **Social Theory in Contemporary Asia**
Ann Brooks

62. **Foundations of Critical Media and Information Studies**
Christian Fuchs

63. **A Companion to Life Course Studies**
The social and historical context of the British birth cohort studies
Michael Wadsworth and John Bynner

64. **Understanding Russianness**
Risto Alapuro, Arto Mustajoki and Pekka Pesonen

65. **Understanding Religious Ritual**
Theoretical approaches and innovations
John Hoffmann

66. **Online Gaming in Context**
The social and cultural significance of online games
Garry Crawford, Victoria K. Gosling and Ben Light

67. **Contested Citizenship in East Asia**
Developmental politics, national unity, and globalization
Kyung-Sup Chang and Bryan S. Turner

68. **Agency without Actors?**
New Approaches to Collective Action
Edited by Jan-Hendrik Passoth, Birgit Peuker and Michael Schillmeier

69. **The Neighborhood in the Internet**
Design Research Projects in Community Informatics
John M. Carroll

70. **Managing Overflow in Affluent Societies**
Edited by Barbara Czarniawska and Orvar Löfgren

71. **Refugee Women**
Beyond Gender versus Culture
Leah Bassel

72. **Socioeconomic Outcomes of the Global Financial Crisis**
Theoretical Discussion and Empirical Case Studies
Edited by Ulrike Schuerkens

73. **Migration in the 21st Century**
Political Economy and Ethnography
Edited by Pauline Gardiner Barber and Winnie Lem

74. **Ulrich Beck**
An Introduction to the Theory of Second Modernity and the Risk Society
Mads P. Sørensen and Allan Christiansen

75. **The International Recording Industries**
Edited by Lee Marshall

76. **Ethnographic Research in the Construction Industry**
Edited by Sarah Pink, Dylan Tutt and Andrew Dainty

77. **Routledge Companion to Contemporary Japanese Social Theory**
From Individualization to Globalization in Japan Today
Edited by Anthony Elliott, Masataka Katagiri and Atsushi Sawai

78. **Immigrant Adaptation in Multi-Ethnic Societies**
Canada, Taiwan, and the United States
Edited by Eric Fong, Lan-Hung Nora Chiang and Nancy Denton

79. **Cultural Capital, Identity, and Social Mobility**
The Life Course of Working-Class University Graduates
Mick Matthys

80. **Speaking for Animals**
Animal Autobiographical Writing
Edited by Margo DeMello

81. **Healthy Aging in Sociocultural Context**
Edited by Andrew E. Scharlach and Kazumi Hoshino

82. **Touring Poverty**
Bianca Freire-Medeiros

83. **Life Course Perspectives on Military Service**
Edited by Janet M. Wilmoth and Andrew S. London

84. **Innovation in Socio-Cultural Context**
Edited by Frane Adam and Hans Westlund

85. **Youth, Arts and Education**
Reassembling Subjectivity through Affect
Anna Hickey-Moody

86. **The Capitalist Personality**
Face-to-Face Sociality and Economic Change in the Post-Communist World
Christopher S. Swader

87. **The Culture of Enterprise in Neoliberalism**
Specters of Entrepreneurship
Tomas Marttila

88. **Islamophobia in the West**
Measuring and Explaining Individual Attitudes
Marc Helbling

89. **The Challenges of Being a Rural Gay Man**
Coping with Stigma
Deborah Bray Preston and Anthony R. D'Augelli

90. **Global Justice Activism and Policy Reform in Europe**
Understanding When Change Happens
Edited by Peter Utting, Mario Pianta and Anne Ellersiek

91. **Sociology of the Visual Sphere**
Edited by Regev Nathansohn and Dennis Zuev

92. **Solidarity in Individualized Societies**
Recognition, Justice and Good Judgement
Søren Juul

93. **Heritage in the Digital Era**
Cinematic Tourism and the Activist Cause
Rodanthi Tzanelli

94. **Generation, Discourse, and Social Change**
Karen R. Foster

95. **Sustainable Practices**
Social Theory and Climate Change
Elizabeth Shove and Nicola Spurling

96. **The Transformative Capacity of New Technologies**
A Theory of Sociotechnical Change
Ulrich Dolata

97. **Consuming Families**
Buying, Making, Producing Family Life in the 21st Century
Jo Lindsay and JaneMaree Maher

98. **Migrant Marginality**
A Transnational Perspective
Edited by Philip Kretsedemas, Jorge Capetillo-Ponce and Glenn Jacobs

99. **Changing Gay Male Identities**
Andrew Cooper

100. **Perspectives on Genetic Discrimination**
Thomas Lemke

101. **Social Sustainability**
A Multilevel Approach to Social Inclusion
Edited by Veronica Dujon, Jesse Dillard, and Eileen M. Brennan

102. **Capitalism**
A Companion to Marx's Economy Critique
Johan Fornäs

103. **Understanding European Movements**
New Social Movements, Global Justice Struggles, Anti-Austerity Protest
Edited by Cristina Flesher Fominaya and Laurence Cox

104. **Applying Ibn Khaldūn**
The Recovery of a Lost Tradition in Sociology
Syed Farid Alatas

105. **Children in Crisis**
Ethnographic Studies in International Contexts
Edited by Manata Hashemi and Martín Sánchez-Jankowski

106. **The Digital Divide**
The internet and social inequality in international perspective
Edited by Massimo Ragnedda and Glenn W. Muschert

107. **Emotion and Social Structures**
The Affective Foundations of Social Order
Christian von Scheve

108. **Social Capital and Its Institutional Contingency**
A Study of the United States, China and Taiwan
Edited by Nan Lin, Yang-chih Fu and Chih-jou Jay Chen

109. **The Longings and Limits of Global Citizenship Education**
The Moral Pedagogy of Schooling in a Cosmopolitan Age
Jeffrey S. Dill

110. **Irish Insanity 1800–2000**
Damien Brennan

111. **Cities of Culture**
A Global Perspective
Deborah Stevenson

112. **Racism, Governance, and Public Policy**
Beyond Human Rights
Katy Sian, Ian Law and S. Sayyid

113. **Understanding Aging and Diversity**
Theories and Concepts
Patricia Kolb

114. **Hybrid Media Culture**
Sensing Place in a World of Flows
Edited by Simon Lindgren

115. **Centers and Peripheries in Knowledge Production**
Leandro Rodriguez Medina

116. **Revisiting Institutionalism in Sociology**
Putting the 'Institution' Back in Institutional Analysis
Seth Abrutyn

117. **National Policy-Making**
Domestication of Global Trends
Pertti Alasuutari and Ali Qadir

118. **The Meanings of Europe**
Changes and Exchanges of a Contested Concept
Edited by Claudia Wiesner and Meike Schmidt-Gleim

119. **Between Islam and the American Dream**
An Immigrant Muslim Community in Post-9/11 America
Yuting Wang

120. **Call Centers and the Global Division of Labor**
A Political Economy of Post-Industrial Employment and Union Organizing
Andrew J.R. Stevens

121. **Academic Capitalism**
Universities in the Global Struggle for Excellence
Richard Münch

122. **Deconstructing Flexicurity and Developing Alternative Approaches**
Towards New Concepts and Approaches for Employment and Social Policy
Edited by Maarten Keune and Amparo Serrano

123. **From Corporate to Social Media**
Critical Perspectives on Corporate Social Responsibility in Media and Communication Industries
Marisol Sandoval

124. **Vision and Society**
Towards a Sociology and Anthropology from Art
John Clammer

125. **The Rise of Critical Animal Studies**
From the Margins to the Centre
Nik Taylor and Richard Twine

126. **Atoms, Bytes and Genes**
Public Resistance and Techno-Scientific Responses
Martin W. Bauer

127. **Punk Rock and the Politics of Place**
Building a Better Tomorrow
Jeffrey S. Debies-Carl

128. **Bourdieu's Theory of Social Fields**
Concepts and Applications
Mathieu Hilgers and Eric Mangez

129. Global Management, Local Resistances
Theoretical Discussion and Empirical Case Studies
Edited by Ulrike Schuerkens

130. Migrant Professionals in the City
Local Encounters, Identities and Inequalities
Edited by Lars Meier

131. From Globalization to World Society
Neo-Institutional and Systems-Theoretical Perspectives
Edited by Boris Holzer, Fatima Kastner and Tobias Werron

132. Political Inequality in an Age of Democracy
Cross-national Perspectives
Joshua Kjerulf Dubrow

133. Social Networks and Music Worlds
Edited by Nick Crossley, Siobhan McAndrew and Paul Widdop

134. Gender Roles in Ireland
Three Decades of Attitude Change
Margret Fine-Davis

135. (Sub) Urban Sexscapes
Geographies and Regulation of the Sex Industry
Edited by Paul Maginn and Christine Steinmetz

136. Advances in Biographical Methods
Creative Applications
Edited by Maggie O'Neill, Brian Roberts and Andrew Sparkes

137. Social Cohesion and Immigration in Europe and North America
Mechanisms, Conditions and Causality
Edited by Ruud Koopmans, Bram Lancee and Merlin Schaeffer

138. Digital Publics
Cultural Political Economy, Financialization and Creative Organizational Politics
John Michael Roberts

139. Ideology and the Fight Against Human Trafficking
Reyhan Atasü-Topcuoğlu

140. Rethinking Serial Murder, Spree Killing, and Atrocities
Beyond the Usual Distinctions
Robert Shanafelt and Nathan W. Pino

141. The Re-Use of Urban Ruins
Atmospheric Inquiries of the City
Hanna Katharina Göbel

142. Reproductive Tourism in the United States
Creating Family in the Mother Country
Lauren Jade Martin

143. **The Bohemian Ethos**
Questioning Work and Making a Scene on the Lower East Side
Judith R. Halasz

144. **Critical Theory and Social Media**
Between Emancipation and Commodification
Thomas Allmer

145. **Socio-Cultural Mobility and Mega-Events**
Ethics and Aesthetics in Brazil's 2014 World Cup
Rodanthi Tzanelli

146. **Seeing Religion**
Toward a Visual Sociology of Religion
Edited by Roman Williams

147. **European Citizenship and Social Integration in the EU**
Jürgen Gerhards and Holger Lengfeld

148. **International Migration and Ethnic Relations**
Critical Perspectives
Edited by Magnus Dahlstedt and Anders Neergaard

149. **Stigma and the Shaping of the Pornography Industry**
Georgina Voss

150. **Religious Identity and Social Change**
Explaining Christian conversion in a Muslim world
David Radford

151. **God, Politics, Economy**
Social Theory and the Paradoxes of Religion
Bülent Diken

152. **Lifestyles and Subcultures**
History and a New Perspective
Luigi Berzano and Carlo Genova

153. **Comedy and Social Science**
Towards a Methodology of Funny
Cate Watson

Socio-Cultural Mobility and Mega-Events

Ethics and aesthetics in Brazil's 2014 World Cup

Rodanthi Tzanelli

LONDON AND NEW YORK

First published 2015
by Routledge

2 Park Square, Milton Park, Abingdon, Oxfordshire OX14 4RN
711 Third Avenue, New York, NY 10017

Routledge is an imprint of the Taylor & Francis Group, an informa business

First issued in paperback 2018

British Library Cataloguing in Publication Data
A catalogue record for this book is available from the British Library

Library of Congress Cataloging in Publication Data
A catalog record for this book has been requested.

ISBN: 978-1-138-86008-7 (hbk)
ISBN: 978-1-138-34478-5 (pbk)

Typeset in Times New Roman
by Taylor & Francis Books

Contents

	List of figures	xviii
	Poem	xxi
	Preface and acknowledgements	xxii
	Introduction	xxiii
1	Cosmographies of riches and cosmologies of desire: A cultural-as-political perspective on Brazil	1
2	Aesthetics and practical action: Euro–Brazilian clashes and harmonisations	21
3	Complementary articulations: Characterising ideal human types and communities	47
4	The ceremonial script: From tropicalism and *Brasilidade* to cosmographic mobilities	67
5	A defeated people: The loss of riches and the return of debt	98
6	The script of post-colonial desire: Positive excess, negative reciprocities	119
	References	128
	Index	165

List of figures

Figures

4.1 The mega-event's giant female *Brasilidade* 'deconstructed' 71
4.2 The closing ceremony's *Carnaval* atmosphere: samba schools and *foliões* 86
4.3 Brazil's cosmopolitan statement on peace and solidarity 88
4.4 Articulating FIFA's peaceful message: technology's heart and soul 89
4.5 Articulating the beautiful football 'cockfight': international and national singers, Brazilian dancers and the much-desired 'gold' *porta bandeiras* 93

For Majid

Poem

My home is my name,
that blossoms the indomitable.
The physical word
in my disembowelled howl.
My home is to own myself.
[…] And to burn
beneath the sleep of time
and its lyrics of debris.
Withdrawn to playful arteries
I listen to memory sing
in a living room of dry lagoons.
[…] From the dock wiped clear of waiting
nights keep vigil to the clashing
of African drums.
My home is my skin.
From cockfights
in which salt
gives water muscles.
Comes the sun –
and the blackest black
mated to the flesh;
and mills for grinding sugar cane
and men in supplication;
and impositions of the whip
and centuries of untangling phonemes
to add to the boil.
To me with whom they sailed their way
to the sea of the Antilles; lacerated.

Salgado Maranhão, *Blood of the Sun: Poems*, translated by Alexis Levitin, 2012

Preface and acknowledgements

As is the case with most monographs, a lot of conceptual work 'recedes' in one's mental warehouse, and never sees the light of the day. The book's collaborative, interactional nature merits acknowledgement, as the most important proto-hermeneutic sample one can extract from this study. A world of thanks goes to my companion in life and ideas, Majid Yar; his chapter editing, expert cooking and jokes proved therapeutic. A second thank you goes to our extended Greek and Pakistani families, which are constantly reproduced in Skype and telephonic sites; they have been part of my preliminary ethnographic notes. I would like to thank the two anonymous reviewers for their constructive comments, which helped me improve the manuscript and the title considerably. I am also grateful for the support I received from Emily Briggs, Associate Editor at Routledge, and the publisher's editorial team. All images are credited to Jimmy Balkovicius.

The monograph is, in part, the result of my inhabiting a quite diverse academic unit, with different research centres, and an equally diverse university. Occasionally, some of my peers' voices creep into the text, modified by the process of writing. Although it is intended as a mediation of ethical considerations over any mega-event's aesthetic content and context, as a book that does not respect the boundaries between political and artistic analysis, it may acquire diverse readerships. Although I endeavour to retain no control over the study's public interpretations, I invoke a priori the usual disclaimer.

Introduction

The first chapter is meant as an introduction to the study's themes: the general context of the 2014 mega-event, its ceremonial parameters (opening and closing ceremonies), the content of the celebrated game (football) and its public reception in Brazil. The 2014 World Cup is placed amongst Brazil's strategic developmental priorities. Hosting mega-events so as to be ranked amongst the world's political and economic leaders is supposed to propel the country to its own unique modernity (heretofore 'trans-modernity'). The actual aims of the strategy are defined in civilisational terms: proving to others that Brazilian culture holds the key to world progress and global mobilities (of talent, technologies and artstyles). Football and artistic ceremony occupy central roles in this argument as 'riches' that the European hemisphere should not monopolise.

The chapter frames the study in a combination of globalisation and mobility theory: it outlines Brazilian perceptions of a global 'cosmography of riches' – a term originating in contemporary anthropological theory but reframed as a geopolitical concept for a study of phenomena of historical and contemporary mobility in Brazil. This spatio-temporal depiction of symbolic capital includes commerce, technological innovation, human talent and material mobilities (produced artefacts); its representation as a cognitive map dates back to colonial movement into South America. Such movement bequeathed Brazil with novel ideas of travel as tourism, which challenged and enriched domestic, indigenous 'moorings' or conceptions of (home)land. Hence, the cosmography of riches would ultimately over-determine Brazilian 'cosmologies', ordering native social experience in comprehensible patterns of human interaction. The chapter concludes with the observation that such imported cosmographies provide us with the mega-event's 'deep (political-cultural) plot', a scenario explaining government policy and popular reactions to its staging beyond the ephemerality of accusations concerning governmental 'corruption' and overspending. The plot's core is defined by creative reactions to global value hierarchies, as it turns foreign capital (football and European art) into domestic heritage. Such creative reactions are superimposed onto domestic understandings of civility that recognise one's humanity and merit only through kinship and family recognition.

Chapter 2 isolates the civilisational 'connectors' between Brazilian and European cosmologies so as to comprehend better how and why these clash or harmonise. As such, it implements globalisation critiques on structural hybridisation (e.g. the clash of European–South American civilisations) on the Brazilian case. This allows us to consider the role of interpretation and use of European structures of thought in Brazil from colonial times to date. Methodologically, the chapter invites us to examine how the hermeneutics of the 'new mobilities paradigm' relates to more established structural hermeneutic theory in cultural sociology ('the strong programme'). It is suggested that instead of divorcing the quotidian (football and its social trajectories) from elitist aesthetics (the extraordinary, sacralised ceremonies and their aristocratic histories), we should consider how the two work in unison to define Brazil's 'heritage kinaesthetics' (modes of cognitive and embodied movement as heritage) and 'performative synaesthetics' (recurring discursive performances through sensory combinations).

It is argued that though Western European epistemologies (prioritising vision and organisation of the social via ocular technologies) certainly affected Brazilian perceptions, Afro-Brazilian cultures of slavery (prioritising multi-sensory harmony via combined cognitive and embodied movement) are present in Brazilian styles to date. Both the art of football (*futebolarte*) and the officially sanctioned ceremonial spectacle tend to negotiate these clashes and harmonisations. Clashes or harmonisations of art are informed by another essential split in Brazilian culture, between 'heritage' (as inherited culture, a property of the 'national family') and 'legacy' (as legal pacts on what should be protected for the 'people' in the domain of law, beyond the 'suspect' practices of familial networks). It is argued that conceptions of heritage and legacy are both local and global phenomena because the communities that uphold them can be both fixed and mobile.

The chapter concludes with a reconsideration of aesthetics as an aspect of domains of practical action – loosely defined in Brazilian contexts as mobility styles. The prioritisation of the Brazilian body as fluid nature (in Afro-Brazilian cosmologies) but also as surface of inscription (in Western, European cosmologies) was crucial for the enactment of Brazilian aesthetic-practical action in 2014. More precisely, it is argued that Brazilian heritage kinaesthetics and performative synaesthetics oscillated between acceptance and appropriation of foreign codes as forms. The shift from aesthetic codes (beauty as justice, goodness and order) to forms (beauty as phenomenally sanctioned feminine gentility and aristocratic 'whiteness') is part of what is known in the social sciences as the 'Brazilian dilemma'. Enacted on global (ceremonial, mediatised and activist) stages, this dilemma should be considered as Brazil's aesthetic statement on public appearances as socio-cultural depth. The argument filters anthropological theory through globalisation (of sports) and cultural sociological theory so as to develop a new mobilities scholarly discourse.

The third chapter further develops connections between globalisation (structural hybridisation theory) and mobility theories (the global movement of artstyle and national style via technology and mega-event performance). The previous chapter's emphasis on Brazilian civilisational mobilities and moorings is further developed in a proposal to consider social lifeworlds and artworlds as co-produced. First, it is suggested that in the World Cup context we deal with 'articulations', a double understanding of art as communicative action and as form of communication (oral, scriptural, digital, aural and embodied) that activates community-building mechanisms. Forms of communication over-determined divisions between 'civilised' and 'uncivilised' cultures in colonial times. In contemporary contexts they seem to over-determine practices of communal connectivity and bonding. There are criss-crossings and interactions between the two forms of articulation, but the communities that operate in the World Cup's ceremonial and social stage are either highly mobile and affiliative (actors, singers and event stage organisers) or more rooted and filiative (government agents, citizen activists and Brazilian football fans). The World Cup's ceremonial stage, which is created by blends of filiative and affiliative networks, is officially endorsed, but can also deviate from social norms and domestic cosmologies. However, even the event's unsanctioned public stages (of street protests and football fandom) display both sedentary and nomadic traits. Brazilian football fan reactions to the national team's defeat by Germany allow us to examine how the nomadic and fluid nature of fandom can be modified by the injection of values rooted in Brazilian land and heritage. The chapter considers the circulation of symbols of popular culture and banal nationalism in sports contexts. These symbols are also accompanied by rituals in mega-events, which tell us something about the culture of those performing them. The chapter suggests that public stages of ceremony and popular protest alike, and their performative synaesthetics, call into being particular human types or 'characters'. These supra-human archetypes tell us a story about Brazilian styles of social conduct. As the 'protagonists' of Brazil's deep plot, they draft the national community's mode of 'being in the world', and making friends or enemies.

Chapter 4 focuses on the content of the 2014 World Cup's opening and closing ceremonies. Instead of providing art theory, it prioritises the uses of art analysis for the study of Brazilian social problems and their global significance. It suggests a meaningful gap between the opening and closing events' articulations of Brazil's progression through civilised time and space. More specifically, it explores how audiences are moved from the opening ceremony's colonial (African slavery) and contemporary 'traditional' (the Amazonas) contexts to hypermobile environments of touristified consumption and cultural industrial production. The opening ceremony's emphasis on centuries-long customs and rituals dichotomises the stage's symbolic cosmography in temporal terms and into local, circular and colonial, linear templates. The engagement of Amazonian and Afro-Brazilian communities with foreign cosmographies of riches is symbolised in the ceremony by a globe. As

Brazil's dialogically formed cosmological centre, the globe introduces in the country all these technologies that saw Brazil to (trans-)modernisation – amongst them, football. The rest of the ceremony focuses on processes of Brazilian trans-modernisation, which is narrated to audiences through Brazilian personages, their performances and struggles to turn 'nature' into 'culture'. The concluding act, dominated by blends of foreign celebrity singers and performers, suggests that Brazilian trans-modernity ought to be governed by the principles of equality, freedom and respect for the other without compromising the value of national bonding.

The switch from idealisations of domestic realities to European and Western legacies of equality guides the closing ceremony's dominant audio-visual and kinaesthetic art forms. Here the local and the particular are replaced by the global, and Brazilian aesthetics are mostly reduced to forms for global intelligibility. From projections of 'fair play' in a parade of all World Cup national teams (represented as ornamented female personages), to the staged struggle between the two finalists, Germany and Argentina (represented by two football celebrities displaying their artistry), the ceremony retains the formalist elements of Geertz's 'Brazilian cockfight'. The mobilisation of gender and race as ideal types in articulations of national styles is blended in musical and kinaesthetic performances, in which foreign celebrities (Shakira, Carlos Santana) and domestic performers (samba schools, Ivete Sanghalo) celebrate hybrid music and choreography. With an eye to mobilities into Western markets, these pop-rock and *axe*-samba-belly dancing artstyles articulate the twin cosmetic projects of the mega-event's filiative and affiliative communities.

Chapter 5 is meant as a contribution to the development of the stylistics of fan movements, which readers are prompted to consider as part of global cultural mobilities. As an aspect of mobility theory, it considers disorganised fan protest as a form of tourist-like pilgrimage in a context (World Cup) that can be national, regional and transnational; banal and commoditised, but also serious and semi-sacralised; and simultaneously characterised by fixity and change in cultural values. Pilgrimage is discussed as part of globalisation and mobility theory here, to commence an analysis of the stylistics of Brazilian fan reactions as by-products of social movements.

The chapter turns to the national scene to examine two pivotal moments in the 2014 World Cup: President Dilma Rousseff's (online) public address before the programmed football matches on the one hand, and Brazilian reactions to the national team's match loss to Germany (hence exclusion from the World Cup final), as well as the final match between Germany and Argentina. The chapter highlights the widespread uses of samba in street enactments of a Brazilian 'cockfight' between football enemies, alongside desperate gestures of flag burning, mourning and protest after the 'loss of the Cup'. All these phenomena are examined within the problematic of heritage kinaesthetics and performative synaesthetics, as they articulate the Brazilian non-networked 'individual' in collective terms (the 'defeated nation'). It is argued that the twin return of stereotyping football enemies (Argentina, Germany) on the one hand, and of enemies of utopian law (government and capitalist football business) on the other, brings resentments to the fore. Rarely escalating into full-blown violence (such as that displayed in the 2013 *favela* riots over mega-event overspending), these emotions provide creative anchorage to more peaceful or less violent (fan) 'protests'. The football defeat thus assumes cosmic proportions as an articulation of failing to 'get one's returns' but, luckily, watching one's arch-enemy (Argentina) having a chance to do so (in the final), and also failing.

Post-defeat and final fan reactions are articulations of Brazilian trans-modernity, which is characterised by interpretative discourses of Western civility: the 'acclimatisation' of aristocratic 'goods', such as the English game of football, into the slowly industrialised 'tropics' of Brazil (urban but also progressively mixed-race and working-class communities). Articulations of Brazilian trans-modernity's heritage kinaesthetics were highly ritualistic. They involved marching, dancing and mild street embroilments with rival football fans and police as forms of tourist-like pilgrimage to Brazil's imaginary heritage domains. These rituals draw upon *futebolarte*'s and *samba-arte*'s social histories of inequality and the triumph of working-class black masculinity against all social odds. Fan clashes typify these rituals in the form of national heroes, which can also regionalise the cosmography of riches, presenting Brazilian identity and memory as more fragmented than external viewers may assume it is. When considered as a popular triumph against national and global hierarchies of value, Brazilian heritage kinaesthetics prompts fan crowds to venerate the roots of the nation's slave ancestry through discourses of 'debt'. This debt (unpaid to ancestors by colonial usurpers of Brazilian riches) transmutes in 2014 into a discourse of legal responsibility to Brazilian citizens, still unpaid by an overspending state.

The concluding chapter recapitulates the necessary components of Brazil's 'deep plot', which date back to constant losses of resources to foreign 'usurpers'. The plot involves a seamless narrative across popular and state domains of a double 'debt' to the country's martyred ancestry. It suggests that modern Brazilians ought to remember and claim compensation for this unjust past, but also directs this compensation to the Brazilian imagined community's living members, who should be treated with respect according to the law. Whereas the first debt rekindles ethnic communion and the problematic network practices of Brazilian 'persons', the latter transposes legal rules from Brazilian trans-modernity's utopia to the real, living Brazilian cultures. The custodians of the colonial heritage are articulated as black masculinised personages, tricksters who claim without giving back; the custodians of the law are feminised personages, who offer (national style and artstyle) in excess, thus reversing the debt, and expect to be reciprocated.

Gender, race and class are crucial in social symbolisations. The chapter concludes by stressing how any culture's aesthetic principles should not be contemptuously treated as inessential 'bourgeois projects' or stereotyped as effeminising techniques of self-presentation in international political domains. By the same token, the aesthetic principles of black working-class masculinity should not simply be regarded as dangerous analogues of terrorism, protest or nationalism. As respect guides the pursuit of foreign cosmographies, both styles/personages come into being by distortions of traumatic memory, so both merit attention. The active ('healing') potential of these styles points to those hidden structures of complaint that, if ignored, can transform into malignant populism. Brazil's historical trajectory provides such an example of cosmopolitan desires that are constantly left partially articulated, prompting citizens to claim and demand without any interest or intention to give or reciprocate.

1 Cosmographies of riches and cosmologies of desire

A cultural-as-political perspective on Brazil

On 12 June 2014, Brazil opened the 20th FIFA (Fédération Internationale de Football Association) World Cup with a spectacular ceremony. Framed in the colours of the Brazilian flag and with the motto '*untos num só ritmo*' (all in one rhythm), the 'Cup of Cups', as President Dilma Rousseff would name it, had a logo as *belo* (beautiful) as its host. Created by Brazilian design agency 'Africa', the logo's winning design originated in the iconic photograph of three victorious hands together raising the world's most famous trophy. The design was meant as an uplifting message of humanity's interlinking and of 'Brazil warmly welcoming the world to Brazilian shores' (FIFA.com n.d.a). It is unfortunate that its two key emotive elements – victory and union – would crash on the same shores three weeks later, in a humiliating 7–1 loss by the national team to Germany. It was only the second time (the first being in 1950) that Brazil had hosted the competition, after an unchallenged selection in 2007, when FIFA decreed that the tournament would be staged in South America (FIFA.com 2007). The country's supremacy in World Cups was epitomised in five titles (1958, 1962, 1970, 1994 and 2002), and hosting the 2014 mega-event seemed like a natural development. However, things simply did not go according to plan (to host and win the event). At first, the realisation that the spectacle Brazil had staged for the 31 qualified competitors in 64 matches across 12 of its revamped cities would not be matched with such global applause induced bafflement, tears and anger amongst fans, filling the streets with mobs, and international press with unwelcome comments about the country.

Reading this disarray as a disconnected incident is, at least, unhelpful for a country that continues to invest in its past and dream of a better future for all its cultures. To do a decent job we must investigate such attitudinal fluctuations within a temporal horizon that expands and contracts so as to accommodate South America's shifting cultural politics. The politics unfold theatrically, but are not theatre for mere entertainment and 'mere aesthetic embellishments'; they are 'the thing itself' (Geertz 1980: 120). To consider ceremonial performances separately from such political staging, as if art floats in an empty cultural field, is also incorrect. However, the study also takes an extra analytical step: it is my intention to examine the polished performances of the ceremonial spectacle and its political elite, and the less 'decorous', emotional reactions of football folk side by side, as part of narratives of *Brasilidade* or 'Brazilian-ness'. The statement suggests that we deal with global phenomena, so it should not be signposted as a methodological nationalist exercise. Instead of regarding them as isolated examples of national specificity, I stress their complex positioning in moving systems of power, culture and chrono-spatiality. As a multifarious study (of art, politics, social protest and even finance-scapes), the book addresses thematic questions that fall under the ambit of the 'new mobilities paradigm' (Hannam et al. 2006; Sheller and Urry 2006). Having as its starting point the two social events in the duration of the Brazilian World Cup, it traces the historical and contemporary temporalities and spatialities of mobility regimes, technologies, and practices in the country, considering their place in movements for social rights and justice (Sheller 2014a).

The interrelationships of globalisation, mobility and football can be traced in the ways each country refracts its specific historical, cultural, economic, political and social conditions through global complexity systems, occasionally prompting those to adapt, but quite often adapting its own needs and planning to them (Tomlinson 1996, 2005; Tomlinson and Young 2006; Giulianotti and Robertson 2004, 2007, 2009; Urry 2003; Sheller 2014a). These needs are shaped by the inescapably political character of proximity (neighbours, friends and foes) and mobility (of the country's cultural capital), as well as their complementary nature (Adey 2006). I define the politics of mobility as part of an arts system that encompasses the art of power 'and the possibilities to set up strategies in order to enable, constrain, or even enforce conditions of physical and virtual proximity between people, objects, and information' (Pellegrino 2011: 2).

I will outline Brazil's socio-historical specificity in more detail later; suffice it to mention here that football is for the country an example of successful appropriation of colonial capital, both symbolic and material. Andrews and Mower (2012) also remind us that global sporting landscapes are characterised by a plethora of highly localised game forms rooted in the place's socio-cultural relations. The relative immobility of their participants and the idiosyncratic nature of localised sporting cultures are complemented by the progressive 'sportisation' (Maguire 1999; Walmsley 2008 in Presenza 2013: 126–7) of modern societies. Sportisation, the development 'from local variation to international standardization', has fundamentally transformed sport (Bottenburg 2001: 2), by establishing a modern, rationalised, and bureaucratised global sporting landscape out of the patchwork quilt of highly localised sport forms that proliferated in the pre-modern era. This progressive association between societal and sporting development made football cultures globally mobile, allowing national styles of play to join regional and global circuits of cultural mobility.

Hosting a mega-event of World Cup proportions could only activate such background processes, implicating it to regional and global competitions for economic and socio-cultural 'progress' (Deichmann 2007). These competitive agendas are often framed in the bifurcated language of 'civil society' and 'corporate social responsibility' in contexts of urban development (Giulianotti 2012). Such responsibilisation clashes with the cosmetic practices of mega-event management, setting agendas of housing and poverty reduction against those of media expenditure and 'pretty' spectacle deliverance. Mega-event management as an urban development strategy is an important element in policies of stimulating economic growth and job creation (Pillay and Bass 2008: 330). The international literature on such events is more sceptical about pronouncements of positive economic and legacy impacts: imponderables on economic expansion (Owen 2005; Humphreys and Prokopowizc 2007) and optimistic dependence on the host's various 'attraction elements' (Ritchie 2000; Horne and Manzenreiter 2006) often lead to disappointment for the citizens, who have to foot the bill. This leads with mathematical accuracy to complaints about displacement of public funds, and cuts that ultimately affect those least likely to enjoy benefits from mega-events (or even attend them): the urban poor, aboriginals and people in country districts a long way from the city (Whitson 2004: 1227–8).

The separation of football from the politics of leisure may also impoverish attempts to consider the norms and values of Brazilian culture in transnational spaces. For one, football's fandom enclaves, its mega-event ceremonies and audiences are quintessential 'travelling cultures' with socio-cultural roots and cosmopolitan routes (Clifford 1997; Hannerz 1990, 1996); while mapping post-national conditions of being and belonging, they also tell us stories about native conceptions of the good life, happiness and solidarity. Such Brazilian scriptures of harmony, in particular, in which mind, body and soul are in unity, have unprecedented historical depth (Korstanje 2011); they contain stories of coerced and free human movements from East to West, North to South, Europe and Africa to the Americas. In contexts of host-guest encounter, scriptures of harmony should be understood not within a framework rooted in history (e.g. De Kadt 1984) but of memory as a *fluid precondition* of historical discourse (Lash and Urry 1994: 224, 233). Brazilian cartographic imaginaries re-worked – indeed, continue to do so – imported ideas of modernity in folk, pop and elite moulds, through centuries of colonial violence and into a time in which the country emerged as a free but disorientated 'nation'. The 2014 mega-event's opening ceremony and the Brazilian mourning of football defeat become chrono-spatial windows to the Brazilian culture's emotional and material movements in the world. Performed Brazilian-style, these movements are recorded in music, rhythm, theatrical performance and (un)choreographed protest in equally important ways for a social scientific observer.

There are good reasons why amongst the study's master terms are linguistic variations of harmony, beauty and well-being. In Chapter 2, I explain how everyday words such as *belo* (*-a*) and *lindo* (*-a*) dig up a centuries-long tunnel into the Brazilian popular psyche. Such words allow the cultural investigator to explain why deep and thick descriptions of Brazilian culture are 'beautified' so much in global public spaces that seem to turn into spectacular surfaces. Revising Geertzian epistemological convictions, I reconsider why Western conceptions of surface are connected to problematic depth (see Giesen 2011). Truly, however, we cannot divorce the cosmetics of current Brazilian mobilities from their past economic and social histories, as they comprise the heart of the country's current underdeveloped development. The paradox of 'underdeveloped development' goes back to clashes of intimate Brazilian economic relations and external modern capitalist structures as well as with the way these subsequently conditioned social relations in urban areas. The privileged position of the city – in Brazil and other Latin American contexts largely a colonial product – continues to incorporate indigenous socio-cultures into metropolitan visions of economy and the ideas of 'good life', without always considering if these visions are locally compatible.

Global civilisational hierarchy and offshoring

There is a 'deep plot' (à la Geertz's (1973) 'deep play') in this instance, including practices of offshoring native socio-economic capital that would come back to haunt the World Cup's staging as a promise of national betterment (Silk 2001; Hogan 2003; Tomlinson 2005; Urry 2014: 91). As was the case with the Beijing 2008 Olympic Games, the government would be blamed for prioritising cosmetic appearances over human rights to bolster its international profile (Worden 2008; Tzanelli 2010). Economics, culture and politics go hand in hand in diachronic analyses of the Brazilian deep plot: the conversion of the north-east, the Minas Gerais interior, the north and the centre-south (Rio de Janeiro, São Paulo and Paraná) into export economies and their incorporation into global developmental networks produced satellite local economies dependent on the whims of foreign markets (Gunder Frank 1966: 7–8). The focus on urban industrialisation meant that only particular cities such as the heavily industrialised São Paulo could relatively 'progress', especially in periods devoid of foreign influence (World War I and II), without nevertheless shaking off their intellectual and philosophical roots in Europe. As both Russell-Wood (2002b) and Cannadine (2002) explain about Portugal and Britain, respectively, although their colonies and varied populations beyond the seas were conceived of as one vast interconnected world, their cultures were earmarked as the civilisational opposites of the colonial metropoles: hierarchical, corporatist and enervated (see also Marchetti 2011: 19, for contemporary comparisons). Yet, many of these attributes were either fictional, or (as is the case with Brazil) the result of colonial control. The rapid post-industrialisation of some cities in South American regions, combined with the accelerated global mobility of potential consumers and capital investment also suggested their reinvention as entertainment and consumer nodes in a sustainable manner.

However, the ubiquitous shift in strategies of urban governance from civic managerialism to urban entrepreneurialism (Andrews and Mower 2012: 4) is yet to benefit Brazilian culture. Over the last few years Brazilian cities have successfully participated in inter-urban competitions (the Olympic Games and the FIFA World Cup) for elite sporting mega-events, with the anticipation that these 'will become motors of capital investment accumulation … anchors of urban (re)development … [and] an important component of place marketing and promotion strategies within today's globalized economy' (ibid.; see also Ramchandani and Coleman 2012: 258). The basic four key business motives for sponsoring sport (image enhancement, increased awareness of the product and the firm, hospitality opportunities and product trial or sales opportunities; see Crompton 1995) are more or less covered by Brazil's strategic planning. Combining the Olympic Games with the World Cup bid makes sense in long-term policy planning: bundling different events in a portfolio might bring together segments of the population that might not otherwise meet; target and reach diverse market segments, hence increasing the size of a host community's events market; and respond to diverse community needs, such as improving quality of life, building identity, or promoting healthier lifestyles (Ziakas and Costa 2011: 152).

In a post-colonial federation, domestic and international recipients of rhetoric and policy have to be managed differently. Here our step back has to be complemented with a step down and into the Brazilian 'deep plot' of globalisation, which is still conditioned by the norms of honour and impeccable public self-presentation. If Brazilian President Luiz Inácio Lula da Silva's successful Rio 2016 bid achieved Brazilian compliance with other organisations integral to the transnational economy (the World Trade Organization, the United Nations and the G20), winning the 2014 World Cup bid confirmed the country's influence beyond and within 'the football pitch' (Phillips 2009). What it did not achieve was to demonstrate its ability to ameliorate internal ethno-racial and class inequalities (Vinod 2006). Our step down has to be followed by an inspection around the domestic socio-cultural environment: Lula's policy has played a significant role in post-1970s articulations of *abertura*, the nation-wide project of 'opening up' – in practice, the gradual, ten-year process of democratisation on which Brazil embarked after the end of the 1964–85 dictatorship (Valente 2012: 150).

Abertura would soon be implicated in increased open movements across open borders that are 'often out of sight and involve elaborate forms of secrecy' – what is commonly known as offshoring (Urry 2014: 8). Otherwise put, though Lula's policy appeared to bring mega-events 'home', it also enabled opposite cultural flows to foreign political and economic centres that subsequent governments could not keep out of control. The pursuit of foreign 'riches' (football, mega-event management) as prestige-building mechanisms entangled regional urban development in programmatic statements and planning on transportation, new aeromobilities and communication nodes (Kaufmann et al. 2004; Kaufmann 2011) as well as risk (terrorism) management strategising (Jennings 2005), but the actualisation of social utopias is still only a rhetorical device in political speeches (Andrews and Clift 2012). Evidence of intensified surveillance mechanisms of the Beijing 2008 (Tzanelli 2010: 234) and London 2012 calibre (Urry 2014: 91–3) is provided by the Brazilian government's pledge to invest US$900 million in security forces (surveillance vehicles, CCTV cameras and helicopters) so that the tournament would be 'one of the most protected sports events in history' (Morley 2013).

As I intend to explain in more detail in subsequent chapters, Brazil's 'deep plot' combines the need to be mobile with the necessity to survey, inspect and control (Foucault 2007). I do not argue that Brazil's contemporary socialist governance is a continuation of its twentieth-century dictatorships, only that the latter is such a heavy heritage to supersede. In fact, it may be better to consider Brazil's authoritarian heritage alongside wider needs to synchronise domestic visions of technology with those of the oft-called 'developed world'. Rebuilding stadiums to accommodate new technology installations and locative media (De Souza e Silva and Sutko 2010; De Souza e Silva and Frith 2011; De Souza e Silva and Sheller 2014) complied with new architectural mobility regimes, in which multisensory communications can be achieved simultaneously on micro- (audience participation in ceremonies and matches) and macro-interactional (global broadcasting) levels (see also Jensen 2013, 2014). Yet, the locative nature of these media complexes remained reliant upon the country's global cities such as Rio de Janeiro, which acted as telecommunicative 'nodes' (Castells 1996, 2004; Sassen 2001, 2002; Tzanelli 2013b, 2013c).

Such nodes connected to other transnational capitalist pathways, with various consequences for the streamlining of World Cup ideoscapes. Thus, the International Broadcast Centre was located at the Riocentro in the Barra da Tijuca neighbourhood of Rio de Janeiro (FIFA.com 2014b). HBS (Host Broadcast Services), a subsidiary of Infront Sports & Media, provided coverage for the finals for the fourth consecutive time (FIFA.com n.d.b), whereas official equipment provider Sony built 12 bespoke high-definition production 40 foot-long containers for each tournament venue's equipment. Each match utilised 37 standard camera plans, including Aerial and Cablecam, two Ultramotion cameras and dedicated cameras for interviews. The technology used to capture the HD footage included 224 Sony HDC camera chains, 64 Super Slo-motion camera chains, 36 Sony switchers and 820 Sony Professional monitors (RedShark News 2014). The broadcasting rights for the tournament – including television, radio, Internet and mobile coverage – accounted for an estimated 60% of FIFA's income from staging a World Cup and were sold to media companies in each individual territory either directly by FIFA, or through licensed companies or organisations such as the European Broadcasting Union, Organización de Televisión Iberoamericana, International Media Content, Dentsu and RS International Broadcasting & Sports Management (FIFA.com n.d.c).

Architectural and televisual innovations should be considered alongside the organising networks' new ways to 'read' the football field as a space in which certain rules apply for all. Surveillance crops up again in the 'deep plot': the introduction of the biological passport with the help of the Swiss Laboratory for Doping Analysis (FIFA.com 2014c) also allowed for the elimination of the personalised factor (e.g. neutralisation of deviance through autobiographical sentimentalism) from accounts of failed testing (see also Yar 2014a). More importantly, for the first time at World Cup finals, match officials used goal-line technology and vanishing foam for free kicks (FIFA Quality Programme 2014). The goal-line technology had trials in the Confederations Cup of the previous year. Developed in Germany, the chosen Goal Control system featured 14 high-speed cameras, seven directed to each of the goals (Yahoo News n.d.). Data were sent to a central image-processing centre, where a virtual representation of the ball was output on a widescreen to confirm the goal, and referees were equipped with a watch that vibrated and displayed a signal upon a goal. The technology mapped spatial and temporal rules onto audiovisual templates to 'discipline' the bodies of football players (Foucault 1979, 1980). Just like new architectural mobility regimes, these new para-surveillance technologies also ensured that the global fans and audiences of the matches could comprehend the referees' decisions, thus blending macro- with micro-interactional communications.

As explained above, Brazil's plot accommodates surveillance and the desire to be mobile. Amongst the mobility forms this encourages is travel and the ability to attract travellers. In any case, mega-events are often hailed for providing ample opportunities in the tourism sector. It has not been long since the 500th anniversary of Brazil, which 'served to highlight how travel has played an important part in the country's heritage and conquests' (Santana 2000: 424). The tourism sector has acquired renewed significance also in the economies of other South American countries after their transition to democracy, the consolidation of economic blocs and the improvement in basic services, such as health and education. The 1960s and 1970s political disputes, military coups, armed guerrilla conflict and internal terrorist violence did little to lift these countries out of economic instability, and it was only in 1997 that Brazil in particular ranked in America's top 20 destinations (decisively backed by federal governments). Brazil's variable climate zones ensured that certain cities, such as Rio de Janeiro, attracted more tourists than the Amazon or the Pantamal, which are slowly gaining ground with adventure tourists and eco-tourists. Estimates place visitor arrivals during the World Cup at healthy levels, appeasing Minister of Sports Aldo Rebelo.

More specifically, the FIFA Fan Fest in the host cities received about 5 million people, and had about 1 million guests from 202 countries (Passarinho and Matoso 2014). Extending the football event to popular artistic activities has been a strategy that proved successful for the national visitor economy for a third consecutive World Cup tournament. Prominent examples of FIFA Fan Fests in each of the 12 host cities throughout the competition were those staged in Copacabana Beach of Rio de Janeiro, which had already held a Fan Fest in 2010, and São Paulo's Vale do Anhangabaú, and the first official fest on Iracema Beach, in Fortaleza (FIFA.com 2012a). The sites were chosen as traditional settings for celebrations. According to Ronaldo, member of the local organising committee board, such celebrations 'bring together people from all social backgrounds. As Brazilians, we have always had the custom of cheering for our national team in large popular festivals all over the country' (Brazil World Cup Fan Camp 2014 2012).

Climate and urban infrastructural variables played a role in sports venue selection, as the 12 World Cup cities were not just tourist destinations but also training facilities for the competing teams. These were: Estádio do Maracanã in Rio de Janeiro; Estádio Nacional Mané Garrincha (Brasília, Distrito Federal); Arena de São Paulo (São Paulo); Estádio Castelão (Fortaleza, Ceará); Estádio Mineirão (Belo Horizonte, Minas Gerais); Arena Fonte Nova (Salvador, Bahia); Estádio Beira-Rio (Porto Alegre, Rio Grande do Sul); Arena Pernambuco (Recife, Pernambuco); Arena Pantanal (Cuiabá, Mato Grosso); Arena da Amazônia (Manaus, Amazonas); Arena das Dunas (Natal, Rio Grande do Norte); and Arena da Baixada (Curitiba, Paraná). Five of the chosen host cities had brand new venues built specifically for the World Cup. The Estádio Nacional Mané Garrincha in the capital, Brasília, was demolished and rebuilt, and the remaining six stadiums were extensively renovated. The same Brazilian cities were also home to the participating teams at 32 separate base camps. Of these venues, seven were new and five renovated. They covered all the main regions of Brazil and created more evenly distributed hosting than the 1950 finals in the country (Monteiro 2009). Most teams opted to stay in the south-east region of Brazil, with only eight teams choosing other regions; no team chose to stay in the north region or the central-west region (BBC Sport 2014a).

Mobility and technology are status symbols in the Brazilian plot; as signs of synchronisation, they also generate transnational interpretative anchors, making strangers do the advertising for the host. Take, for example, how British broadcaster BBC encapsulated the host cities' cultural capital in its own short documentary on 'Brazil's soccer cities' (BBC Sport 2014b). Narrated by a blend of Brazilian and British reporters, it featured six of the hosting sports hubs. The selection revolved around branding discourses distributed between centres (the Brazilian capital (Brasília), the future Olympic host and cosmopolitan-tourist destination (Rio de Janeiro) and the country's financial centre (São Paulo)), and peripheral, tropical zones (Recife, Manaus and Salvador). The colourful presentations were framed around discourses of travel and mobility: the slum and Carnival capital for Rio; the coastal artistic metropolis for Recife; the country's power base for Brasília; the Amazonian beautiful but progressively industrialised Manaus; the home of African capoeira for Salvador; and the industrious, concrete but cosmopolitan São Paulo.

Though the economy benefited from visitors for the duration of the World Cup, it is admittedly difficult to distinguish between temporary tourist and business influx and more permanent results. Generally, tourism benefits from FIFA World Cup mega-events, which draw a significant number of domestic and international tourists (Lee and Taylor 2005). Notably, nevertheless, such tourists are more inclined to visit urban regions than out-of-the-way areas of national significance. This trend corresponds to other forms of tourism mobilities, such as those to sacralised sites (Korstanje and George 2012). If we are to grant Brazilian cultural self-perceptions a truly cosmopolitan perspective, we cannot hinge just on tourism and travel's economic benefits; the significance of both needs to be localised and globalised – in short, spatio-temporalised. The World Cup's 'deep plot' connects land to ancestry via narratives of Brazil's living human communities, generating raw material for the performances, aesthetics and style that we explore in this book.

Spatialised guilt and ancestral honouring: the underdevelopment of development

Ancestral beings, land and tourism mobilities belong to the same narrative matrix in Brazil. The 'matrix' is constitutive of a fusion of cosmopolitan horizons that incorporates folk practices performed 'from below' and domestic elite practices structured 'from above' (Knorr-Cetina 1999 in Meyer and Molineaux-Hodgson 2010: 2.1–3). It is important to stress again, for reasons exceeding those of marketing, the paramount importance of the physiography, culture and history of the destination (Ashworth and Voogd 1994; Crouch and Ritchie 1999; Slater 2004; Lichrou et al. 2008). Both within the host society and for guest communities, tourist destinations are not just physical spaces but also fluid and dynamic contexts shaped by collective memory in 'a symbolic order of meaning as a form of material production' (Meethan 2001: 168; McCabe and Stokoe 2004). We can safely assume that the athletic/tourist visitors' (including fans, football players and reporters/journalists) consumption of the World Cup venues is affected by mythologies, fantasies and histories deeply rooted in them but also globally reproduced and disseminated in various print and electronic formats (Selwyn 1996; Tzanelli 2007). These myths and fantasies flow freely in global representational channels as 'narrative morsels' to generate the tourist destination (Bendix 2002).

Narratives of place and culture projected by the global media and in ceremonial contexts are not mere meaning structures; they are also power structures, as meanings we ascribe to places affect the lives of their inhabitants (Santos 2004). Both individuals and social groups 'connect (auto-) biographical storytelling to landscapes so as to consolidate socio-cultural identities' (Tzanelli and Yar 2014: 7). We may indeed talk about cultural 'topophilia' (Tuan 1974) or love of place in its various narrative forms. Topophilic rites promoting rural innocence or even utopian visions of place, untouched in our case by usurpers and colonists, reach their digital apogee in the enclaves of Brazilian trans-modernity: the global cities of Rio de Janeiro or São Paulo, which act as dual spaces of travel and popular protest (Sassen

2001). There are also audiovisual links to make in the 2014 World Cup televisual tourist contexts, where the post-colonial city becomes a repository of phantasmagorical images, readily available to global flâneurs and tourist visitors for inspection, consumption and reinvention in personal narratives (Giddens 1990; Patke 2000). The explosion of tourism-inducing urban filmographies is closely connected to postmodern adulation of contemporary 'speed cultures' including those of the specialised (televisual) tour (Savelli 2009: 151) and the video-recorded urban protests (Tzanelli 2012c, 2013b).

In fact, landscapes riddled with horrific crimes harbour a feeling of guilt that underscores tourist fascination with them as much as it provides protesters with a core oppositional discourse to power. Such so-called 'guilty landscapes' include in European modern contexts concentration camps that turned from war crime sites into global visitor destinations (see Armando 1998 in Reijnders 2009: 175). Due to their legacies of slavery, Brazilian urban sites enclose material and symbolic guilty landscapes, ready to be consumed by tourists and venerated by postmodern pilgrims. There is a 'thanatourist' or 'dark tourist' dimension in the global consumption of Brazilian cityscapes that even BBC reporters encapsulated in their journalistic tour. Generally, thanatourism focuses on human visits to locations wholly or partially motivated by the desire for actual or symbolic encounters with death (Lennon and Foley 2000), but post-colonial phantasmologies (the ghosts of ancestral slaves) can also be invoked either as tourist spectacles or as 'debts'. The developed world and native populations alike are called upon to discharge these 'debts', by displaying for ancestry some respect through ritual (Turner and Turner 1978; Derrida 2001).

My connection of consumption, tourism and protest is based on their intrinsic reference to excess, the death drive and the ability of both to recreate the social in material and utopian terms (Mannheim 1968; Marcuse 1955; Korstanje and George 2012). Dann and Seaton (2001) note that slavery as 'dissonant heritage' has left its mark on tourism across the world. Thanatourism's connection to cultures of indebtedness and discourses of political reparation implicate it in the conditions of post-coloniality that I analyse in this book. DaMatta's (1991: 113) call to consider how mediatised programs dramatise merit and hierarchy through performance, 'the programs themselves linking the formal power of broadcasting stations and advertisers with that of the masses', is crucial. Not only do mediatised events such as those of the 2014 World Cup reinforce pre-existing societal asymmetries present in day-to-day economic life, but they also emulate the principles and time frame of life and death in the form of rites of passage (birth, initiation, decline, resurrection, etc.) (Van Gennep 1960; Korstanje 2012). Such blends of native and global activism with tourism have been brought together under the tenet of secularised pilgrimage to sites of social significance and of strong ocular properties (Graburn 2004; Urry and Larsen 2011; Tzanelli 2013b).

The observation connects to Eliade's (1989) argument that material and immaterial sites partake in political mythologisation and collective identity building. Political sociology informed by Eliade often turns to anthropologists Arnold van Gennep and Mary Douglas (1966) to examine how whole political units (national communities, states) enter sacralised rites of passage to validate their insertion into new international alliances (Turner and Turner 1978). The shift from examinations of experiential authenticity to national authentication is not as straightforward, but as 'rites of passage' is a flexible term exemplifying social-cultural ambiguity, it is constantly open to interpretation in the social sciences. The next chapter explains why the regulation of Brazilian culture by the norm of honour may lead to devaluations of 'authenticity' as an attitude that clashes with coherent self-presentation in public (Geertz 1980: 13; Giesen 2011: 170). Although contextual analyses of meaning may highlight Brazilian difference vis-à-vis Western thought, for the sake of what Geertz (2000: 48) has termed 'anti anti-relativism' (a post-colonial 'racialism', no doubt; Stocking 1982: 176) we must acknowledge that its structural logic comes close to Goffman's dramaturgical analysis (but see also Lichterman 2011: 80–4).

To avoid such mishaps, I argue that within the same spatio-temporal frame Brazilian socio-cultures become flexible interpreters of their own condition and global standing. The book's two World Cup *événements* teach us that when a post-colonial culture finds itself in late capitalist domains, it can produce different versions of the same social event in, by and for different groups (domestic and foreign). Shakespeare's conviction that all the world is a stage is even more relevant in contemporary contexts, in which corporate and locative complexes mediate the social (Tzanelli 2013b; De Souza e Silva and Sheller 2014). Naturally, there is no social stage or drama without social actors, who in our case are 'recruited' from both elite and lowbrow social sectors to populate ceremonial and popular scripts, respectively. Where orientalist stylistics allowed colonial authors to superimpose discursive coherence over cultural polyphony even in Latin American domains (Said 1978; Sheller 2003), these days new media complexes often encapsulate local creativity alongside highly polished artistic and political performance, displaying it without fully interpreting its depth.

These audiovisual 'snapshots' of popular performance might be as cunningly 'staged' as their state-sanctioned ceremonial counterparts, allowing social scientists to investigate '*carnivalesques* of revelations' (Tzanelli 2011: chapter 2) – 'simulacra of sociality' (Herzfeld 2005: 6–8) natives can knowingly arrange in clusters of 'signs' that appeal to the expectations of external audiences. The concept of 'native' or 'local' can also be reductive, and is used in this book with a great deal of 'poetic licence' for lack of more appropriate terms. The 'local' can also be regional in the grand scheme of things: South America's post-colonial dependency on its tourist economy accentuates its peripheral status, trapping its diverse localities in 'the clutches of [a] transnational global economy' intent on unrestricted development (Spivak 1993: 21).

Such social simulations may unwittingly point to the source of collective embarrassment. Their aim is to maintain, Western-style, a political secrecy, which is associated with nationalist emotion and is constitutive of the politics of ressentiment, masking the 'serious' and 'mature' as 'humorous' or 'puerile'. This is part of a global, now broadcast game of impressions that can civilise even the denigrated 'pop' or folk. Ideas of 'play' come to the fore to question connections between the healing properties of performance, the commercialised spectacle of football and whole imagined communities' ability to plan their own destiny (all explored via Brazilian understandings of *jôgo*). Indeed, one may parallel in this instance ethnographic and committed political journalist intentionality – bearing in mind their intellectual differences – to note that any expectations to contribute to developmental policies can be appropriated by natives who have their own concerns and ideas about what truly needs to be developed and how (Bowman 1996: 4; Picard 1997). Especially for the snapshots of sociality provided by old (newspapers) and new (via Internet) media sources, observers have to know how to decipher a cultural grammar of local relevance to match analogous native performances (Geertz 1973: 13; Loizos 1975; Warnke 2011: 49). Perception, memory and experience, the triadic points of performance in such mediatised settings (on ad hoc ethnographic encounters see Tomaselli 2007: 48, 52), are difficult to manage when native 'scripts' have been prepared for global audiences.

I suggest that we place the romantic hues of *felicidade* (happiness, prosperity) and *saudade* (nostalgia) of the World Cup's ceremonies alongside those of the defeat's grim militarism on the same canvas, if we are to understand how what DaMatta (1991, 1995) dubbed the 'Brazilian Dilemma' works. This dilemma couples the lofty principles of equality and communal solidarity with the instrumentalist needs of individualism, inequality and internal social hierarchy that mirror global hierarchies of value (Herzfeld 2004, 2005). Together these reiterate a narrative of a fallible human nature struggling to retain its utopian holism. The advent of industrial modernity snatched away this 'World Cup' dream from the Brazilian human, leaving its post-colonial imagined communities stranded in a permanent limbo, waiting for their own redemption on the global stage. Until that moment, the safe keepers of their pride, the state and its subjects, ought to make ends meet in an imperfect world of conflict, crime and 'sin'. Needless to add that the narrative is mapped onto the nation's geopolitical co-ordinates – heavily marked by colonial and post-colonial migrations, flows of ideas, commerce and various technologies that make Brazilian 'modernity' work (see also Bærenholdt and Granås 2008 on Northern European peripheries). Brazil's plural demographics are, today, displayed as spatial rifts: north-eastern urbanity is dominated by black slave heritage, but its Amazonian areas remain indigenous; placed next to the European enclaves of southern areas (from early modern and colonial Italian and German migrations), Brazil's human mosaic echoes the Babelian chaos.

Sadly, regional economic development and mobility of the country's cultural capital abroad remain mostly in a reverse relationship: exoticism sells well to foreign financial centres and tourist visitors, but the profit is streamlined to the developed areas. Thus, the utopian scenario's inbuilt pragmatism dictates the employment of the very same practices of offshoring that constantly bring the nation and its custodians (governments) under global showers of criticism. The loss of a football token (2014 World Cup) that was staged only thanks to constant welfare cuts, under-investment in public services and rumoured underhand dealings with various transnational mega-event partners is implicated in the sustenance of a cultural narrative as much as it is feeds suspicion in networks of global systemic governance. More dispersed than ever before, this governance diverts the attention of nations on the verge of a developmental break to the chronic traces of their economic problems. As I endeavour to explain in the following chapters, both the Brazilian ceremonial spectacle and the rebellious atomistic narrative of the 2014 World Cup defeat provide palliative treatment for the symptoms, instead of looking for radical cures. The emphasis on deferred vengeance and the restoration of a prelapsarian holism strips the nation of its hard-earned rewards to date, promoting what Andre Gunder Frank (1966) has termed 'the underdevelopment of development'.

Offshoring and the cosmography of riches

To connect the issues I presented in detail above to the Brazilian 'deep plot', I stress again that the World Cup stage concerns the efficient communication of national and transnational 'governmobilities' (Bærenholdt 2013), or 'the production of normalized mobile subjects and governance through mobilities' (Sheller 2014b: 4). Such debates have to be introduced for two (seemingly contradictory) reasons: one pertains to the increasing intrusion of surveillance technologies in our everyday lives – so much so, that humans are deemed to turn into mindless automata, obeying the law of civil etiquette, without personal planning-cum-emotion or desire beyond the maximisation of ruthless personal gain (e.g. see Ellul 1964). The second reason follows on from the first and concerns the alleged demolition of wider economies of desire and reciprocity in these governmobility environments – for, surely, all social environments have their norms and values. As Polanyi explains, 'realistic thinkers vainly spelled out the distinction between the economy in general and its market forms; time and again the distinction was obliterated by the economic *Zeitgeist*' (Polanyi 1977: 6). As Sahlins (2013a: 164) further clarifies, 'rational choice theory has to give itself the culture a priori, inasmuch as it is the cultural order that makes the material action rational, but hardly the rationality that makes the culture'.

There is, indeed, continuity between the politics of surveillance and the poetics of cultural-moral economy, insofar as the latter explains not just why (causal links) but how (style) and to what ends (*telos* or end) people pursue things in rational ways (Sahlins 1976; Bourdieu 1977; Reddy 1984; Gudeman 1986, 2009; Sayer 1999, 2000, 2003; Tzanelli 2011). This leads us to reintroduce the cultural organisation of material life to hitherto unexamined connections to so-called 'hedonistic', erratically expressed 'excess' pursuits (whether these be consumerist or revolutionary, but preferably both in startling contemporary combinations) of whole communities. I do so by adapting Sahlins's (2013a) anthropological term the 'cosmography of riches' to the interdisciplinary environments of globalisation and mobility theories.

My own understanding of cosmography closely follows mobility theory's focus on cosmopolitan pluralism. After my own hermeneutic jiggling, the term refers to the *grafí* or inscription of *kósmos* as a beautiful (original meaning of the word), good world: a patchwork of social universes that allow humans to enjoy the good life. Cosmographies of riches establish a dialogue between geometric space and anthropological space 'in the sense of "existential" space, the scene of an experience of relations with the world in the part of a being essentially situated "in relation to a milieu"' (Augé 1995: 80). Instead of 'anthropological space', I use the broader concept of 'cosmology' in a non-reclusive fashion associated with the sociology of religion. The term refers in the study to the ways in which human experience is socially ordered and framed, alluding thus to Campbell's understanding of the dynamics of social relations at large but also to Evans-Pritchard's (1940) emphasis of social ordering on the basis of intra-group rivalry and antagonism (Campbell 1964; Herzfeld 2008). Such antagonisms – no less present in contemporary Brazilian socio-cultural outlooks – give meaning to the good life through communal values, such as those of kinship and the 'family' – no less responsible for global stereotypes and accusations of Brazilian corruption. After all, kinship entails 'participation in the being of the other rather than differentiation of the self' (Sahlins 2013a: 168), a mutuality of being based on sharing and love that prevails in various cultures (including the Brazilian) to date. Kinship suggests ontological continuities ('we are part of the same body-ness') as well as the ways these are epistemologically articulated in post-national (especially political) spaces.

When reading the Brazilian dilemma through the two chosen World Cup instances, we are reminded that the West constantly silences the importance of kinship in its own cosmologies (Herzfeld 1992). Only belonging can protect one from an inhospitable world – a fact that Western etiquette cannot escape, but reproduces in televised political scandals and celebrity romances all the time. Urry (2014: 14) argues after Simmel that if all social relationships 'rest upon the precondition that people know something about each other' (Simmel 1906: 441), large-scale 'civilised societies' have to devise mechanisms of reciprocal concealment to control damaging information flows. However, is this concealment mechanism the effect of Western modernisation and the great 'civilising process' (Elias 1982), or do all communities use gossip and scandal to regulate socialities (Gluckman 1963)? The principle of concealment is, in fact, embedded in banal practices of 'cultural intimacy', the recognition of those aspects of a cultural identity that 'are considered a source of external embarrassment but nevertheless provide insiders with their assurance of common sociality, the familiarity with the bases of power that may at one moment assure the disenfranchised a degree of creative irreverence and at the next moment reinforce the effectiveness of intimidation' (Herzfeld 2005: 3).

In a plutocratic world, capital is pursued in its varied forms (as money or prestige) in interconnected ways, so humans have to devise complex ways to conceal the less licit or fair aspects of their transactions from enemies and those they cannot trust ('non-family'). Utilising a combination of Urry's take on transparency and Herzfeld's cultural intimacy allows me to explore the Brazilian pursuit of foreign riches beyond what Simmel discusses as 'dealings with foreign money' (Simmel 1906: 492), as a practice that breaks down the artificial barriers of method between the elites and common citizenry (Gellner 1983). The ability of the powerful to escape embarrassing scandals (Bauman 2000: 11, in Urry 2014: 19) does not detract from the fact that post-colonial states, such as that of Brazil, base their cosmologies on tribalist conceptual frameworks that developed in opposition to imported institutional structures (see Gellner 1969; Urry 2014: 178). To explore the nature of contemporary Brazilian culture, we must treat with equal respect anthropological investigations into situated Brazilian micro-cultures and macro-sociology as a 'panoramic perspective' (Czeglédy 2003: 17) that favours comparison and investigation into different paths to modernity (Lessnoff 2002: 10–1; Skalník 2003: 206).

Evidence of this is provided in the ways contemporary hospitality norms are framed in the 2014 World Cup context, which had to ensure transcultural communication. The event's constant appeal to ideals of the domestic hearth or the mobile ethno-national family is an essential component of contemporary hospitality norms. Especially the ceremonial marketing of Brazilian culture as a touristic landscape assists in the circulation of this neither fully natural nor wholly cultural 'heritage'. What is 'on offer' in these hospitality circuits is sociability in its purest form as another aspect of money (Hart 2009). Close to nationalist discourse, this model of hospitality is based on the visitor's respect for the Brazilian past, while pushing for more banal consumptions of place based on food and sports activities. Hence, even though, practically, World Cup-induced hospitality conforms to business and managerial imperatives ('the provision of the "holy trinity"': food, drink, accommodation; Lynch et al. 2011: 4), normatively, it still draws on political and moral imperatives that regulate Brazilian landscapes and histories as forms of heritage in need of the right custodianship and marketing by the right centres and people. The mobile national body is therefore Brazil's tourist body, black and familial. Alas, misunderstandings abound, such dialogues mistake morphological discourse grounded in experience for superficial statement, while simultaneously ignoring the plain fact that desire for individualistic happiness is more likely to be socially condemned or ostracised as a crime against humanity. Also poignantly, they allow treatments of the body in such ways that they end up endorsing outdated, 'First World' primitivist and racist fantasies.

The last comment also propels one to connect cosmographies of riches to cosmologies of recognition – what global and, by example or interpretation, national histories denied to native bodies-families. The denial of recognition partakes in systemic and sub-systemic violence, as well as the inclination of social institutions to sacralise dying as a spectacle – for bodies, especially those of darker hues, are signs of humanity's finitude, hence accepted only when they partake in processes of 'museumification' (Korstanje 2014). It has been repeatedly argued that the cross-cultural situation of the powers of life and death in cosmic realms allows for 'objectifications of such otherworldly powers in the form of the "magical property" or "prestige goods" that comprise the monies of life-giving, status endowing, and society-making transactions' (Sahlins 2013b: 171; Tzanelli 2013b: chapter 1). For Brazil, the story runs in various 'archaeological' streams from the beginning of modern ages to date in no single direction. Indeed, following the Discoveries, both the constant and volatile aspects of Brazilian cosmology interacted with European cosmographies, promoting competition and prestige hunting to a native value. Contemporary Brazilian oscillations between Western and South American perceptions of secrecy originate in this interpretative momentum.

Early modern European cultural production focused on the design of maps and globes for commercial gain: depicting 'new sources of wealth and trading opportunities – and … gaining advantage over political rivals vis-à-vis political control of newly discovered lands', gave visual meaning to the rivalry between Spain and Portugal to control the Eastern spice trade (Gunn 2003: 116–20; Jardine 1997; Jardine and Brotton 2000). 'As maps and globes compelled the viewer to reflect upon the nature of the world-as-a-whole and their place within it, the political-economic disputes of the time were prime movers in the fostering of new forms of global consciousness' (Inglis 2010: 13). Maps were visionary experiences of 'revelation' in European cultures permeated by Christian dogma. The famous *mappamundi* or world map was an artistic inscription of the phenomenal world, the belief that visionaries could see into world surfaces and grasp 'an inner reality of which the world's outward, visible forms were but appearances' (Ingold 2010: 18). Unfortunately, native engagement with the inner and outer worlds was thought of as a unity through modes of sensory holism. The pretty cosmic 'faces' (literally *mappa*) that these strangers introduced can be associated with the origins of *contemporary* Brazilian prestige hunting as a belief in 'appearances'. This hunting for prestige was bound to fuse with native cosmological understandings, which saw in honour the only possibility to acquire public recognition.

Cartographic representations of the Americas as spatial networks under European jurisdiction concealed the unevenness of actual hegemony. Especially the Portuguese aimed to master the natural environment (seas, winds, sky, stars, Sun), and to carve out a reliable mode of communication and transportation so that 'a small number of people in Lisbon might influence events half-way around the world' (Law 1986: 235). However, the colonial centre's actual control did not extend beyond the *ecumene*, the immediate area over which European settlers asserted mastery. We should consider the *ecumene* as both an actual sphere of geopolitical control that was progressively shaped more according to European standards of civilisation and progress, and the visionary figment of an expansive European civility based on classical models of governance (e.g. Inglis and Robertson 2005). Beyond the *ecumene* was the sphere of influence, 'an intermediary area in which European or Euro creole traders, hunters, and other boundary crossers interacted with native peoples, serving as advance agents of settlement and contesting the presence of European rivals' (Turner Bushnell and Greene 2002: 2). However, Western modernity's onset in the South Americas would encroach even on spheres of influence, ultimately fashioning their cultures according to ecumenical rules. For progress would soon poison ecumenical imaginaries with the need to 'redeem' anything exotic (e.g. *éxo*, outside immediate influence) from modernity's vanishing spell (Ivy 1995).

Modern industrialisation and urbanisation enhanced this mode of engagement with nature by means of urban segmentation and the simultaneous romanticisation of indigeneity and rurality in the context of Lusophone nation building. Brazil followed suit by simultaneously 'anthropologising' its ethno-cultural peripheries and promoting its industrial-urban centres to zones of post-colonial progress (see DaMatta 1995 on Brazil's peripherality; Russell-Wood 2002b on Brazilian social sciences and racial prejudice; Herzfeld 2002 on crypto-colonialism and Europe). Such processes are not particular to Brazilian nation building, as the Greek and Thai cases (of multiculturalist assimilation) suggest. Ultimately, all national centres also desire 'the resources, the potency and potentiality, the "alien power" of the periphery, the wild, the forest. Both center and periphery seek to restore "vitality" in the exchange of powers' (Turton 2000: 25–6; Tzanelli 2008: 48–67, 99–126).

Though it is wrong to provide a linear narrative of contemporary Brazilian cosmopolitan desires, the invasion of European cosmographies in the New World certainly introduced alterations in local epistemologies (Firth 1961: 152; Dumont 1975: 156). The hermeneutic consequences of this invasion in Brazil have been transposed today onto the more opaque plain of global capitalist networks, where the country has to advertise its economic prowess without losing its cultural, political and intellectual autonomy. The present study rescues one structural similarity between colonial and capitalist conditions: the fact that external material value attained significance in productions of internal social value as transaction of ancient memory with the power of beings beyond national lands, in the exotic overseas world and the foreign provenience. Even money, as we will see, is implicated in such transactions as part of a 'creative diagram' of hierarchical power systems by being 'both the sedimented embodiment of accomplished power and the transactional mechanism for its attainment' (Parmentier 2006: 76). This transformation of material into social value is evident in representations of Amazonian people in the 2014 World Cup's opening ceremony, suggesting that Brazilian imaginaries are not immune to control mechanisms of foreign valuables and the conflation of appropriations of foreign identity with ethnocentricity (Harrison 1990, 1993; Hugh-Jones 1992; Barth 1969). It also affected (folk and elite) metropolitan claims of football as an exclusively Brazilian value good in the same context. On the one hand, this stresses structural depictions of order, but on the other it considers interpretative mechanisms in Brazilian culture's 'thick description' (Geertz 1973: 14).

The description suggests that social variables (race, class, gender) are only part of an invisible whole and cannot provide satisfactory explanation for the presence of cosmographic mobilities in the country. To adapt Shils's (1975) reflections on centres and peripheries, centrality may involve an order of symbols, values and beliefs as well as networks of institutions that define society's sacred centre, but post-colonial societies comprise centralities and peripheralities. Outside the reach of immediate internal and external control, peripheries form pockets of approximate independence, and may even retain their value systems. Their relative independence guides their twin romanticisation by national and tourist imaginaries in contexts such as those of the 2014 World Cup. Such peripheralities are imagined as self-contained spaces, because the centre wishes to preserve its cosmological autonomy from other centres. In reality, as a figment of central imaginaries, the autonomisation of socio-cultural peripheries conceals the desire to appropriate foreign cosmographies of riches. Presented simultaneously as the national centre's origins and the original 'gift' to world civilisation, peripheries sustain the desire for foreign cosmographic hunting as 'claims' to a once plundered property by the powerful.

Urry's argument suggests that there is a loose connection to be made between early modern productions of *mappaemundi* as a synthesis of global geography, world maps, dream theory (cosmopolitan desire) and the contemporary development of networks of power that operate 'from above' (hierarchically) and afar (via new technologies) (see Cosgrove 2003: 860; Szerszynski and Urry 2006; Tzanelli 2013b: 68–9, 76–7). Cosmographies of riches are always mapped onto cosmologies of national desire. They communicate with what is called 'grobalisation' ('the imperialistic ambitions of nations, corporations, organizations, and the like and their desire, indeed need, to impose themselves on various geographic areas') and 'glocalisation' ('the interpenetration of the global and the local, resulting in unique outcomes in different geographic areas'): the 'grobal' and the 'glocal' (Ritzer 2006: 338, 337; Andrews and Ritzer 2007: 137–8). Yet, by just focusing on grobal and glocal processes, we miss the epistemological particularities of localities, as well as their historical and cultural depth – a 'mistake' matching that of representing 'modernity' as the only mode of perception available to world cultures (see Eisenstadt 2001). It would, for example, be wrong to disregard that the contemporary technological innovations propagated by Brazil through the mega-event's staging connect to the ways colonial routes cut through South America before the dawn of European modernity (see Holton 2007 on the historical depth of globalisation) – or, more correctly, the ways such connections are imagined and narrated in creative ways by Brazilians today.

Here, imaginative movement *prescriptively* directs multiple flows from the global (with the old colonial centre as its *Urtext*) to the local, concealing the fact that mobilities are always enabled by the latter (Turner Bushnell and Greene 2002: 19). Historiographic and cosmographic accounts of this intentional 'error' concern the study of revolutionary changes in communications, transportation and mobility that Portuguese navigators, politicians and merchants created in the forging of the nascent Lusitanian empire. A yet younger generation of scholars (Rodrigues and Devezas 2007; Devezas and Modelski 2006) would argue that 'the Portuguese sailors, soldiers and commercial personnel of early modernity were true "pioneers of globalization", forging radically new methods, modes of thinking and forms of action, in the creation of long-distance forms of control and movement that were wholly unprecedented' (Inglis 2010: 4). Such claims ran parallel lives with memories of a European 'debt' to Brazilian culture that cannot be discharged (Sahlins 1972; Tzanelli 2008; Argyrou 2013). The 'situational value' (Appadurai 1986: 5; Sahlins 1965: 153) of Brazilian culture in global cosmographies of riches grants it the status of the global cosmological core, once ravaged by the Portuguese centre and used for its own prestige-building purposes (Russell-Wood 2002a: 108). The tale of unfair self-aggrandisement at the financial cost of the colonial periphery was channelled in contemporary narratives of neoliberal expansion with varied reactions. What is more important is that as a version of Brazil's colonial and early capitalist history, it exerts emotional attraction to the 'civilised world' and is used in transformations of Brazilian exoticism into a valuable commodity. Naturally, the idea that the Portuguese 'gave birth to globalization' (Rodrigues 2008: 9) downplayed the importance of the mobilities of slavery in favour of a technologisation of the world originating in Western modernity. As we will see in later chapters, this technology facilitated a Brazilian code switching from depth to surface, which can address the cosmetic demands of visitors better than the actual needs of Brazilian citizens.

Attention to this baffling Brazilian formalism has been connected to 'evidence' that 'south of the Rio Grande and below the equator' things just 'run on samba, *pisco* [blink, wink], *Caudillismo* [militarism], Carnival, and a kind of historical belly laugh that echoes through a "living museum"' (DaMatta 1991: 270). Today we know that in colonial Brazil, what was legal and illegal depended less on the act than on the individual's status and the context of the alleged transgression, and what was sinful or virtuous was defined on compromises between imported religious (Christian) beliefs and community standards (Kiddy 2000: 55; Russell-Wood 2002b: xv). As a result, in a society multicultural and multi-ethnic by necessity, 'appearances' would come, over the centuries, to acquire the same weight as 'being' – a legacy of the tumultuous colonial age (Goldschmidt 1998: 10). The production of discourses on the 'living museum' – still part of North American and Western European cultural perceptions of Brazilian *habitus* – promotes linear historicity without explaining the roots of secrecy in South American 'money economies' or the Brazilian ambivalence towards an individualist ethos (see Urry 2014: 18–20, on '*qualculation*' and citizen surveillance).

We must go the extra mile in order to comprehend that dichotomies between 'public' and 'private' spheres, individual and person, or *rua* and *casa* (street and house) (DaMatta 1991: 35), allow Brazilians to survive in a world of ruthless bureaucracy, where they need to possess the knack to transform nameless public functionaries into people with names, 'friends who can help' (Barbosa 1995, on *jeitinho*). I do not condone Brazilian cultures of secrecy, but suggest that its roots shed extra light on the Simmelian cultures of secrecy that Urry (2014) so eloquently analyses. For this reason, I endeavour to show how Brazilian cosmography's financial flows are connected to both filiative (based on blood relations) and affiliative (non-kinship and professional networks) relations, as where the economy is 'embedded' in society and subject to its moral laws, 'monetary relations are rather unlikely to be represented as the antithesis of bonds of kinship and friendship, and there is consequently nothing inappropriate about making gifts of money to cement such bonds' (Parry and Bloch 1989: 9). Such 'gifts' require *personalised* (family and family-like) relations, rather than individual (isolated) gestures of 'good faith'. Not only can the split between 'individual' and 'person' connect Brazilian value hierarchies to colonial epistemologies as 'cosmographies of riches' (DaMatta 1995: 275), but it explains how it is possible for a society still demonising (racialising, orientalising) its rogues, to grant the self-same *personae* with the mantle of celebrity in its globally broadcast imaginaries (ceremonies); under what conditions it attributes corruption to charismatic politicians; and why, against these odds, it still involves all of them in global monetary and cultural mobilities.

2 Aesthetics and practical action

Euro–Brazilian clashes and harmonisations

Brazilian stylistics: a panoramic view

Bærenholdt et al. (2004) have noted that places enclose performances defining them as (tourist or mega-event in our case) destinations. Considering their ceremonial-artistic and popular performances as aspects of their identity enhances those places' tourist reflexivity and produces their unique 'aesthetic grammar' – a grammar imprinted on their social landscape and hospitality potential (Lynch et al. 2011). Southern places-destinations, such as parts of Brazil, have informed colonial narratives of tropical utopias, which originate in European imaginaries of a prelapsarian cosmos. Originally, Europeans framed this fictional cosmos on island logic, reclusivity and social-as-natural holism – all the things damaged with the passage of Western industrial modernity (MacCannell 1989; Greene 2000). The fictional imaginary of perfection continues to guide tourist imaginaries, as these are manufactured by state and industrial stakeholders, transnational corporations, and maintained in individual tourist discourses. On the realist plane, Brazilian tourism policies have to refute this utopia openly as a counter-world to modern everyday existence and tourist consumption (Henning 2002: 183–4). It is no coincidence that as much as the country's artistic cosmopolitan ethos is characterised, like that of the Caribbean, by an interweaving of adventurous narratives of 'physical movement and imaginative migration' (Wardle 1999: 524–5, in Sheller 2004: 14), its ceremonial projections in mega-events cannot shake off the aesthetics of 'sedentary' *indigenismo*. This domesticated version of cosmopolitanism – what Aravamudan (1999: 6–7) terms 'tropicopolitanism' – maintained a dialogue with the former colonial and late capitalist powers on the nature of Brazilian character. Hence, the aesthetics of Brazilian tropicopolitanism are not altogether disconnected from the Western European 'beautiful' world image (Heidegger 1975, 1967) and the picturesque renditions of cultural nature as a way of 'world making' (Duncan 1999: 153; Dann 2002: 6).

We still inspect historical records to diagnose contemporary peculiarities. Brazil's place in European imaginaries of consumption proves crucial in this conjunction, as the country still retains the function of a global mobility node: a former colony, a destination for migrant groups from Europe, Africa,

Asia and the Americas, and a cultural 'melting pot', it was debated as an extension of the Darwinian terra nova, but also as an anthropological paradise. Its connection to the outside world by sea (the continent's basis of industrial life) and to inner life-worlds by land and rivers (the basis of family and communal life) consolidated its twin global profile as a South American regional centre (Schmitt 1996, 2006). Taking a leap forward, one may also add that the need to be seen as a strong emancipated nation is still better achieved for Brazil at the level of imaginary, utopian movement that art facilitates (Tzanelli 2014). It is significant that this move takes place in the spiritual domain when the pragmatic obstacles of recognition seem insurmountable: as Chatterjee has noted in a comparable case, the crucible of emancipatory post-colonial nationalism is the ideational sphere of culture that allows transcendence of the domains of civilisation and technology, where the post-colony is always found short of expectations (Chatterjee 1993: 3–5). Artistic expressions of this shift are actualised in mega-events through ameliorations of clashes of folk and subaltern (indigenous, slave) with high cultures (European, colonial) for the benefit of global tourist guests in ways that are impossible in realist contexts (Moreiras 1999: 133; Moreiras 2001: 252; Popovitch 2011: 37–9).

Here we can recall how Brazil's plot combines the need to move with the urgency to survey and control in order to understand the significance of hosting a mega-event. On the realist scene modern Brazilian governance ensured the country's much-debated political transition from a 25-year military dictatorship (1964–89) to a neoliberal democracy. This transition defined institutional organisation in three interconnected spaces: the military, the political and the bureaucratic (Nervo Codato 2006). Brazil's colonial experience generated links between the antiquated colonial stereotyping of cannibalism and another sort of visual 'anthropophagy', the voracious consumption of native exoticism. Visual anthropophagy became characteristic of Western Borgesian travellers, who could fall in love with the land and become natives, thus turning their journeys into 'darkness' into an educative experience (Tzanelli 2008: 178; Tzanelli 2013c). It seems futile, then, to talk about tourism and artistic expression independently from capitalist structuration and neoliberal expansion in the country; both over-determined conceptions of hospitality and collective self-perception in terms of civilised transaction with colonial/tourist incomers.

Memory always informs the present, so it is useful to examine colonialism's implication in the birth of Brazilian trans-modernity. Atlantic pathways such as those of post-colonial Brazil are good examples of the ways individual societies were woven into complex relations of global interdependence (Benjamin 2009). In federalised Brazil's case, uneven transitions to democracy in the 1970s harboured a fragmented governance model in which administrative maladjustment and the overall ill-defined functional boundaries between branches of the state became sources of infinite conflict, prompting bureaucrats to strengthen their ties with external 'allies' and 'clients'. The shameful military *getulismo* (authoritarianism), which took its name from the practices of Getúlio Vargas, became one of the permanent features of Brazilian society, which would later want to be seen as civilised Western-style. One of the main characteristics of *getulismo* is the so-called *jeitinho*, the practical skill of getting what one wants with little effort and at the expense of others, because one is a networked person (DaMatta 1991: 138–9). Though incorrect to build hypotheses on linear genealogies, *getulismo* mirrored the collective behaviour of both early Portuguese colonisers, who revelled in administering prestigious 'brotherhoods' in the Brazilian tropics (Russell-Wood 2002b: 136–9), and of African, Afro-Brazilian and indigenous slaves, whose limited guild presence was under constant surveillance by colonial bureaucracy. Both coloniser and colonised were socially organised in newly developed urban areas under strict kinship rules. Especially domestic arrangements and kinship ties were viewed by scholars as products of adaptive socio-cultural change rooted in systems of Afro-American beliefs and values, transmitted from generation to generation and comprising a cumulative collective experience (Durkheim 1969, 1992; Gutman 1976). Their transposition into purely organisational domains as network capital, or as values of 'corporate responsibility', was also originally conditioned by Portuguese bureaucracy.

There were good reasons why kinship bonds would provide the basis for network socialities, and why, by turn, these necessitated shadowy dealings with colonial bureaucracy. Afro-Brazilian practices of godparenthood (*padrinazgo*) or co-parenthood (*compadrazgo, compadrío*) provided slaves with the opportunity to establish an organisational network, when all other developmental possibilities were denied to them. Not only would the expansion of the filiative (blood-based) into an affiliative (non-blood) network would provide more flexibility in their negotiations with power, but it also enabled guild consciousness to flourish in post-abolition contexts. As was the case in many Mediterranean societies that experienced foreign rule (e.g. Campbell 1964: 218–24, 255; Herzfeld 1985: 20, 98, 106; Herzfeld 2001: 310–1), godparenthood developed into an interpretative mechanism of networking and became the passport to status acquisition by association with those who had achieved social recognition (Russell-Wood 2002a: 132; Russell-Wood 2002b: 188). The homological likeness of these practices to Vargas's surviving legacy is evident to date, suggesting that *getulismo* and *jeitinho* are not 'coloured' in a racist fashion, but derivative of hybrid (native and foreign) structures of experience. This experience views bureaucratic apparatuses as external to cosmological arrangements when they are definitional of Brazilian cosmological organisation.

This tension between desires for civility and real 'cultural intimacy' (Herzfeld 2005) prompts regional policy makers today to favour disorganised capitalism, allowing for continuities between (liberal) ideological discourse and (crypto-authoritarian) political practice, leading to a 'deficit in citizenship'. The onset of industrialisation and increased urbanisation transposed in big cities old citizenship struggles originating in the age of slavery. The strong tradition of Brazilian social movements was inextricably associated with the designated cradle of *Brasilidade* (Brazilian-ness) in the north-east – a region considered both 'underdeveloped' and multicultural within the nation-state. Social movements' historic connection to the Church fostered a philanthropic ethic that placed emphasis on the protection of vulnerable groups, sustainable development of international networks, human rights and the environment (Barreira 2011: 153), and was geared towards ideological alliances between Christianity and activist Marxism (Garrison 1996: 250).

However, the imported Cartesian cogito of European Christianity did not sit well with the native unity of mind and body that defined especially Afro-Brazilian ontologies. Using conceptions of *feitiçaria* (Portuguese *feitiço*: fetish) to define not only African religions, but also native lifestyles (Thornton 1988), Europeans projected their own mindset on Afro-Brazilian society, considering all rituals of social cleansing as 'witchcraft', works of a Devil who deceives the faithful with his simulacra (Russell-Wood 2002b: 114–5, 137–9). Places like Rio de Janeiro were dubbed by the Inquisition an 'inferno; a Babylon corrupted by the pernicious effects of slavery; a land of perdition; a Godless land whose people were libertines, listless, physically and morally weak and degenerate' (Russell-Wood 2002a: 110). For European incomers, the earthly world was marked by deceit, and perceptions could be used by the unfaithful; for Brazilians, the world was a natural *and* spiritual given and humans were part of both. Because 'being in the world' connects to knowledge pathways (epistemologies) (Schütz 1945), from the outset Brazilian self-presentations split between a (racialised) urgency to polish and whitewash civil surfaces and the agential project of acknowledging the country's ethno-cultural polyvocality but cultural-ontological unity. To be plural but one, is a Brazilian translation of organic solidarity (Durkheim 1997), a version of Herder's (1744–1803) romantic nationalism that views the national body as a coordinated whole of its living components (Smith 2000). Let us not forget that ethnic embodiment is regarded as a form of primitive orality that can be inscribed upon, manipulated and re-invented by the skilled (Derrida 1976: 84). I return to this in the following chapter, where I discuss the role of technology in Brazil as an interpretation of European notions of the corrupt networked person.

Notably, just like the London 2012 handover ceremony to Rio, the 2014 World Cup's ceremonial show focused on the ways the 'abject' Brazilian body of subaltern dancers choreographs – literally and metaphorically – Brazil's national body as a contested commodity (Radin 1996). The country's artistic pool is supported by past and present migrant mobilities from Europe and Africa, with traditions of embodied labour. However disadvantaged (if not because of their disadvantaged social standing), such human resources, institutionally recognised as subjects akin to Bauman's (1998) 'vagabonds', hardly lose the character of the journeyman and woman and never the ability and will to strike (Deleuze and Guattari 1988). Given Brazilian insistence to consider art and politics in unison, although I recognise artistic independence from the bureaucratic realm, I will not fully disconnect artistic concerns from the cultural contexts in which they are born. Artistic indifference to context is never apolitical; on the contrary, it constitutes a unique politics with a traumatic record in Brazil.

Connell (1995, 1987) reminds us that gender as a social category interacts with race, class and sexuality, and he uses the ancient Greek term *cathexis* to describe the gendered character of sexual desire and the practices that shape that desire in the 'gender order'. His analysis draws upon Freud's mechanical conceptions of *Bezeichnung* – a German translation of *cathexis* that refers to the functioning of psychosexual energies and the subject's investment of libido (Freud 1982: 381–2). I argue that Connell's intersectional theory defines Brazilian artistic creativity. The applicability of 'lashing out' mechanisms on group behaviour is as old as the project of critical theory but here I am more interested in *la longue durée* disconnections between politics and art that create and recreate economies of signs and the European economy of thought (Lash and Urry 1994; Argyrou 2013). The Brazilian artistic scenes of samba, Carnival and capoeira are haunted by the memory of political oppression, but when performances begin to travel the world, 'artistic caravans' become preoccupied with the translatability of such particular national *leitmotifs* rather than overt productions of political statements. 'Travel' itself is *cathexis*: it works as a liberation from the past, opening up new entrepreneurial horizons. Exotic interiorities and marginalities (the ceremony's indigenous people and flora) might commonly project vulnerable or uncouth modes of social being (see Mannheim 2003 on 'social volition'), but in World Cup ceremonies they can also be accommodated into non-paternalistic cultural self-presentations.

For this reason the structures and forms of the ceremony were borrowed from everyday life rituals of extraordinary cosmological proportions. These rituals abstracted masculine and feminine habitus and produced movie-like simulacra of Brazilian sociality to enter a dialogue with global audiences. Geertz's discussion of Balinese cockfight rituals as both amplifications of the 'narcissistic male ego' (Geertz 1973: 419) and grand cosmological statements social institutions use in political discourse is a useful starting point (Smith 2008). To distance themselves from harmful associations with Brazil's authoritarian past and make sense to global audiences, the artistic directors included in their narrative domesticated forms of abject but marketable socialities and intimacies. In this conjunction the poetics of the nation-state (as in Herzfeld 2005) and artistic poetics (as in Wolff 1984, 1987) commenced a dialogue replete with conflict and revisions. In what follows I argue that this troublesome Brazilian 'dialogue' rested its case on the bureaucratisation of performance genres (samba, capoeira) which framed national self-narration within the nation's culturally fragmented domain and outside it as tourist commodities.

The rejection of bureaucratic tropes not only defined artistic ceremonial genres but informed the tropicopolitan content of fan reactions to Brazil's loss to Germany. As is the case with Moroccan society, interpersonal communication in Brazil is agonistic and characterised by the struggle to seize what is coveted or recover what is lost (Geertz 1983: 114). Such Brazilian styles were framed around ideas of (masculine) violence and (feminine) eroticism, and enacted a critical thanatourist journey based on pastiche and embodied mobilities (Geertz 1973; Alexander 1987; Trondman 2011: 154). Freud's and Marcuse's (1955) pairing of *éros* with *thánatos*, and Dann and Seaton's (2001) examination of slavery as 'dissonant heritage' in global tourisms are pivotal for an examination of the teleology of artistic tourist desire here. A striking homology develops between the migration of Brazilian communities outside the national domain and the global mobility of subaltern, lumpen genres outside Brazilian bureaucratic discourse that thrives on emotional withdrawal and performative irony (Sarlo 1988 in Popovitch 2011: 42; Nietzsche 1996; Scheler 2003; Tzanelli 2011). The political conditions in the country have altered significantly over the last decade, but the historical phantom of violence still looms large, constantly re-activating mechanisms of withdrawal from the national public sphere.

It is true that Brazilian human demography is very diverse and often regionally disconnected, with ethnic groups observing different customs, religious beliefs and lifestyles. Rio's and São Paulo's own ambivalent status (as regional social and financial articulations and post-colonial phantasmagorias far away from North American and European cultural industries) is reflected in the ways their artistic sentiments promote policies of 'reaching out' to national peripheries and marginal discourses so as to fuse and traffic them abroad as new 'world cultures' (on which, consult Nagib 2011). The process of 'reaching out' to traffic repositories of ethnic memory is recognised as a global manifestation of post-colonial artistic movements with a mission to transmute earlier proletarian and folkloric modes of socialist realism into forms of what became part of magical realism in Latin America. The handover's cultural mosaic is not immediately available to global audiences and the ceremonies artistic directors and performers have to find effective ways to communicate its complexity. As a result, they have to speak in playful riddles on behalf of the country's most desired cityscapes and those who have no voice, despite their ceremonial representation. This responsibility resembles what Rancière recognises in the politics and ethics of academic work, which should undermine the privileged position of those who wish to speak for others, 'be it the proletariat, the poor, or anyone who "is not destined to think"' (Rancière 2004: xii). De Sousa Santos (Barreira 2011) speaks in this cultural context of a 'sociology of absences', the ability of institutional frameworks to erase or amplify disenfranchised voices that escape through cracks of officialdom into global spheres. The terms 'absent presence' and 'sociology of absences' do not point to the discourse of slavery per se, but revert instead to traces Borgesian travellers redeem as tourist tokens (Thompson 2012: 42). The idea of a looming 'absent presence' can also be considered regionally, as the margins are always subjected to anthropologisations by the centre, which thinks of itself as more attuned to European imaginaries of civility (Herzfeld 2002). It is worth remembering that hybridity is as much an artistic as it is a political tool (Nederveen Pieterse 2006a). It is this continuity between art and politics that turns the art of football into the most important stamp on Brazil's cosmopolitan passport.

The curse of beauty: gender (dis-)symmetry, racial-class hierarchy and the Brazilian human

Harmonising tropicopolitan and cosmopolitan perceptions of the world has been one of Brazil's cosmic projects. This amounted to the creation of civil society (a *pólis*) through replacement of *kósmos* with the tropics. However, if Western European civility was beautiful in the sense that it was good and virtuous – the twin heritage of Aristotelianism and Neoplatonism (Aristotle 1924, I, book B, chapter 8: 198b–199b; Aristotle 1946) – Brazilian civility would turn a cosmetic surface into cosmic value. Appearances matter in a culture regulated by hierarchy: when to be (a respected person) is based on them, surface becomes replete with meaning – it becomes an interpretative mechanism of socio-cultural reality and the good and beautiful world. For these reasons, what amounts to 'Brazilian Truth' encompasses visions of a nascent culture, always ready to mature into a beautiful product. Currently, this mirrors globalisation imperatives and the urgency to develop: this young entity is playful like a childish tourist, dexterous like a pre-conscious body and in need of putting into new digital frames that favour what Ong (1982) describes as 'second orality'. However, where modern colonisers instilled in the country the machine of scripture from outside, post-modern natives installed a spectacle machine originating in the country's urban centres.

This clash within the Brazilian cultural project is nicely encapsulated in the ancient Greek term *ómorfos* that denotes the beautiful being (the equivalent of Brazilian *belo*). As opposed to *õraíos*, the beautiful of time that comes to pass and to *kallós*, the aesthetically and morally ideal being that conforms to Kantian notions of beauty, *ómorfa* beings appealed to the Pythagorean principles of symmetry and the architectonics of image, so to speak (the Brazilian *lindo/a* as part of human *physis* or nature). With an emphasis on surfaces and form, Pythagorean discourse communicates with Lucretius's combination of body and emotion that inspired Spinoza's observation on power geometries and the physical effects of human affects (Adey 2010: 164–5). Brazilian ethno-cultural dispositions to *omorfiá* created a philosophical medley that at least in the contemporary discourse on sports confuses nurtured skills with ethno-racial (black) capacity (Bales 2004). The same discourse would inform Brazilian national identity that framed civilisational beauty in terms of what we know as 'style' or character (Born and Hesmondhalgh 2000: 20–1). However, European colonisation produced a bifurcated narrative of identity as otherness, a heterological trope akin to that we encounter in the ill-defined domain of the Caribbean (De Pina-Cabral 2008: 234–5; Sheller 2003, 2004).

This bifurcation challenged the native search for 'typicality' in everyday situations, propelling adjustments to perceptions of socio-cultural reality that guided future native action (see Schütz and Luckmann 1973: 241). First of all, the Brazilian world of 'actual reach', the immediate knowledge of Brazilian social environs, began to be viewed by natives as both an intimate internal territory and a cosmetic surface for external consumption. Although centuries after colonisation Brazilian modes of art are still engaging in Western-style counter-colonial games (Dikötter 2008; Law 2010), globalisation imperatives replace the memory of slavery with narratives of lifestyle consumption, cinematic and tourist mobilities. Foreign observers espoused and globally disseminated the demonic trope of native anthropophagy to validate representations of specific human types, but Brazilians used them to validate thanatourist practices (Dann and Seaton 2001), so as to honour ancestry. Following Mbembe's (2003) analysis of 'necropolitics' which recognises the power of death as a state of non-existence, Tate (2011) suggested that oscillation between terror, love and romance allowed for the production of a critical post-colonial discourse in which choosing to die (as native sacrifice) responded to the Western tourism, sex trafficking and racist idealisation. This sacrificial revolt betrayed the natives' inability to inhabit the world of 'attainable reach': to comprehend but also fully and equitably participate in Western anthropophagies (Schütz and Luckmann 1973: 40). In many ways, Kantianism landed on Brazilian soil the moment European settlers discovered this otherworldly, 'demonic' *topos*, at once fearful and *ómorfos* in their writings.

Brazil's metaphysical background resurfaces in the 2014 World Cup ceremonies and the episodes that followed the defeat of its football team. Though tempting to consider both instances as mere examples of global consumption of sports, the exotic venues and the host, they merit consideration as contexts in which rituals blend the quotidian with the sacred to re-narrate experience. Ingold (1996) and Lowenthal (1985) remind us that we are all too inclined to populate the past with people like ourselves, pursuing the same aims and responding with similar feelings, albeit dressed up in different cultural costumes, that 'otherness is … reduced to the cosmetic variety of consumer choice' (Ingold 1996: 204). However, ceremonial Brazil emerges in both instances as *linda maravilhosa* (marvellously beautiful): through a cosmetic spectacle of dance, music and celebrity appearances in the World Cup ceremonies, and through pop displays of national style in reactions to the loss of the Cup. The blended (elite and pop) spectacle is based on the very intersectional paradox that defines identity essentialisations in the 'Brazilian dilemma' (DaMatta 1991): globally Brazil is *linda*, a beautiful feminised being travelling the world in her easily translatable cosmetic form; nationally, its peripheries are *lindas* as exotic entities in need of ecosystemic conservation under global laws. However, the country's image is further broken down into less civilised, dark and masculine fragments. These fragments partake in global cultural circuits only as a 'new black aesthetic' (Denzin 2002), but in the national domain, they codify a national crisis. The crisis uses an intersectional vocabulary that colours the otherness of class, gender and ethnicity in moral terms. To respond to European moral imperatives, a male and coloured working-class-ness would emerge as Brazil's uncivilised demon.

The harmonisation of Brazil's civilisational hierarchy with global hierarchies of value was not a straightforward process: what in domestic domains translated into a binarism between art and craft had begun as a split between *epistéme* and *téchne* in European thought (Stiegler 1998; Parry 2003; Frabetti 2011). Heavily influenced by a fictionally uniform Hellenic heritage, comprising a textual palimpsest 'salvaged' by African, Byzantine and Renaissance scholars, early Western European philosophy would not identify itself as a technology. Ancient Greek understandings of knowledge as *epistéme* (from *epístamai*: standing on top, knowing well, mastering) had issued a divorce from fifth-century Athenian understandings of *téchne*, the Sophist rhetorical skill of constructing political arguments. The Sophist's skilfulness came in direct conflict with the Socratic search for truth via *maieftikí*, the art of searching for the truth in the form of self-knowledge (*gnôthi s'aftón*: know thyself). Contemporary Greek interpretations of *maieftikí* as midwifery resemble the leap from European to Brazilian hermeneutics of *téchne* as proto-national craft, 'giving birth' to imagined communities as biological beings-in-the-world – useful these days only as an exotic tourist commodity. As nationalised and commoditised folklore 'associated with the emergence of national consciousness and glorified as the repository of ancient skills' (Herzfeld 2004: 5), Brazilian *téchnes* comprised a complex of crafts and mannerisms of disreputable nature (samba and *malandragem* being part of the same complex).

What proved to be the real turning point in the split between ancient Greek understandings of téchne and *epistéme* was Aristotle's (1984, book 6: 3–4) definition of the 'technical being' as a being with no end in itself, hence a tool to serve someone else's ends. The demotion of the *technítis* or technical human to an instrument echoes both Weber's *Zweckrationalität* ('instrumental/goal rationality'), a type of social action that involves the calculation of the most efficient means to the desired ends (Gerth and Mills 1948: 56–7), and Marx's critique of human alienation from labour and production tools. Indeed, the onset of modernity and industrialisation conceded *téchne* as technology with utilitarian value, but also led to dehumanising associations of labour with capitalist profit making. However, in the contexts of the Discoveries and colonisation, ancient Greek conceptions of *téchne* would also encompass technologies of writing, which philosophers such as Plato (1974) had associated with amnesia. The loss of memory or *anámnesis* was predicated on the suggestion that writing technologies, including the art of poetry, were instrumental, hence crafts in the service of power that drift humans away from the truth. Unlike that of Plato, European modernity's self-establishing essence of technology is focused on mastery (*Herrschaft*), which is responsible for the division of the world into subject and object (Moran 2012: 267–8). To reconstruct both Foucault (1980, 1989) and Derrida (1976), *téchne* has come closer to modernity's epistemic objectives of articulating the object of mastery, hence subjecting it into alien 'power grammars'. This is how Brazilian understandings of technology as an imported colonial good would be accommodated into native cosmographies of riches: while retaining their original ambiguity as a craft, written speech and its accompanying (embodied) ritual would be placed at the service of regional centres that controlled indigenous and slave peripheries.

However, nationalisation and trans-modernisation would also prompt urban centres (Brazil's capitalist nodes) to utilise téchne in education, literature and the *belles artes*. Following Western rules, these *téchnes* have become part of post-modern *epistemic* or knowledge economies in the service of national prestige, but their origins in technological labour as working-class culture, tightly connected to peripheral custom and African cosmologies does great disservice to this objective, if not manipulated into a palatable civilised performance. Just as mechanical technology masters the natural environment, such *téchnes* can master Brazilian nature or character (*Brasilidade*). The technics of Afro-Brazilian crafts can only meet the world as polished art, which is as alien to those centralised technology represents as Vargas's bureaucratic surveillance.

We should not dissociate the ceremonial spectacle's provision of such conflicting representations from academic and political discourses of Portuguese 'exceptionalism': on the one hand, Eurocentric myths about the Portuguese explorer who promoted singlehandedly a distinctive 'globalist vocation' (Inglis 2010: 7) forget the centrality of Lisbon's migrant groups clustered in trading and technological innovation (Genoese, Florentines, Flemings, French, German, English and Castilian Jews) (Gunn 2003; Newitt 2005). On the other, they attribute particular progressive traits (pragmaticism, entrepreneurialism, technical know-how) exclusively to the very Lusophone cultures of conquest that would reappear in early Brazilian representations of the Portuguese conquest as 'friendly' and 'mild'. It is this 'mildness' that the coloniser habitually attributed to the 'weaker sex', which, like the colonised lands, could be moulded into more 'palatable', aesthetically pleasing forms for consumption (Enloe 1990; McClintock 1995). This invisible subjection still manifests in more contemporary rejections of the idea that art and spirituality are 'endemic to economic activity, rather than superfluous or in opposition to it' (Molotch 2003: 13), and suggest that making and appreciating art are for those to whom we can assign 'the unessential tasks: women and effete or neurotic men' (Molotch 2004: 343). Thus, despite their usefulness as a domestic mastery tool, even the arts have today to be subjected to the craft of politics, so as to gain public recognition – masculinised pursuit in the country. The matrix of the Brazilian 'gender order' is based on such contradictions so as to gauge global against national needs.

As 'ornamentation' and, by association, art and design are stereotyped as 'feminine preoccupations' (De la Fuente 2007: 419), the European orientalisms of South America are wilfully equalised to colonial cultural 'ornamentalisms' (Cannadine 2002). Since the colonial experience had cast women slaves as more portable property, endorsing concubinage and interracial marriage partnerships as convenient commerce in human flesh (Russell-Wood 2002b: 162–3), artistic ornamentalism in Brazil would never shake off its connotation as prescriptive mobility. Although art and heritage were tied to Brazilian (home)land as property through such processes of naming and claiming, contemporary artscapes would come to 'do' the 'dirty job' other domestic (political) 'operators' could not openly claim 'at home': trafficking in ideas and talent abroad. To complement this stereotypical logic, the 'male brutishness' of Brazilian football would be considered a global stylistic asset and transformed into the guardian of post-colonial nationalism. Here we tap into the opposite terrain of denigrated working class-ness and its ambivalent role in contemporary consumption styles that are used as models of happiness and well-being (Bauman 2007a). Emphasising Brazilian football's 'black masculine ethos' compares to the ways in which appearances control ideas of beauty phenomenally. Today we associate these assumptions with Gobineau's conviction that 'true', 'pure' races are always both aristocratic and male, whereas inferior races are inevitably corrupted by female procreation practices (miscegenation, creolism) (André 1985). In football's case, the onus of social visibility – again a globally sanctioned visibility through talent trafficking – merely replaces conventional notions of (feminine) beauty with projections of the right, nationally honed 'style' of play, displayed only by gifted players who can attain access to desirable positions (Machado-Borges 2009; Skeggs 1997, 2004). Machado-Borges (2014) convincingly debates how visual mechanisms at play in processes of social categorisation in Brazil link physical appearance, morality and social hierarchies. Bearing the damaging effects of Lusotropical perception, Brazilian popular cultures tend discursively to link bodies, physical appearance, morality and social hierarchies. The emphasis of the Brazilian World Cup ceremonies on cosmetic appearances is therefore deeply ingrained in the country's racist and sexist legacies that feminise and racialise the desire of those lacking in status for inclusion in world politics (Nederveen Pieterse 2006b; Tzanelli 2011).

In conclusion, it may not be incorrect to consider the importance of gender, class and race/ethnicity as a unity in Brazilian self-presentations. By this I do not mean that we should have recourse to traditional intersectional studies, but view intersectional performativity as an essential self-presentational tool. The Brazilian Geertzian 'cockfight' and its cosmetic dimensions remind us that cultural politics has its own aesthetics, which draws on the aesthetic politics. I can only draw on the ways Brecht's politicised art builds on an extremely complex and cunning equilibrium between forms of political pedagogy and artistic modernism to explain the gendered structure of the 'Brazilian dilemma', stressing the latter's emphasis on fragmentation and hybridisation as a response to modernity's cultural alien-ness (Brecht 1964). Brazil's Brechtian theatre has an epic flair that nevertheless undermines the legitimacy of 'great art' even in state-sanctioned ceremonial environments (e.g. Rancière 2004: 57–8). Intersectional symbolisations in everyday performances and utterances, but also exceptional ceremonial contexts draw on immediate social experiences of classification.

Take, for example, Cannadine's (2002: 6–8) contentious argument that British perceptions of the colonised were not over-determined by processes of orientalisation-as-racialisation (e.g. Said 1978), but instead replaced race with class hierarchies, because these appealed more to British social experience 'at home'. If anything, this suggests that social variables such as class entered the coloniser's perceptual spectrum, as much as they affected that of the colonised. Cannadine's emphasis on phenomena links cultural symbolisation to status, which is desired by Brazil in global politics. I argue that symbolic intersectional characteristics are constitutive of Brazilian self-presentations in 2014, and their historical depth ascribes Brazilian-ness with formalistic characteristics. To complete the country's socio-cultural discourse on civility, we need to unpack the politics and metaphysics of Brazilian *futebolarte.*

Futebolarte*'s deep play in Brazil*

Football represents Brazilian identity's opposing stereotyped pole, which emphasises its mobile black male qualities. Yet, as I endeavour to explain, both gendered narratives share the racist and class subtext ascribed to tropicalised identities of the 'lower orders'. Moreover, as explained before, it is incorrect to dissociate the game and its popular imaginaries from the aesthetics of the mega-event's ceremonial art, just because sport is not 'artistic' as, unlike art, it is purposive: it always involves the aim of scoring and winning (Best 1995: 380–1). Inglis and Hughson's (2000: 283) argument, that 'sport stylistics' as form of play embodied in players is intrinsically aesthetic, matches my argument that football stylistics tends simultaneously to fulfil aesthetic, pragmatic and political ends. Football stylistics often partakes in nationalist teleologies, which in our case are rooted in the very cosmologies of homeland of the 2014 ceremonial scripts. The emphasis on home territory provides ceremonies with spatial contours that are experienced in a semi-religious fashion, just like the player experiences and enacts the virtual space of the football field. Otherwise known as zone 14, this field is entered only by charismatic initiates, skilled football players who can perform a sort of magic by 'floating' through the field of play, eluding the gaze of spectators and scoring masterful goals (Coghlan 1990). One may argue that the 'reciprocal relationship between the space of zone 14 and aesthetic play' (Inglis and Hughson 2000: 286) corresponds to Pierre Bourdieu's analysis of art, power and what he terms *illusio.* We are already exploring Brazilian *futebolarte*'s phenomenological dimensions that will expose the game's 'magic' as another version of *Brasilidade*'s practical-as-poetic knowledge: the embodied experience of being and acting as a Brazilian.

Bourdieu (1998) warns that 'habitus' and 'field' are ontologically complicit, because different power alliances collude (*collusio*) in *ex post festum* rationalisation of a tacit form of belief – what he terms, in a manner compatible with Merton's (1948: 506) sociology and Geertz's anthropology of style (Alexander 2004; Giesen 2011: 172–4), *illusio*. He would suggest that 'the competitive game is a polarised "field of force" … consisting of opposed positions determined by reciprocal relations in a network of objective relations … rooted in an unequal distribution of different forms of capital: economic, cultural, social and symbolic' (Albertsen and Diken 2003: 3). Instead of considering *collusio* in relation to straightforward habitus transfers from plane to plane, I examine it in terms of a more spontaneous distribution of character or disposition (*dispositif*) outside the main fields of domination. Habitus transfers from artworlds to lifeworlds might be restricted to monetary imperatives (cash flows), whereas the customary immanence of cultural disposition in the arena and the ceremonial field transcends monetary imperatives. Like magicians, football players score a goal in distinctive national styles, performing an 'athletic *Candomblé*', so to speak, corresponding to Brazilian dispositions. This theatrical or magical exposure of *dispositif* or habitus is also constitutive of the ways Brazilian cosmologies are presented ('interpreted') as African-European on the ceremonial stage. Like Geertz's (1973) 'deep play', football-artistic magic 'tricks' audiences into believing that *Brasilidade* truly exists as an autonomous mode of being and mastering one's nature into culture. Schiller's *Spieltrieb* or 'play-principle' gestures towards the same reconciliation between the main antinomies of human life (the rational capacities of Mind and the sensuous components of Nature) in a synthesis producing Beauty (Miller 1986: 91–2; Inglis and Hughson 2000: 291). *Futebolarte* is therefore a less conscious but fully inculcated aspect of the art of being a Brazilian.

However, Brazilian culture *arte* and *futebolarte* are not enacted only in visual fields (Merleau-Ponty 1962), but on a kinaesthetic plane that defines Brazilian heritage at large. Brazilian *futebolarte* thrives on a convergence of the mental and the material, or the imagining terrains and physical environments, in what appears to be a holistic ontology (Ingold 2010: 16–7). Though these meditations are grounded in a fundamental distinction between 'inside' and 'outside' forms of knowledge, they turn to kinaesthetic ('perambulatory') practices for thought composure. Nevertheless, in contemporary technological athletic fields, football professionals tend to filter other senses through the gaze. Merleau-Ponty's anti-Cartesianism replaced divides between Mind and Body with a *problématique* over Abstraction and Practice as perception and sense. There have been cultures around the world (amongst them some of Afro-Brazilian origins), whose philosophical matrices were based on multisensory perception and varied ideas of 'visibility'. Magic's tangible qualities, for example, over-determine, in African cultures, connections to the world of nature and that of spirits in multisensory ways (see McCreery 1995).

The myth of Afro-European play as Brazilian artistry is crucial, so we should not drop stereotyping from the 'panoramic picture'. Yet, the fact that other rival football nations do not enjoy the composition of Brazil's 'ethnic mix', is not in itself an explanation of Brazil's decades-long pre-eminence in the game. If we adopt this line of explanation of Brazilian supremacy we resort to racist fantasies of a nation that owes its successes 'to the "animal suppleness" of the blacks and the "amazing flexibility of their ankles"' (Mason 1995: 122). Other characteristics attributed to Brazilian play may also invoke suspicions of racial prejudice: these include the reputation of Brazilian players for alleged 'spontaneity' or even 'surrealism' compared to the 'organised physicality of the Europeans' (ibid.: 123) that would come back to haunt Brazil's historic 2014 loss to the Germans. Though compatible with the tropes of *saudade* and *felicidade*, such discussions redeem *Brasilidade* as an anti-European phenomenon, marked in the football field by what Brazilian sociologist Gilberto Freyre (1945: 421, in Foster 2003: 74) saw in 'a conjunction of qualities of surprise, guile, astuteness, swiftness, and at the same time the brilliance of individual spontaneity'. Writing during a two-decade dictatorship, Freyre came to represent a major paradigmatic shift in Brazilian social sciences. His argument that *futebol* is no less than Brazil's racial heritage, 'a tropical hybrid (European technology infused with Amerindian and African psychic forces)' (Freyre 1964: vii–viii, in Foster 2003: 82), transposed tropicopolitan discourses into the game's 'social field' (Bourdieu 1993).

This discourse capitalised on binary stylistic oppositions between European Apollonian (tactical, teamwork-based, rationally organised) and Brazilian Dionysian spirits (spontaneous and individualistic, closely associated with blacks and mulattoes) (Freyre 1964: vii–viii, in Foster 2003: 83). The formulaic opposition corresponds to tourist modes of mobility that in (post) modern environments promote seemingly paradoxical combinations of individualistic play and consumerist pilgrimage on the one hand, and collective activist action on the other (Graburn 1977, 1983, 2004; Tribe 2008; Tzanelli 2013b). Freyre's nationalistic intention to rehabilitate the *mulatto* in national consciousness was predicated on a Darwinian-like theory of 'Luso-tropicalism', the Portuguese quality of 'plasticity' both towards the environment and in attitudes towards people of other 'races' (Russell-Wood 2002b: 11, 14–8). Despite football's involvement in celebrations of *Brasilidade*, the pursuit of foreign riches would eventually dictate the slow replacement of native fluidity, spontaneity and 'ballet-like elegance' with 'European training methods and more "scientific" forms of strategy' (Levine 1980a: 455) – closely related to the game's professionalisation in 1933–4. This change is of both social and cosmological proportions: socially, it ensured that more poor black players could enter the game, even if it simultaneously reinforced their economic and tactical subjection to the Europeanised football-run elites. Cosmologically, it complied with an old Luso-Brazilian conviction concerning cultural capital, which would reappear in post-1960s tourist milieux: movement from Europe to the 'tropics' is acceptable only as either a pleasurable (travel, holidays, artistic and pedagogical activity) or a commercial pursuit (colonial or capitalist domination) (Sheller 2003, 2004; Loizos and Papataxiarchis 1991: 226). In tropicalised contexts, reverse movements from Brazil to Europe would be considered as migration of the underdeveloped professionals to the world's former centre (Europe, later North America) in search for riches (a football career).

Football's 'delayed' alignment with European cosmographies can be traced in the way the game was imported and adopted in Brazil (1894) at a time when the old monarchical regime ended and the country entered a non-slave-based period (1888) of republican government (1889). The ensuing transformation of a rural, agrarian society into an urban and industrial one led in the first decades of the twentieth century to massive internal migrations from the country to the cities and the subsequent formation of an urban proletariat. Though brought to Brazil by English immigrants, football was initially adopted by sectors of the new educated urban elites, who disapproved of the participation of blacks and *mestizos* in the game. However, the elites' defence of an all-white, highbrow football was challenged in 1923, when the *mulatto* working-class Vasco de Gama became the Rio de Janeiro champion, and then in 1933, when the game was professionalised and players began to receive salaries. The change signalled nation-wide shifts from regimes of conspicuous leisure (in which football was an amateurish elite pastime) to regimes of conspicuous consumption (in which the game became a spectacle for all, and incorporated lowbrow working-class players as objects of consumption and *ersatz* celebrities) (Veblen 1899, 1904).

A national 'archaeology' of Brazilian football leads straight back to the symbolically gendered subtext or 'archplot' of the country's tropicalised cosmography of riches. The 1930s experienced the death of the Old Republic and the birth of a state headed by President Getúlio Vargas. Vargas's emphasis on political centralisation and his preoccupation with national integration as Brazil's developmental pathway was also coupled with planning over labour matters as a strategy of control. These changes were grafted onto the 1934 Constitution and its 1937 Mussolini-inspired revision through provision of a minimum wage, set working hours, the right to union representation, social security, the establishment of a judicial body for arbitrating conflicts between workers and bosses, and the harmonic accommodation of the different social-ethnic groups (Gordon and Helal 2001: 144). Vargas's desired 'national unity' was strongly influenced by fascist corporatism and European nationalist trends, thus implicating the game in revisions of Brazilian cultural 'profiling'. From now on, 'appearances' would matter more and more in global presentations of the country's 'racial democracy'. If Freyre's (1964) intellectual corpus represented colonialism's 'racial miscegenation' as the core of Brazilian national prowess, sporting journalist Mário Rodrigues Filho's reporting transformed football into a sport appealing to the expectations and tastes of the public, thus achieving its acceptance of Vargas's corporatism (Leite Lopes 1997). Filho's unequivocal defence of football professionalism as 'a means towards the emancipation of blacks, a necessary condition for the constitution of football as a national sport', and his involvement in the construction of Estâdio do Maracanã to host the 1950 World Cup as a 'glorification' of

Brazilian love for football (Filho 1964 in Gordon and Helal 2001: 157) provide a link to the present study's 2014 context.

As European football tactics were strongly endorsed by the dictatorship – responsible for contriving the team's slogan, 'In sport as in life, integration brings victory' (Murray 1996: 121), and appropriating its song, '*Pra Frente Brasil!*' (Forward Brazil!) as the theme tune to promote its program at political rallies and even in television commercials – their mode as exogenous intervention into Brazilian everyday life gradually became enmeshed in ideas of bureaucratic surveillance. The regime's censorial policies were such that even Pelé himself was shamelessly used by the football establishment and the military regime from 1970 to endorse their doctrines, embody their values and rally national pride (Foster 2003: 83). Questioned by a Uruguayan journalist in 1972 about his country's military dictatorship, he responded: 'There is no dictatorship in Brazil. Brazil is a liberal country, a land of happiness. We are a free people. Our leaders know what is best for [us], and govern [us] in a spirit of toleration and patriotism' (Levine 1980b: 244). Brazil's political leaders had paved a rocky way to synchronisation through rather tight regulation of sporting activity. Before the 1988 Constitution, which abolished the 1944-founded Conselho Nacional de Desportos (CND) with the objective of 'orientating, fiscalising and incentivating [sic] the practice of sports in the country' (Gordon and Helal 2001: 145), football clubs were organised into regional federations. These federations were subject to the rules of the Confederação Brasileira de Desportos (CBD) and, after 1979, the Confederação Brasileira de Futebol (CBF), with the CND acting as their normative agency (but with executive powers to intervene in federations and clubs).

This highly specific combination of authoritarian technologies of power, increased bureaucratisation of social life and maintenance of kinship values had grave consequences for football. The turbulent transition to democratisation did not ameliorate the crisis, as by 1994 the game was solidly structured around practices of *Caudillismo* (militarism) and *jeitinho*, which individual clubs had to employ to survive the global onset of liberalism. By the end of the 1990s and the beginning of 2000s, scandals involving football's administrative elite and accusations of corruption and fraud aimed at Wanderley Luxemburgo, the former manager of the Brazilian national team, reached their zenith in two Parliamentary Commissions of Inquiry (CPIs), one in the House of Deputies and one in the Federal Senate, which aimed at investigating the nature of contracts between the CBF and the Nike multinational corporation. The CBF also asked the Fundação Getúlio Vargas (a non-governmental organisation for socio-economic research) to provide a *Plano de Modernização do Futebol Brasileiro* (plan for the modernisation of Brazilian football), which the commissions found to be characterised by a lack of professionalism, credibility, manager and referee qualification training, appropriate salaries and leadership (Gordon and Helal 2001: 140). Based on a series of 'facts' translated with the help of Western ethical vocabularies, but little consideration of Brazil's cultural idiosyncrasies, the reports dictated a path to athletic modernisation as *synchronisation*: the alignment (*sýn*) of local temporal (*chrónos*) needs with those of the 'developed world' (also Tzanelli 2011: 141–2).

As synchronisation presupposes movement, it obliges individual humans and communities to traverse spatial frames: this is how mobilities are actualised, after all (Cresswell 2001, 2006, 2010). However, when the state and its supporters tried to blend the Brazilian *time*frame into alien *spatial* coordinates, they produced a cosmographic discourse that recognised *kósmos* as a cosmetic entity. Otherwise put in football language, Brazilian racial democracy could 'walk' the high road of celebrity in global domains if it were 'sold' to the developed world as unique Brazilian 'style', part of an immanent national character that developed over the centuries on a single temporal platform (Tarde 1903; Fabian 1983; Tonkonoff 2013). A typically Brazilian 'style' of football allegedly expressed specific traces of the Brazilian 'character' or 'spirit', which placed particular emphasis on the theory of harmony between European and African, white and black. The idea that Brazilian football appeared, on the pitch, as a sort of 'dance', which expressed characteristics such as cunning, art, musicality, *ginga* (swing) and spontaneity (Gordon and Helal 2001: 146) comprised Brazil's particular character and capitalised on images of the athletic, sexualised body as a celebrity mechanism. The Brazilian 'style of play' might be individually expressed, but remains representative of a hidden ontological whole. By collecting titles across different spatial frames, the Brazilian artistic-athletic body would manage to carve a place of its own among nations (Gordon and Helal 2001: 147–8; DaMatta 1982, 1995; Lever 1983). In this phenomenal concoction, traumatic memories – their *tempos Brasileiros* – had to take a back seat to allow the nation's inclusion into the dominant 'world picture' (Heidegger 1967; Lash and Urry 1994: 230). Both domestic (political and administrative) and international (criticism) pressures would result in the post-1982 exodus of *futebolarte* abroad, with many talented players joining European teams and seeking naturalisation on professional grounds (also Veblen 1914).

Time, heritage and the ritual nature of Brazilian well-being

In this concluding section, I wish to explain how ceremonial art and football interlink; how they link with popular protest in understandings of Brazilian heritage; and how all three partake in conceptions of well-being. There is a differentiation to make between inside and outside, the rule of kinship and the rule of law, so as to understand how the Brazilian dilemma works in the study's transnational sites. Official conceptualisations of heritage in conventions ratified by the United Nations Educational, Scientific and Cultural Organization (UNESCO) split it into intangible/immaterial ('the practices, representations, expressions, knowledge, skills – as well as the instruments, objects, artifacts, and cultural spaces associated therewith', from the 2003 Convention on the Safeguarding of the Intangible Cultural Heritage of

Humanity), and tangible/material ('sites that bear witness to multiple cultural identities, are representative of minority cultural heritages, are of founding significance or are in imminent danger of destruction', from the 1973 Convention on Heritage Monuments and Sites) (see UNESCO 2003; UNESCO Culture Sector – Intangible Heritage 2003). It is markedly difficult to legislate over intangible cultural heritage in countries scarred by racist ideologies.

The very divide between tangibility and intangibility resembles Merleau-Ponty's (1965, 1968) perceptions of space, which correspond to European cosmologies. His phenomenology of space distinguishes between geometric and physical space – simply put, an abstract space based on the formal criteria of rationality, and a practical space, generated on the basis of the exigencies of human life. Though this distinction applies to other cultures, Merleau-Ponty's conception of practical knowledge and reflexivity prioritise visuality over other sensory connections to the world. Surely, people mobilise other sensory outputs to comprehend the phenomenal world (see also Crouch 2009)? We know today that post-colonial space was prescriptively defined by visuality, as all social phenomena and human beings attained social identities and recognised subjectivities on the basis of European phenotypical hierarchies (Law 2010).

Generally, we may argue that the production of discourses of 'heritage' and 'legacy' in national and transnational sites are connected to collective memory work of the kind we find in post-colonial Brazil. These regulate communal narratives of cultural and intellectual property in contemporary industrial settings, where transnational, national or regional agents have to agree on the use and consumption of tangible and intangible heritage. The functionalist dilemma is a clandestine structural question that collapses into biological discourse: as Geertz (1980, 2000), Gellner (1983), Smith (1995: 98) and Habermas (1996: 495) warn us, the 'nature' of culture is not an innocent metaphor but a political model of belonging. In line with strategic oscillations between ethno-racial and civic understandings of citizenship, conceptions of 'legacy' and 'heritage' condition identity battles in the era of global digital reproduction. Legacy is a gift of a chattel or an item of personal property by will (Tzanelli 2013a: 2). In legacy arrangements the rule of law precedes the rule of kinship: law is a prerequisite in formalising (making public and visible to external observers) intimate arrangements (posthumous transfer of property to kin). Once the transfer of property is completed, the act of transaction becomes a form of intergenerational reciprocity. Only in this way does legacy form a continuation with heritage as the process of inheriting, whereby the beneficiary (heir) is legitimated as an actor in transactions by publicly recognised kinship affiliation.

In-heriting refers to pure exchange (Mauss 1954): the 'gift' of will becomes magically inseparable from the donor, who transfers it only to those with whom (s)he shares a bloodline (Shohat 1992: 109). Where giving is involved, we deal with tropes of debt to ancestry: in Brazil's case, landscapes, performances, ethnic styles and national characters function as 'gifts' conditionally lent to foreign visitors or redistributed by rituals within the national community. In both instances, recipients are left in debt to phantoms to whom they can never reciprocate. Families live and die, and their deceased members survive only through remembrance till a time all living members are no more. To preserve memories, we need *mnemonists* who record the chronicles of social groups in oral or written ways. Such collective memories become public through substitutions of images for ideas that may be inaccessible to outsiders. Freud called this phenomenon 'screen memories', but opened his thesis up to other – yet unexplored – sensory possibilities, when he claimed that these image memories should be seen as part of the linguistic apparatus of human experience. Given that for Freud the role of screen memories is to foreclose traumatic experiences (Freud 1965: 42–5), a synaesthetic orchestration of their blocking remains a possibility. Different cultures have different sensory-as-aesthetic hierarchies, so their *mnemonists'* function must be harmonised with them.

The term 'heritage' is of European origins, but today it regulates global notions of time as linear progression through space (Hewison 1987, 1989; Harrison 2005; Butler 2006; Sloterdijk 2009). The development of technology (Hussel's *Technik* or 'techicity') into an instrument constitutive of human progress was also implicated in such hermeneutic fixities of temporality. We could trace modern conceptions of time in the Galilean principles of celestial movement, but thinking of temporality as an irreversible, teleological-evolutionary movement (testimony to human finitude) would take us back to Enlightenment philosophies of nature (Adorno and Horkheimer 1991). Enlightenment conceptions of time found their apogee in Heidegger's Aristotelian division between *chrónos*, the mechanical and quantifiable time we read in clocks, the time of everyday life, and *kairós*, the sacred time, the site of myth, in which real(ist) spatio-temporal constrictions cease to define the subject's experience (Tzanelli 2011: chapter 3). *Kairós* and *chrónos* would come to represent the slow and fast mobilities of contemporary capitalist environments, further implicating technology's *chronic* speed in discourses of humanity's 'impure' – yet efficient – nature. Heritage as defined by imagined communities borrows from *kairotic* registers, to preserve (for intangible heritage) and conserve (for tangible) the nation's myths and memories (Smith 1999; Anderson 2006: 192, 195), but such derivative European temporal models do not cover the Brazilian experience.

It is more accurate to argue that under the pressures of synchronisation, heritage can become the maiden of nationalism, which revels in making religious icons. Although it is counterintuitive, collective protests, which damage national prestige (hence the impeccable Brazilian cultural image), are meant as attempts at restoring the imagined community's holism and solidarity. The deployment of 'civilising rituals' and 'theological languages' during moments of national bonding (e.g. mega-events) and crisis (the loss of the Cup) ironically reproduces the model citizen out of Brazilian *indignandos*, who take to the streets to burn and loot with a vengeance. Ritual looting is performative in Butler's (1993) terms: it reveals the ways in which subjects are both subjected to discursive manifestations of power and emerging. Lest the mistake is committed of jumping from ontological to cultural categories, let me clarify that Butler did not develop the concept of performativity to analyse whole communities that are formed in historical time. Nevertheless, this book borrows from her thesis the idea that although subjects repeatedly perform the teachings of discourse, the experience of repetition ceases to be mechanical: 'as the appearance of power shifts from the condition of the subject to its effects, the conditions of power (prior and external) assume a present and futural form' (Butler 1997: 16). In the case of World Cup riots, the Brazilian indignants are not necessarily reacting for neatly defined objectives, concerning political strategising. They may also react against all those intermediaries who are responsible for the 'moral spoliation' of Brazilian personhood – even though 'persons' are by definition enablers of suspect social practices. Indeed, expressions of indignation in popular protest of all kinds (including the less violent reactions to Brazil's 2014 defeat) are signs of 'resignation' from the social world, as the protesters feel and act as wronged individuals (DaMatta 1991: 24).

The observation will provide a novel view on Brazilian performativity as the country's embodied heritage, explaining simultaneously the principles and meaning of key ceremonial acts (explored in Chapter 4). Resignation is performative withdrawal from the secular world, usually associated with religious pilgrimage. The European pilgrim, in particular, could renounce the social in search of esoteric truths through a spiritual journey (Adler 1992). In Catholic religious systems such as that of post-colonial Brazil, the soul might continue to be seen as superior to the body and the renouncement of the social might reinforce personage over the apodictic reality of the individual (DaMatta's 1991: 181–2). Unlike the conciliation between 'body' and 'soul' in the Protestant ethic (Weber 1985), imported Catholic cosmologies in Brazil led to associations of work with the slavery of the soul. The Brazilian 'technical human' is morally corrupt, but *he* is a crafty demon because *he* makes ends meet, thanks to *his* flawed humanity as a *Malandro*. However, Brazilian heritage is separated from technique only superficially (in cosmetic, 'surface' terms), as in reality, networked persons borrow from the 'impure individual's' disposition.

For clarification, I use the term 'technique' to refer to inculcated dispositions, and 'technicity' to refer to the general properties of technology as human (electronic and material) prosthesis (Gallope 2011: 48–9). The difference between individual and person is not of real essence but of positional power to control appearances with the use of technology. The paradoxical couple of masculine labour with harm begins to make sense even beyond old, religiously endorsed conceptions of work as cunning or 'devilish' craft: more recent global tourist flows to Central and South America continue to reproduce understandings of service as servitude, leading to perpetrations of problematic host-guest reciprocities (Simoni 2008, 2013). The renouncement of the social by means of peaceful protest exposes these continuities between personage and individualism, by both reproducing heritage ritualistically and opening up the public sphere to legal revisions.

Contemporary continuities between consuming and communing are crucial in such reproductions and revisions. The presence of the renouncer as an intermediary (between the *caxias* or law-abiding compromiser and the *Malandro* or male rogue) character in Brazilian culture (DaMatta 1991: 208) can describe the mode and style of upheavals such as that following Brazil's 7–1 defeat. Just as the former European pilgrim routes are now populated by tourists, armed with 'devotional texts' (Horne 1984: 1–6), touring sports fan cultures are in possession of devotional rules to the national team. These rules look to restoring the national team's honour by collective rituals. The rituals respond to urges to 'build' *lieux de mémoire* (sites of memory) for the national team's history, because few *milieux de mémoire* (real environments of memory) survive in post-colonial countries that experienced slavery; hence, these rituals are meant as acts of repossessing one's lost heritage from its 'usurpers' (Nora 1989; Maleuvre 1999: 59). Football discourse in Brazil is implicated in this conundrum of forgetting its real 'roots' in favour of stressing its domestic social routes (so as to fabricate exclusive national roots and repaying debts to ancestry). Such heritage urges can falsely attain the mantle of well-being as recuperation from past suffering; as such, they are an *essentialised* part of what it means to 'be human' (Alexander et al. 2004). Yet, the restoration of a people's 'heritage to dignity' for the creation of just futures (e.g. Derrida 2002: 5) is, like beauty, in the eye of the beholder.

Brazilian society in particular is dominated by a basic opposition between 'seeing' and 'doing' because of spatial-as-moral differentiations between home (invisible to outsiders) and street (visible to all). This opposition also determines the realm of work, where actors/labourers are supervised by employers (DaMatta 1991: 106), thereby losing the privilege to act privately. In order to understand Brazil's inclusion in global cultural politics, we need to understand how its heritage is performed in embodied ways in its twin transmodern spaces: the private *casa* and the public *rua*. The former corresponds to symbolisations of privacy – hence, what is revealed to knowing insiders – and the latter to globally accessible cultural registers (Herzfeld 2005; Tzanelli 2008, 2011). Ceremonies and protests may be signposted as public, when they are replete with private meanings and performances; or, they may be subjected to state surveillance but evade translations by the national and transnational (FIFA) technological eye. There are layers of privacy and intimacy in enactments of Brazilian custom, but we may safely attribute to the country's heritage a uniform bodily dimension.

Dimitrova Savova's (2009: 550) deployment of the term 'heritage kinaesthetics' to explain 'the moving bodily practices that set the built environment alive and are a counterpart of heritage aesthetics, or the immobile quality usually ascribed to a historic site', complements my argument for a synaesthetic approach to the World Cup ceremony as well as fan reactions to the Brazilian loss of the World Cup. Not only does kinaesthesia (sensory-aesthetic movement) attribute the need and practice of image making with embodied, multisensory expressivity, but it can also be applied to urban studies (De Certeau 1988) and tourism theory, to counter human sciences' occulocentrism (Crang and Franklin 2001; Urry and Larsen 2011). The move to an experimental empirical domain facilitating multisensory and emotional movement is a prerequisite for the development of a new mobilities agenda that does not divorce politics from aesthetics and culture (Büscher and Urry 2009; Büscher et al. 2011; Thrift 2011). In spaces traumatised by colonialism and racism, embodied mobilities continue to define even those 'material ecologies of home' that partake in global traffic (Tolia-Kelly 2010).

The embodied mobilities of Brazilian ceremony and protest, as well as their attendance by domestic and foreign observers, are discussed with the help of the term 'performative synaesthetics'. This allows us to explore the mind-body complex of performativity: deriving from a real disorder (synaesthesia as replacement of one sense with another), it points to a productive re-ordering of narrative pathways through combinations of image, movement, touch, smell and sound (on performativity, see Butler 1993; in tourist studies, see Ateljevic et al. 2007; on synaesthesia in sociology see Tzanelli 2011: 19; and in neuro-philosophy see Sacks 2011). These synaesthetic organisations of perception induce pilgrimages that combine the monetary capital of arts (e.g. the generation of tourism or other consumable styles) with the emotional and spiritual investment of artists and audiences in values that exceed this capital (Thrift 2006). Synaesthesia or combined sensory engagement translates into cognitive, aesthetic and emotional consumption of place though synergies of text, music and image (Tzanelli 2014: 17). The body's material and symbolic implication in synaesthetic performativity is crucial, as ceremonial routines often develop into 'the *choreographic* form of the community that sings and dances its own proper unity' (Rancière 2004: 9, emphasis in original).

Especially where combined audiovisual technologies are involved, a tourist *synaesthete*, whose senses (*aésthesis*) are coordinated (*sýn*) to perceive and appreciate the world's beauty, is interpellated with the help of various 'authorised' discourses (Urry and Larsen 2011: 19). These include education *à la* Grand Tour, group solidarity within the tourist group, pleasure and play, heritage and memory, as well as nation. The last discourse has been pivotal in the advertising of touristified countries as brands, the more general role of establishing lineage as identity and the development of heritage-conservation tourism as part of a cultural nationalism programme via state-sponsored institutions. The discourse of 'nation' becomes enmeshed into those of tourist play and memory, which are nevertheless connected to a particular version of group solidarity of universal appeal: the family idea(l).

In Brazil, kinship networks influence domestic visions of the good life. To live well, *eudaimoneîn* in ancient Greek, connects with understandings of distribution in European political philosophy, but with a twist. As Brazilian socio-cultures are hierarchical, persons cannot be morally pure beings and individuals are, by definition, corrupt 'technicians'. Afro-Brazilian cosmology is based on the communication of good (*eu*) demons with the human world, who return as ancestors to collect debts from living family members through remembrance rituals. Such rituals involved in tribal societies the excavation of the bones of dead ancestors and their use in the production of concoctions for family members to share. Such rites 'are usually carried out very discreetly … but even when they are practiced in more overt forms it has to admitted that … moral condemnation of such customs implies … a belief in bodily resurrection' when such rituals are not based on Cartesian dualism and are meant as an incorporation of ancient powers (Lévi-Strauss 1974: 387–8). Needless to add that ritual anthropophagy in the Amazonas is a literal rendition of posthumous anthropophagy as thanatourism. The Brazilian demons were human beings before becoming spirits, but they linger as a posthumous interpretative vehicle in this world. Their posthumous value is to harmonise this world's riches with otherworldly powers through recognitions of the past. This balancing act ensures that the living enjoy a good life, free of reminders of forgotten obligation; in many respects, anthropophagy forms the moral basis of the contemporary person's nature.

The root of the original Hellenic act of *daimonáõ* (being possessed by demons) in *daíõ* promotes the idea of providing through distribution, but the bodily dimensions of Brazilian ritual are lost. All the same, giving relates to meanings of pre-classical demonic justice, as another derivative of *daimonáõ, datéomai* communicates expenditure through shared consumption (*daíõ*: divide). In fact, ancient Greek *eudaimonia* connects directly to *dámimi*, the act of providing meals in socialising symposia, but also the public function of the ancient *dẽmos*, whose presence in the *agorá* was connected to expenditure and discursive exchange. If we consider Geertz's (2000) conviction that linguistic communication produces our humanity, then we should not dissociate consumption from public and private rituals in Brazil and also in Brazilian venues used to promote global flows. In contemporary, hypermobile environments Aristotelian *eudaimonía* as the vision of good life, welfare or prudential value, and consumption, complement understandings of the human condition (Tribe 2008: 17). In hyper-neoliberal contexts of mass consumption, such as those of mega-events, *eudaimonic* consumption is often recast as a kind of enjoyment (Fennell 2008: 221). If ancient enjoyment (*euthymía*) was centred on tranquillity and virtuous activity (as in Plato's *Republic*; Haybron 2008: 19), pleasurable postmodern consumption of sporting and ceremonial spectacles encourages the projection and generation of good affects to performers and viewers. These affects are constitutive of the wider mobility networks of mega-events, including those of Appadurai's (1990, 1991) ideoscapal paradoxes: the clash or harmonisation of local or global values with the help of emotional flows.

Brazilian *felicidade* as *eudaimonía* is therefore another rendition of Brazilian *physis* with the help of non-natural mechanisms, such as those of artistic performance. However, the global performance of Brazil's *physis* needs to be harmonised with other technical discourses that communicate relevant global concerns. Here we note how the urgency to synchronise can lead to medleys of human nature with the environment: notably, an underlining theme in the 2014 World Cup has been the harmonisation of *felicidade* with sustainability, especially environmental sustainability – a tall order to meet, which dictates the replacement of the domestic rule of kinship with that of international law. The 1992 Rio Declaration on Environment and Development (2012) is based on the principle that:

> Human beings are entitled to a healthy and productive life in harmony with nature ... all states and all people shall cooperate in the essential task of eradicating poverty ... states shall cooperate in a spirit of global partnership to conserve, protect and restore the health and integrity of the Earth's ecosystem ... cooperate to promote a supportive and open international economic system that would lead to economic growth and sustainable development in all countries, to better address the problems of environmental degradation ... [and] develop national law regarding liability and compensation for the victims of pollution and other environmental damage.

The latter forms a continuation with Principle 22, which evidently guides the World Cup ceremony's political agenda: 'Indigenous people and their communities and other local communities have a vital role in environmental management and development because of their knowledge and traditional practices. States should recognize and duly support their identity, culture and interests and enable their effective participation in the achievement of sustainable development' (ibid.). Below I return to performative renditions of this principle in 2014. For the moment, it is worth stressing that like other developing nations, Brazil does not escape the discourse of a global environmental crisis that has secured a strong presence in the anxieties and expectation of industrial societies, provoked legitimation crises in national governance systems, and even led to welfare or public deregulation as unquestionable by the 'non-technical' citizen (Lorente and Alonso 2014: 3).

The conflict between idealised indigeneity as national heritage and a consumable for the romantic gaze, ear and nose, occasionally falling prey to regional 'warlords', cannot be avoided in such risky times (Beck 1992, 1999; Giddens 2009; Urry 2011). Tensions between multiple mobilities of local custom and *physis* and sustainable tourism principles suggest that the governance of vulnerable destinations in Brazil should be grounded in local community dialogue (Dredge 2010; Dredge and Jamal 2013). However, it must be borne in mind that in the paradigmatic contexts of liquid, mobile and fluid capitalism (Bauman 2007b), narratives of scale can also become discursive devices to obscure or resolve tensions between particular interests and natural mechanisms.

World Cups are characterised by fusions of local and international styles of communication, but as their venues are dedicated in the performance of host culture, the (art)style on which sustainability discourses focus is that of the host. The propensity to move from artistic to general aesthetic practices allows political discourse to shed light on ways of doing and making that are allegedly common to the community (Rancière 2004: 8, 19). The inclusion of environmental sustainability in the 2014 World Cup's programmatic statement was evidently connected to the sustainability of Brazil's heritage kinaesthetics. This was expressed both in ceremonies and in urban spaces in various ways, but in all instances the emotive dimension persisted. It has been noted that football identities can give rise to authentic micro-societies characterised by a set of distinctive discourses and social practices (Armstrong and Giulianotti 1997). Despite their local roots, 'such micro-societies are embedded in transnational social networks that span the entire planet' (Feixa and Juris 2000: 204). Affects circulate in these contexts extensively: from inducing emotions amongst sport audiences, to experiencing feelings of failure or victory, to narrating one's culture and history as the host, they form the basis of emotional consumption of landscapes, humans and communal identities (Urry 2007: 26). As both Bruner (1994) and Kirshenblatt-Gimblett (1997) have noted, learning occurs via a 'performance epistemology' that prioritises experience – equivalent to the Geertzian cockfight's function as 'sentimental education' (Geertz 1973: 449).

Again, instead of thinking of affect in fixed terms, we should recognise its transformation into emotion that communicates national and global ideals. This means that certain effects, feelings and emotions – in particular, those motivated in our case by pride, obligation and mourning – are not just passing moods, but are motivationally specific: by association with their motivations, they have 'directional casts' and an 'overall course' (Geertz 1973: 97; Trondman 2011: 149). Here we note a convergence between the 'strong programme' and the 'new mobilities paradigm' that transcends the researcher's interpretive explanations (Alexander 2011: 57) and extends to ad hoc interpretations of socio-cultural structures by football fans. Early on, Nigel Thrift (1996, 2007) outlined mobility as a 'structure of feeling', a 'way of addressing people, objects, things and places … [and] authoritarian regimes' (Adey 2010: xvii). As I proceed to explain, touring the world performatively, in ceremonial and popular sites alike, encloses fully articulated emotions that began their journey as feelings of discontent or weakness towards colonial, capitalist or domestic authoritarian power. I am not interested in assessing the accuracy of the material conditions at this stage, only to outline the movement from 'firstness' of feeling to the 'thirdness' of emotion (Peirce 1992, 1998) in Brazilian expressions of identity.

Focusing on ceremonial expressions of identity in particular, one notices that utilitarian promotions of well-being as hedonism give way to narrations of 'nature' (character) fulfilment or capability enabling (e.g. Sen 1999; Nussbaum 2000). Incidentally, 'happiness' (*felicidade*) and joy (*alegria*) provide two conceptions of the good life that rest at the heart of Brazilian culture. By analogy to discourses of the subjective nature of well-being, *felicidade* (a more permanent sentiment) and *alegria* (a fleeting equivalent) voice an Epicurean-like fulfilment of Brazilian nature (see Haybron 2008: 25) in its multiple manifestations. *Felicidade*'s *kairotic* qualities correspond to *chronic* expressivity while 'performing character', generating agential capabilities: as motions produce affective states that consolidate emotional narratives (Bruno 2002; Jensen 2010), we arrive at a kinaesthetic fusion of the body with the various human technologies that give it social meaning (Ahmed 2004; Massumi 2002; Turner 1984). Brazilian kinaesthetics and their performative synaesthetics continue to be based on public artistic narratives that mostly borrow from dance and music (Brooks 2011: 15; Alexander 2011: 62).

As ceremonial spectacles involve nationally meaningful dances, they ensure that the whole community (no doubt, fragmented in real time) is symbolically bonded while telling the story of its own mobility and development in time (Adey 2010: 167). McNeill (1995: 65) explains that 'the emotional arousal of dance (and less energetic forms of rhythmic movement like stately professionals and military drill) was fundamental in widening and differentiating social bonds' amongst and within human communities, and Brennan (2003: 70) adds that mobile togetherness is critical in establishing a sense of collective purpose. Dance routines in the 2014 Brazilian World Cup ceremony are constitutive of the Brazilian nation's emotional communion with its roots. However, they simultaneously enable the external viewers' pilgrimage to the Brazilian social imaginary (Bajc et al. 2007; Cavanaugh 2008). We must be cautious here: as Chapters 4 and 5 endeavour to explain in detail, ceremonial and street dancing – as well as their corresponding musical background – may be drawing on the same structures of experience, but they articulate them in different ways. The articulators of Brazil's 2014 heritage kinaesthetics (artists and protesters) belong to different socio-cultural streams and carry in their performance different motivations and alliances. However, as the next chapter explains, the diverse cosmopolitan profiles of these articulators reveal that components of the Brazilian cosmological template can manifest in blended Western-South American practices.

3 Complementary articulations

Characterising ideal human types and communities

Articulating Brazilian trans-modernity

It is said that one of the commonest Old World fantasies has been the depiction of emergent nations in former colonial dominions' stead as 'cloned' from their Western master's cultural roots. It is as if the human world is nothing but an expanding European kin, complete with a *pater familias*, legitimate and bastardised progeny, and moving towards the same end of socio-cultural self-fulfilment. This is too simple a worldview to accept. In this chapter I want to add to arguments that see in such emergent nations the antidote to totalling Western conceptions of modernity 'as a modernity-without-windows, in which – as usual in Western conceptions – South-North and South-South (or East-West and East-East) flows and influences are either ignored or underestimated' (Nederveen Pieterse 1998: 75). Downplaying the hermeneutic skills of the periphery and its 'underdeveloped' centres is a common political manoeuvre, which sees in *mélange* cultural formations immaturity and in hybridisation the indeterminacy of a novice. The suggestion that we consider the tensions of global cultural, economic and political pathways in terms of multi-polarity (Nederveen Pieterse 2009), multiple modernities (Robertson 1995; Therborn 1995), ambivalence (Bauman 1991) and cosmopolitan dialogism (Beck 2000b; Delanty 2006) is pertinent here, insofar as we also consider that the Brazilian worldview constantly crossed (and continues to cross) paths with Western European and North American flows. This allows us to examine what the previous chapter left unfinished – namely, who acts as the hermeneutician in the study's social platforms, and what they actually interpret.

Taking on board the centrality of multiple mobilities in Brazilian history, I opt for an approach that encapsulates the paradigmatic shift away from a singular vision of modernity, but opt for a different term to analyse it. The notion of 'trans-modernity' describes 'the emerging sociocultural, economic, political and philosophic shift' in the cultural and material development of a pluralised human history (Ghisi in Ateljevic 2008: 280). It promises to plant the seeds of hope and replace colonialism's antiquated world orders, which constantly masquerade cultures in terms of feminised victimhood or macho militarism. It is not coincidental that trans-modernity has borne its best scholarly fruit in post-colonial (Dussel 1985, 1995; Cole 2005) and tourism studies (Ateljevic and Hall 2007), where it has uncovered the performative fallacies of victimisation and passivity that world politics reserves for subaltern groups. The emphasis on centrifugalism and imaginative or embodied travel as activist gestures can apply not just to individuals but whole nations and cultures habitually cast as 'self-immolating entities', so to speak (Spivak 1988). We should not mistake the cosmic for something avoiding banal articulation: such pathological acts of collective 'self-immolation' may appear humorous or trivial, but still guide contextual responses to defeats on the world stage, such as that suffered by the Brazilian football team. As such, they are tired 'styles' informed by modernity's singular teleology of historical evolution and rupture (Rancière 2004: 22–3).

Trans-modernity thus promises the rejection of command, control and conquest as heritage values that 'have turned the world into a competitive and territorial background' (Ateljevic 2008: 282). For post-colonial political formations, such as Brazil, which blend domestic, intimate socio-cultural registers with foreign codes, it also suggests a turn away from flat, horizontal organisations and bureaucratic stagnation so as to become more aware of humanity's vulnerability and interdependency. In other words, where the 'multiple modernities' thesis contributes to globalisation, trans-modern discourse proposes a cosmopolitan ethic. If the suggestion that we consider the presence of 'multiple' or 'alternative modernities' provides a sensitive realist look at world orders, the trans-modern proposal holds the promise of their radical revision. The suggestion is articulated with some humility in the face of what bureaucracy actually is in post-colonial polities such as Brazil: stereotypical complaints about its existence and 'evils' form part 'of a much larger universe that we might call, quite simply, the ideology and practice of accountability' (Herzfeld 1992: 3). Therefore, if bureaucracy belongs to endogenous cultural-cosmological constructions (Handleman 1990), it is epistemologically problematic to consider the diversion of popular rage from the loss of a World Cup to government cuts as mere reaction to bad welfare policies. Such 'unexpected' mobilisation travels down the lane of geopolitics, where rival footballing nations, especially those ridden with post-colonial traumas, compete for global recognition.

The constraints under which the project of building a global biosphere comes at any moment in time run parallel with those under pressures met by post-colonial nations. The 2014 World Cup's performative politics on the pitch, the ceremonial stage and in the streets are manifestations of trans-modern justice and have a poetic potential: they produce and modify Brazilian (Bourdieusian) habitus and transnational (Tardean) dispositions. In other words, the World Cup stage is made up of communities that display particular characteristics, social organisation and cultural outlook. We do indeed deal with the expression of *biomechanics*, the mechanical aspects of social solidarity en route to becoming organised in a more mechanical fashion

(Durkheim 1997). In line with Foucault's (1997b) concept of 'biopolitics' that I explore in the next section, *biomechanics* blends cultural symbolisations of biology into industrial, post-industrial and technological processes – including those of bureaucratisation. However, the mobility of national ideals such as those of the working, industrious man should be placed within the wider global contexts in which they operate. There is, currently, a heated debate concerning the epistemological and methodological boundaries between globalisation and mobility theory, whereas the implication of both in emancipatory post-colonialist projects remains largely unresolved. Gikandi (2002) highlights that post-colonialism and globalisation studies share at least a concern with explaining forms of social and cultural organisation transcending the boundaries of the nation-state, and providing 'new vistas for understanding cultural flows that can no longer be explained by a homogenous Eurocentric narrative of development and social change' (Gikandi 2002: 627). Their discourses of development converge upon the recognition that we should not avoid the reality of colonialism's historical conditions in favour of 'the fantasmatics of colonial discourse' (Young 2001: 160).

On the other hand, it is equally necessary to avoid a return to simplified forms of localised materialism that refuse entirely to recognise 'the existence and effect of general discourses of colonialism on individual instances of colonial practice' (Ashcroft 2012: 3). Generally speaking, as the fields of post-colonial theory and research are characterised by a growing investment in diaspora, transnationalism and cosmopolitanism, their connection to mobility theory cannot be discarded (Marchetti 2011: 27). Sheller, whose work on Caribbean mobilities was heavily influenced by post-colonial theory, today contends that mobilities theory differs from globalisation theory in 'its analytical relation to the multi-scalar, non-human, non-representational, material, and affective dimensions of mobile life' (Sheller 2014b: 6). Yet, this is hardly a point of departure for differentiations, as studies on globalisation and social movements have proved, for example (Melucci 1989; Tzanelli 2013b). Sharp divergences take place mostly at the level of movement per se as a symbolic, political, cultural and theoretical move: mobilities theory always begins with specificity and localised movement, whereas even the study of 'glocalisation' (Robertson 1992) commences observations from a global vantage point. In line with Sheller and Ateljevic's more general stance, I argue that we should consider the World Cup's blended Brazilian and transnational *biomechanics* as trans-modern manifestations: not only did the mega-event's forum bring together different types of community, but it transformed them into situated carriers of discourses of Brazilian and global ethics.

Trans-modernity's foremost task is to find the right vocabulary, cultural grammar and poetic syntax to express particular needs. In order to encapsulate this task, I will employ the term 'articulation' for analytical and methodological purposes. Originally part of the lexicon of music, articulation would convey the formulation of transitions and continuities between multiple notes or sounds. There is a progressive note in this background, in line with Husserl and Heidegger's epistemology. In a more explicit post-colonial argument, Said (1994) spoke of 'contrapuntalism', a method pitching different cultural notes on the same track to produce a whole musical theme. His contrapuntalism is a methodology of knowledge (Chowdry 2007: 103): it conveys different viewpoints, examines the cultural-ethical singularity of different ethnic idioms that music-colonialism's technological machine would recognise only as part of its dominant artistic idioms. As already highlighted, while music can be mobile, it can also induce embedded sentiment – a point connecting to modernist contradictions between Enlightenment belief in modern, universal progress and the Romantic spirit's rootedness in land and ideals that draw from the past to critique liquid modernity (Löwy and Sayre 2001: 10). Music's connection to manipulated but de-mediated environments (Strain 2003) reinstates the power of nature in representations of the social.

The World Cup's articulators are divided into different communities that can also blend and synergise to make art and social statements. Those communities' socio-cultural gradations correspond to movements from, and between, region, nation and transnational sites. Their symbolic movement from and between ethnic and civic spheres corresponds to articulation's applicability to regional, national and global contexts. Etymologically 'articulation' comes from the ancient Greek noun *árthõsis* (connection, joint) to describe the bending of one's joints, but the noun's origins in *arthrõnõ* (verbally articulate) reminds us of connections between Durkheim's embodied understandings of nationhood in terms of human maturity and subjectivity (Tzanelli 2011: chapter 5). Today, this 'physicalisation' of power is constantly countered by the polygenesis of sociality, which manifests in the form of assemblages or multiple competing social compositions such as those of the mobile artists (Tonkonoff 2013: 277). Hence, O'Reilly's (2003: 302) use of the term 'articulation' to explore migration and tourism's moves both separately and together, 'sometimes smoothly and sometimes causing friction', is also pertinent. As a by-product of ethical frictions between transnational and national communities, articulation transcends national boundaries and occurs whenever and wherever we have host-guest encounters.

Notably, the term is also an audio-visual manifestation of literacy: its Indo-European root, *art(h)a* (Sanskrit: meaning, sense, goal, purpose or essence), speaks of organisation akin to that of the African-inspired ancient Greek *kósmos*, 'an iconic expression for "good order"' (Sandywell 2011: 152). Like art, *artha* harmonises one's being with the *kósmos* as virtue and emotional fulfilment. The self-same *artha* complies in world religions such as Hinduism to visions of good governance, because the term also refers to social, legal, economic and worldly affairs. Though born on a different continent, the meaning of *artha* would reappear on European and colonised soil in administrative domains and then in their artistic representations in painting, literature and architecture to *visually* articulate political discourses of power (McClintock 1995). The somehow international context of colonialism would be replaced by organised national bureaucracies that also articulated through pictorial and literary art, history and education (Leoussi 2004). In the age of nations the paradox of literacy, in its print and audiovisual forms, was that it democratised knowledge, while making it complicit to the emergence and preservation of political centres (McLuhan 1962, 1964; Anderson 2006). Herder's views on the socio-cultural organisation of humanity through languages that preserve the uniqueness and purposefulness of national *Geistes* (spirits, essences) (Bhatt 2000) have been a clear rendition of articulation since the modern emergence of nationalism (Goodman 1976).

The contemporary rooted-national and mobile-artistic articulations I explore in the following chapter are attributed to anonymous and celebrity performers of the World Cup's ceremonial show alike. We will see in Chapter 4 how these performers share with national articulators in method: just as the political centre stereotypes subjects to articulate ideal types of citizenry (Gellner 1983), transnational artwork represents the nation's history through ethnic characters and styles. However, mega-events also recreate particular 'human types' as symbols of intercultural communication. Art systems can also be open-ended assemblages that negotiate anti-national and anti-statist forms of thinking, doing and feeling, thus countering what Goldmann (1964, 1980) has recognised as the tragic 'cosmo-vision' (*vision du monde*) of every human society, which is based on the dystopian verdict that nothing and nobody escapes socio-cultural constrictions and rules. At the same time, mega-events are opportunities for the host nation's external recognition via (cultural) industrial growth. Such growth relies on urban 'global financial articulations' (Sassen 2001) such as those of the city, which enable the commercialisation of the arts (Chia-Ling 2004). As a result, technological (i.e. linguistic and mechanical) calibrations of Brazilian trans-modernity aestheticise its multiple realities (Dean 2007) so as to articulate the utopian parable of the imagined community's Edenic 'futural history' – a history produced from the present for the creation of particular futures. The oscillation between real and utopian discourse borrows from Schütz's systematic examination of stratifications of the 'lifeworld' as 'multiple realities', finite provinces of meaning or 'sub-universes' (Henning 2002: 170).

Provinces of meaning are always conditioned by conceptions of self-worth and (in)equality, which can be individual, or, in our case, collective. It is worth stressing that the World Cup's ceremonial and activist performances appeal to the imaginary as a process of social representation that promotes a social aesthetics (O'Callaghan 1995: 22–3). Maffesoli (1993) debates this as an image cluster; at least in the case of sports or patriotic assemblies, it develops into a 'vector of communion' that can be collectively consumed even by neo-tribal groups without shared roots (Maffesoli 1996). The utopian dream is a far cry from the ways Brazilian society functions on the basis of ethno-racial and other value hierarchies, but it is a dream nevertheless. Rather than exploring the conflict of reality with aspiration on a national level in the tradition of DaMatta's (1991) social anthropology or anthropological sociology, I suggest an approach that relates cultural specificity to those old civilisational centres, which are unable to survive new intercultural traffic in their original form.

Still, we cannot avoid considering how even electronically mediated environments might produce zones of privilege and exclusion, as new professional communities and their infrastructural support systems reside in separate physical domains from those of the represented populations (Cronin 2013: 107; Dredge and Jamal 2013: 561). As a 'globally integrated network' (Urry 2003: 12), the 2014 mega-event's industry represents a macro-system with predictable connections that counter space-time constraints (e.g. uses of digital and cinematic technologies in the international market of the mega-event). Yet, as a fluid cultural formation, the enterprise comprises various media forms (film, music, photography and Internet), which produce ideas and aesthetic codes with plural meanings, uses, creative implementations and political applications. Fixing meanings to represent one nation is a haphazard cultural programme that aspires to harmonise what is seen as 'authentically native' (heritage kinaesthetics) with what is seen as the 'global pop'. Evidently, this 'programme' articulates through both local and global technologies, shifting from orality or embodiment to visuality and even to digitality.

Ubiquitous fallen humans: *technopoiesis*, heritage and legacy

It seems that the old European debate on technicity awaits us just around the corner, when we attempt to understand how the 2014 World Cup's communities function and to what ends. The use of tools in articulations suggests an immediate connection between established techniques and available technologies. In this study, it is important to connect those communities' *bio-mechanics* to Brazil's pursuit of a cosmography of riches, instead of generally studying their make. With this in mind, I start by flagging their twin capitalist and nationalist 'ends', adding that especially artistic creativity may have more motivations than I can explore here. My focus on 'art' rather than 'nation' also allows me to consider how transnational mobilities connect to national social (im)mobilities (Cresswell 2001: 25; Hannam 2008: 108). The machinery of global information technologies and its adjacent labour divisions acquire a 'light', tourist veneer as 'playful practices of subjectivity that enable users to slip the moorings of location and materiality' (Kaplan 2003: 209). Just like 'mobility', 'articulation', especially via mobile technological assemblages, like the ones used in World Cup fixtures and ceremonies, provides communities with interpretive resources to understand the global changes occurring in contemporary society (on mobility and interpretation see Hannam et al. 2006; Pellegrino 2007, 2011; Tzanelli 2013b). Articulations provided by transnational artistic communities in mega-events may also offer alternative social possibilities; yet, as Buscema (2011: 44) notes, even the social appropriation of new technological apparatuses – the so-called 'relational machines' – by indigenous migrants, 'represents their ultimate endowment to the *creation of the world* … and to the realization of the multitude' (see also

Hardt and Negri 1994, 2000, 2004). Hence, there can be ideational symmetry in the aims of transnational mega-event artists and common labour, but we should not discard real social asymmetries altogether.

The communities I prioritise in this study are defined by synergies that can be organised (artistic, ceremonial) or spontaneous and disorganised (activist, fan). There are several networks operating simultaneously within them, but these communities usually depend on the rule of heritage or law. I divide them into *filiative*, kin based (including the enlarged fictional kin of the Brazilian 'nation-family'), and *affiliative*, guild and profession based. Filiation and affiliation refer to modes of belonging that organise individual and collective perception of the world around us, thus maintaining the 'provinces of meaning' I introduced above. Today, like yesterday, this organisation is based on various modes and styles of technicity, which started its life as human material prosthesis before becoming a fully recognised extension of the technological body. Even Putnam's (1993) social network theory is transformed via new media routes, as artistic communities operating in new digital contexts are not always bound by regional or national belonging but by shared interests and commercial infrastructures (Averill 1996: 218; Gauntlett 2011: 138; Grugulis and Stoyanova 2011; Manning and Sydow 2011). Capitalist structuration and neoliberal ideology seem to have won according to some radical critics, sucking into their vortex people, technologies and musical practices, and crafting complicity through global interdependencies (Erlmann 1999; Albertsen and Diken 2003: 11).

A Plato-inspired condemnation of *téchne* as contemporary art is rendered obsolete, to some extent: as others noted (Stiegler 2003), writing and digital design or other new technologies are *mnemotechnical* – that is, they use technics to assist memory. In fact, humanity's articulation appears with the use of tools and 'semiotechnologies', not in a de-humanised actor-network event, but in synergies between tool and human, which create (*poieín* from *poíesis*: making) meaning through signs (*semeíon*) (Langlois 2012). There is 'subtle intimacy' between technology and language that resists the instrumentalisation of technical beings, including artists (e.g. Derrida 1981). Therefore, to examine the World Cup's communities in terms of function suggests their instrumentalisation by some sort of intervention. This intervention is not posited outside Western rationality (*lógos*), as the Brazilian nation-state and its satellite communities were born within its logocentrism. If we are to question the Western European logocentricity that dissociated technology from thought (Derrida 1986: 108), we should re-introduce the hermeneutic process (e.g. Derrida's (1976: 27) 'writing') as technology's true epistemic condition (Gardiner 1992: 12, 26; Alexander and Smith 2001; Archer 2003; Alexander 2006).

To resolve these tensions, I employ the term *technopoiesis*, 'the totality of practices and processes of "self-making" available to a community and embodied in the artefacts, techniques and technologies available to a culture' (Hand and Sandywell 2002: 208; Cronin 2013: 11). Tools and practices can of course be mobilised by various social groups for the promotion of disparate causes. Couldry's (2006) suggestion that some notion of commonality – hence the defence of possibility of any shared site – is essential for an emergent democratic politics is pertinent. The 2014 World Cup's communities' technopoesis is based on combined uses of old and new technologies, as their democratic discourses were articulated both by Brazilians and individuals living in different sites and connected with the help of new technologies because of shared interests rather than exclusively because they share ethnonational origins. The difference between the two forms of technopoesis (kinship and profession based) is encapsulated in Ingold's (2000: 142) differentiation between 'genealogy' and 'relation' – or the production of the social via ready-made attributes received from predecessors – and 'progeneration' – or production of the social field through shared capacities and dispositions. National technopoesis looks to the past to replenish its creative repository (Coleman 1988: 102–3), whereas transnational technopoesis produces ways of being and knowing via contemporary experiences and shared interests. The ceremonial spectacle's transnational technopoesis in particular comprised groups of native and international artists. We can call this blend an 'epistemic community', given that it articulated, interpreted Brazil's take on the cosmography of riches. 'Epistemic communities' are networks of experts whose shared beliefs and sentiments are, voluntarily or not, mobilised in national policy planning (Haas 1992). Contractual obligation certainly binds all the members of this community to produce plausible versions of *Brasilidade*, ensuring that the mega-event 'legacy' is over-determined by the country's 'heritage'.

In any case, epistemic communities can display the signs of kinship independently from their contractual obligations, because they tend to move together from one mega-event to the next as 'networked persons' (apropos DaMatta 1991) but reflexive individuals, prioritising their own aesthetic and commercial pursuits (apropos Giddens 1990). Shakira's example in the 2014 closing ceremony is, amongst others, a case in point. Members of artistic technopoetic groups can also draw upon their national networks, transpose national imaginaries into transnational ceremonial templates and assist in further hybridising alien cultures. Rather than considering artistic technopoesis as part of a single 'world culture … one network of social relationships' or many cultures 'without any clear anchorage in any one territory' (Hannerz 1990: 237), I see in them the coexistence of new sub-cultural (pop) elements with more stable ideas of home. Technopoesis relies not only on embodied but also on digital technologies, which fuse experiences and practices of being at home 'while being away', or vice versa (Robertson 1994; Lyall and Bell 2002; Germann Molz 2008, 2012). If being in the world as an artistic traveller means a broadening of the cultural horizons for the Self and Others, then new and old technologies subjected to personal or professional uses bind 'home' and 'away' in novel dialogical patterns (Albrow et al. 1997: 31; Germann Molz 2004, 2009).

The 2014 World Cup's ceremonial technopoesis prompts us not to isolate one form of mobility (travel, virtual and/or terrestrial) from other technological complexes of movement (including the digitised images of dancing or football play as national arts) or its equivalent activist movement and marketable products (the dancer's body, relevant music and paraphernalia). This hides a hypothesis: that there is such a thing as a 'technology of action', involving a combination of physical/embodied and digital movement of people that aspire to present themselves as travellers, activists, artists (masters of dance styles), but also masters of technology (Archer 1996). As societies move towards more integrated mobility systems that combine digital and mechanical movement of ideas, highlighting the importance of some human variables (gender, ethnicity or sexuality) is enmeshed into new socio-cultural considerations, including the significance of mediated interaction in contemporary everyday life (Shilling 1999; Uteng and Cresswell 2008; Kaufmann and Mantulet 2008). Much like Schütz (1945), Scheler (1966 in Albrow et al 1997: 30–1) sees humans committed to relatively stable sets of intentions, which allow us to navigate the world. The structures of our thought are not practically measurable, but help us act on our 'actual milieu', our relatively (in relation to other people sharing our interests) natural (our dispositions) worldview. Whereas structures are more fixed, our actions change the milieu.

In technopoesis, we deal with the classical sociological question of structure and agency then. Note that I used the term 'mechanical movement' as a byword for *biomechanics*: the World Cup's artistic human belongs to a polity and is often mobilised by the nation-state, in spite of, or in line with, their personal beliefs. Also, it is simplistic to approach *biomechanics* only nationally – a point on which Brazil is not different from other nations. It is true that the middle class in developing countries participates in global circuits of advertising, brand names, consumerism and high-tech services, but the exploitation of the most privileged labour in mega-event contexts is a moot point. The idea of exclusion thus has gradations, as it ignores the ways in which developing countries are included in globalisation, while being subject to the global financial discipline. 'Thus, it would be more accurate to speak of *symmetrical inclusion* or hierarchical integration' (Nederveen Pieterse 2004: 30), which always extends to imports of foreign artistic and technical talent to stage the mega-event. The logic of flexible citizenship is, as Ong reminds us, a new mobile calculative technique of governing (Ong 1999, 2006). One also wonders to what extent we can argue that tropicopolitanism forms a secular cosmology that challenges the historical privilege of Enlightenment cosmopolitanism (Aravamudan 1999: 4–5), surviving now in the new aesthetically reflexive subjects that actively monitor the world around them (Beck 1992; Beck et al. 1994; Lash and Urry 1994: 5–6) – notably, another product of Western developmental paths. The issue with the tropicopolitan hypothesis is whether there is 'catachresis' (Spivak 1993: 281) in its use, because its political-cultural flexibility actually licenses the neoliberal mantra of benevolent economic connectivity between North and South (both continentally and within Brazil).

The North–South gap poses multiple practical and moral questions, as global inequality globalises (political, ecological and security) risk (Nederveen Pieterse 2004: 31). However, as a *problématique*, it can also obscure other processes of 'internal colonisation' on minority or indigenous groups (Nederveen Pieterse and Parekh 1995: 8) or 'crypto-colonisations' of peripheries from urban centres or urban satellites by the state's capital, which follow the logic of Western domination models (see also Herzfeld 2002). On this, I explain in Chapter 5 that Brazilian regional self-designations generate 'civilisational' alliances in the South American 'neighbourhood' of nations that draw upon conceptions of risk and animosity originating in precisely those spectral political centres that Brazilians condemn for the murder of their ancestry. Here, the ceremonial script and football as a popular movement seem to recite the same 'plot'. We cannot disconnect the spectacle this book analyses from the new spatial arrangement of politics that expand and develop into (criminogenic or not) networks, flows of ideas and various other interconnected mobilities (Peck 2003; Rumford 2006; Franko Aas 2007; Adey 2010; Urry 2007, 2014). Without collapsing the analysis into a discourse of the 'immanence of mobility' in mega-events such as that of the 2014 World Cup, it is useful to remember that just like the origins of colonial expansion and the partial development of Fordism, mobility has been commensurate with European linkages of spatiality to commercial exchange and filiative reciprocity (Jensen and Richardson 2004; Argyrou 2013; Rumford 2008). Considering athletic mega-events as part of the great European tradition of intercultural dialogue and global peace making (Tzanelli 2004) places the Brazilian spectacle in the context of an expansive global connectivity through exchange of goods – legally or illegally obtained and traded (Castells 1996, 2000; Urry 2003).

The ethics of contemporary consumption have become a lightning rod for new social movements and protest groups that fight for the improvement of the conditions under which things are produced in distant lands such as Asian and South American countries (Enloe 1990; Sheller 2003: 13). It is significant that economic exploitation, scientific investigation, visual consumption and conservation were identified as part of a single project: that of appropriating the physical world into consumption apparatuses and practices (Urry 1995). This project, once inextricably tied to the colonisation of exotic places, is today connected to offshoring mechanisms and secretive financial mobilities (Urry 2014). Urry's Simmelian thesis on offshoring, which presupposes the comprehension of social processes and types in terms of social distance (Simmel and Wolff 1950: 402; Frisby 1992) should also be qualified on the basis of other forms of accessibility, given that consumers of touristified paradises are only allowed to access the spectacle prepared for them, devoid of the mishaps of production processes (Pattullo 1996). As the world is split into more and more post-colonial polities that emerge from old and new imperialist projects, the old 'representational machine' (Greenblatt 1991) that used South America as 'a territory for the projection of … capital, expertise, dreams and power' (Salvatore 1998: 71) is copied in the peripheries it subjugated. What the post-colonies export these days is not just various such representational discourses (modified in various degrees) as their own, but also native human expertise modelled after the image of 'developed' global centres. These exports are reciprocated by imports of expertise and artistic labour that contribute to the production of the mega-event. Many technologies of the Brazilian ceremonial spectacle thus constitute nodes and practices of seeing, narrating, displaying and experiencing the other-native through what Aravamudan (1999: 6–7) saw in 'tropicopolitanism'.

Too far away from Europe and North America to comprise a global mass tourist destination, Brazil has entertained visitor influx in the past, mainly from Portugal and France. In particular, its major urban centres, such as Rio de Janeiro and São Paulo, could not entice adventure tourists, mostly attracted by Amazonian wilderness, which nevertheless remains too inaccessible to foreigners (Jaguaribe and Hetherington 2004: 155). However, electronic trading and other informational mobilities partially shape Brazilian conceptions of globalisation in the tripartite flux of demand-supply-competition (Nederveen Pieterse 2004: 9–10). It is more correct to argue that, like other post-colonial cultures of the region, Brazilian economies are better geared towards competition and networking that regionally depends on a filiative, clientelist ethic, and globally on prestige-building cont(r)acts. We may call contemporary, urban Brazil a 'spectacle-prone' society (Debord 1995: 31), preoccupied with appearances as an economic process – even though 'images' as commodities belong to bastardised colonial philosophies. The focus of the ephemeral marketing of images distorts trans-modernity's project of 'Becoming', rather than 'Being', and a search of unity within difference (Harvey 1989: 359), but even such commercialised spaces enclose critical and corrective voices that may even belong to elite art. Hence, the present study's dual focus on ceremonial and activist performances is the crux of a 'post-international' cultural political agenda that is not controlled solely by state actors but is rhizomatic and multipolar (Rosenau 1990). This mode of acting is simultaneously a mode of understanding and shaping the social that encloses utopian aspirations to blend 'legislating' with interpretation of the social (Bauman 1987; Tzanelli 2010: 225). Yet, as I explain below, its actual performance might reproduce some cosmological structures alongside new, creative touches.

On recreating Brazilian character and the 'person'

The Brazilian system of mobility involves agential practices of meaning making that are performed and communicated through embodied media (Farnell 1999). The ceremony's medium of communication involves blended 'technologies' that correspond to an actor-network theoretical schema but prioritise human ideational and material mobilities. It is as if the ceremonial design aims to modify European conceptions of the 'tourist gaze' (Urry 2002), in spite of its ability to incorporate other types of sensory experience (Urry and Larsen 2011). To the sensory stimuli of the ceremony one should stress the significance of music, which is one of the primary media of intercultural exchange in the South Americas (see Robins 2000 on music transmission and encounter). If anything, this reminds us that 'touring' practices are deeply grounded in multisensory activities and that the visual ones are always constituted through 'the material connection to bodies, space time and objects' (Obrador 2003: 57). The Cartesian divide between mind and body is challenged in both predictable and unorthodox ways: not only does the ceremony showcase *whole ethnic communities as embodied subjects*, who experience the world phenomenally (Merleau-Ponty 1962), but it also illuminates the role of imported, colonial civilising processes as a turning point in the development of *Brasilidade* as 'Brazilian nature'.

Ceremonial technopoesis borrows from philosophical connections between 'writing' or articulation to produce a script for *Brasilidade.* Practices of embodied 'inscription' through performance, but also the 2014 ceremonies' 'indigenous' observations ('readings') on foreign inscription, exteriorise knowledge and produce native interpretations. This first use of tools or technologies is a representation of Brazil's 'technical memory' (Frabetti 2011: 14–5), apparently born, according to the opening ceremony, in the tropics. Its mission was to enable transmissions of individual experience 'from generation to generation', as a 'world of spirits' that defined proto-Brazilian temporality (Stiegler 2003: 159). The imaginary villages of Edgar Allan Poe that DaMatta uses to analyse closed societies, in which time was conceived of as cyclical – 'and it is impossible to think of about social, economic, and political realities without thinking about a circular cosmos' (DaMatta 1991: 247) – approximate Brazilian cosmologies before colonisation. The opening ceremony's procession directed performance around an artificial 'globe', so as to suggest that its leading Brazilian personae (*ethnies*) managed to direct reflection on the other-coloniser in organised, embodied *styles.* The selected styles (dance and martial arts routines) might be contextually different from the mega-event's occasion (football), but when placed in the *kairotic* colonial momentum, they become structurally and ritualistically homologous to national styles of football (Inglis and Hughson 2000). In this respect, I consider some of the selected ceremonial styles as gateways to the domain resided in by the stabilising forces of subaltern Brazilian lifeworlds (Seamon 1980: 162 in Adey 2010: 139). Football, capoeira and dance manage to articulate non-representational characteristics of the mobile body at the moment it performs 'choreographed' activities that only knowing viewers translate into meaningful emotions.

In short, in the 2014 World Cup's ceremonial domains, representations of 'Brazilian character' split into two personae – one addressed to Brazilian and other neighbouring audiences, and another to foreign visitors-tourists. Hence, background knowledge of Brazilian memories conditions the selection of the mega-event's creative capital. If, externally, Brazil as a trans-human persona, or Brazilian types of humans as social beings, correspond to the global economies of tourist signs (Lash and Urry 1994: 230–3), internally they respond to Brazilian society's needs for mythical archetypes and appropriately crafted national plots (Tzanelli 2013b). If sport de-routinises the security of social life, providing audiences with 'controlled doses of excitement associated [with] fear, shame and violence … [so as] to reinforce the sentiment of superiority among competitors' (Korstanje 2012: 4), its ceremony achieves a similar result at a communal, cosmic level. The difference lies in the degree of ceremonial control over the 'script', which is much higher than the control over the end of football games. Football results are supposed to be conditioned by meritocracy (merit as *moíra*, one's fair share) at all times, whereas ceremonial narratives always enhance national *personae*, plots and archetypes with serendipitous qualities for the benefit of the host community. Even humanity's endgame, death, is healed by the expectancy of national 'resurrection' (McKee 1999; Tzanelli 2008). The idea of dying, as well as that of commemorative mourning, echoes the tragedy of democracy, 'where the god is beheld crucified in the catastrophes, not of the great houses only, but of every common home' (Campbell 2008: 27). Death is in this instance something that unites humanity in mourning and celebration. If the athletic hero achieves a domestic 'microcosmic' victory (medal winning, Cup raising) as representative of a hidden whole (the imagined community), the ceremonial hero-*persona* attains cosmic proportions as the abstracted human who joins artwork's 'macrocosmic triumph' (ibid.: 37).

The Brazilian transpersonal character of the ceremony reflects the ways Brazilian social life endorses persons with the essential role of making kinship function healthily. There is little structural difference between the myths of the nation's serendipitous recovery from social ills (including defeats) and the familial-networked person's good luck in life. Mauss's (1954) conception of 'personage' in tribal societies provides the origins of the contemporary person as a highly individualised 'being', an emotionally and psychologically mature individual and a social unit based on collective moral imperatives (kinship). The Brazilian individual has no fate, hence no place in a competitive world of corporations, state networks and regional kinships. However, all individuals know that 'fate' and 'destiny' are 'emplotted' in realist terms – hence a degree of rational planning is implicated in their social positioning. In fact, I argue in Chapter 5 that there is serendipitous association between Brazilian conceptions of the individual and mourning as a public performance – here for the 'nation', there for global visitors-viewers.

This cautions social scientists to consider Brazilian mannerisms as performative events 'emplotted' and 'entailed' by communities in chronic contexts. By 'emplotment' I refer to Ricoeur's (1988: 10) suggestion that there is a formal principle of configuration in artistic genres, such as the novel, against which characters constantly develop their autonomy, so as to confront 'readers' with a question: 'are we faced with illusion or resemblance to reality in fiction?' (Pellauer 2007: 77). Embodied performances (on the ceremonial stage and in the streets) during the 2014 World Cup, negotiate formal emplotments of Brazilian history, therefore they provide interpretative representations of them. Here the concept of entailment proves useful as a system of pre-requisites for technicity to exist (primary entailment) and function (secondary entailment) (Taylor 2010). Entailment suggests that persons and their equivalent ceremonial personage exist only within the structures of kinship, which are, by turn, enabled within the mechanical conditions of the (post-) industrial system. Communities need for their techniques and technicity certain post-industrial tools that only the technological complex of the media can provide. In the 2014 World Cup the media condition the communities' articulation, hence their interpretative-representational possibilities. The social scientist's task is, in a sense, to activate a tertiary entailment: to figure out what Brazilians and foreign artists wish to convey with performances as a social reality. The general task is ubiquitous, because conveying contexts and meanings of articulation is shared with other professionals, including journalists.

Translation is often taken as a straightforward task, when in fact it entails successive interpretations in cultural environments that differ from the original message's 'cradle'. There are always possibilities for sociological comparison, with all the humorous mishaps they produce. Skouteri-Didaskalou (1980) gave the mark of zero to Greek translators of Lévi-Strauss's *Tristes Tropiques*, when they conveyed his master term (*tristes*) in a muddled way, connecting it to so many other words (*malhereux, morne, sombre, sordide*, etc.) he used in the book that it became a floating signifier. The failure to stabilise primary, secondary and tertiary entailment in Lévi-Strauss's discourse divested its translation of the possibility of reaching meaningful understandings of its writer's emplotment of the real tropics, as well as of the tropical context in which they performed their rituals. According to Skouteri-Didaskalou, his translators' simplified rendition of native cosmology excluded from the original title (untranslated in the English version at the author's request) the possibility to consider tropical natives as *fateless* ('Poor Tropics!' – the present study's 'individuals') because of their implication in capitalist development; mournful in performative ways, in rituals of social bonding (hence, as 'persons'); and pain inducing in interactive (centre-periphery, observer-observed) contexts.

The humorous subtext of this confusion emerges, as the reader becomes more disorientated – but the disorientation is also instructive as part of the impossibility to restore a supposed original meaning. We may say that the Lévi-Straussian *tristes* are, like the defeated Brazilian nation in 2014, fathomable only in a fluid plot of performative mourning ('Poor Brazilians! What is in store for their team from now on? What about the national investment in the World Cup?'). Such cultural transliterations stand at the heart of Brazilian cosmographic desires. To follow Skouteri-Didaskalou's (1980: 58) acute observations again, social scientists must read such social events as 'texts' akin to the *Tristes Tropiques* myth of the heroic quest for meaning, magic, immortality and knowledge – all the investigations that frame human existence culturally. The formalist notes of this interpretation match those of Brazilian cosmology after the European conquest, in which appearances are treated as spells one casts on (de facto mediated) reality to manipulate impressions (Warnke 2011: 45). Here we have no choice but to articulate the book's epistemology.

Epistemology, methodology and musical sociality

The mobilities paradigm informs my conviction that we need a realist framework for investigations in social scientific fields – for a realist relational ontology is 'capable of transcending old debates and bridging disciplinary boundaries' (Sheller 2014b: 2). Yet, 'knowing' and 'being' need to be connected somehow – a task for which I use hermeneutics. Any selection of 'artistic texts' – these are ceremonial, activist or, as is the case here, both – is, like reading in a particular discipline, 'programmatic', rather than merely 'representative' (Tanner 2003: ix). Just as traditional ethnographic practice aspires to filter the strangeness and exoticism of a human reality different from our own through anthropological theory (DaMatta 1991: 245; Geertz 2000: 16), artistic approaches to other cultures through their texts and performances aspire to create a social programme. I have no illusions when it comes to my production of particular knowledge about Brazil through my selection of authoritative (e.g. endorsed by authority) artistic texts, and their matching with unauthorised performance practices (by football fans). The contrast underlines Gellner's (1959, 1983; Herzfeld 2005) acknowledgment of false differentiations between 'highbrow' and 'lowbrow' practices and beliefs and the admission that sociological studies of art can be of interest to wider audiences (Inglis and Hughson 2005; De la Fuente 2007).

The actual materials on which the study draws include articles published in the international (Brazilian, Anglophone and Germanophone) press online, as well as YouTube or other public site presentations of the mega-event's ceremonies, interviews with celebrities and politicians and announcements on the official FIFA and Brazilian World Cup sites. The global public spheres in which fan, national, regional and transnational identities emerge are 'staged' with the help of new media technologies (Tzanelli 2007: 17), but the ways these articulations emerge through connections between such spheres or sites deserves additional examination (Nederveen Pieterse 1998: 79–80). Although, methodologically, I do not research through physical sites, I do consider contextual productions of meaning (Büscher and Urry 2009; Büscher et al. 2011). Treating the web as a multi-site that facilitates plural meanings for the mega-event entails consideration of the ways in which the Internet as a medium absorbs and recreates itself through hyperlinked content, breaking this up into 'searchable chunks' while also surrounding itself 'with various other media it has absorbed' (Carr 2010: 91; Anastasiou and Schäler 2010).

We deal with multiple spheres and interpretative agents, including the media industries, the national centre and the community from which the media draw inspiration. The word 'local' or 'community' might distract from 'the intense complexity or micro-politics that all sides are inevitably imbricated within and shaped by' (Meethan 2001: 61). As Dürrschmidt (1997: 57–8) also notes, intense processes of micro-globalisation of global cities may call for considerations of lifeworlds in locality's stead, to encapsulate the ways in which different and similar perceptions of living cultures constantly bleed outside neatly defined territorial (local, regional or national) boundaries. There are intersections and disjunctions between the sub-scenes and imaginaries of these sites (virtual, fictional and real) that I explore as discursive tropes, which are continuously (re)interpreted by various human agents (D'Andrea 2006: 114–5). We deal with a multiple (Errington 2011: 34), rather than neat 'double hermeneutics' (Giddens 1987) of subalterns, artists, tourist business and authorities, to which one must add that propagated by the researcher (Tzanelli 2013b: chapter 1).

I borrow for my reading of the ceremony and its social context from post-positivist epistemologies with an emphasis on critical realism – in particular, its applications in contemporary tourism mobilities contexts (Nechar 2005 in Tribe 2008: 8; Ayikoru 2008). Mega-events such as the Brazilian World Cup are attractors of global sports tourism, so we should problematise the ways their ceremonial spectacles are produced for the global audiences that assume the role of tourists (Tribe 2004: 59). If the production of tourism knowledge is not politics-free, the ways the object of knowledge (the ceremonial Brazil) comes into being are also steeped in political and economic intent. In this respect, I disagree with Hollinshead's (2004: 84) suggestion that 'matters of ontology should always precede the choice of a particular research method': knowledge of tourist destinations also produces (and reinvents) them prior to academic study, especially in ceremonial contexts that tend to modify ontological narratives of place. The notion of place is only deceptively simple and merits problematisation in relation to its human populations, its ecosystems and global political, economic and cultural imaginaries (see also Shurmer-Smith and Hannam 1994; Urry 1995; Cresswell 2004; Edensor 2014). Indeed, there is an ontological complicity between conventional academic differentiations between identity and subjectivity. This conflation could also be sustained in the current study by the fact that researchers who observe and analyse the mega-events' football cultures and rituals are simply 'too close to them' (Augé 1982: 59): proximity brews subjectivisation, enmeshing real events into personal biographies and subjectivities.

If the study's epistemological and ontological aspects are informed by critical realism, which emphasises constructions and productions of socio-cultural realities (hence the power of human narrativity to make socio-cultures; Archer 1995, 1996, 2000, 2003; Smith 2007), then my blend of discourse analysis with hermeneutics provides an appropriate methodological framework (Alexander and Smith 2001). By 'hermeneutics', I refer to the sociological, rather than theological, 'art' of interpretative 'exposure' of social events, as well as their multi-disciplinary contextualisation (see also Inglis 2005; Tzanelli 2011). By discourse I refer to a specific ensemble of ideas, concepts, and categorisations 'that are produced, reproduced and transformed in a particular set of practices and through which meaning is given to physical and social realities' (Hajer 1995). For Foucaultian theorists, rejecting the 'meta-historical deployment of indefinite teleologies' (Foucault 1984: 76–7) produces much-needed histories of the present that are based on tenacious re-arrangements of past experience – or, more accurately put, memory traces that invent one's past anew. Brazil's temporal movement involves the juxtaposition of a series of pasts (the ceremony's different 'acts') to promote a conceptual structure that is still in progress (Rodowick 1997: 160–9; Tzanelli 2011: chapters 3 and 6). The ceremony's retroactive reading of the Brazilian 'archive' has now joined the 'global library of mega-events' (Roche 1996: 325) – a symbolic 'ideoscapal' act of classifying athletic events (Appadurai 1990), so to speak, which should attain material extensions in the future as a record of humanity's peace-making rituals.

The exhibition of tropological traces or performative themes involves ways of displaying the 'Brazilian dilemma' as an intercultural momentum. There is no doubt that journalistic and televised reporting of the tropes (on which the study occasionally draws) provides audiences with a framework 'through which events can be viewed, ordered, interpreted and emotionally glossed' (Tudor 1992: 391). Yet, such commentary-driven processes of 'world construction' as interrelated discourses of ethno-centricity, racism and politics are not provided in a socio-cultural vacuum: journalists in World Cups may carry cultural prejudices, like all humans, but they record the social field's atmosphere (see Alabarces and Rodriguez 1996 in Alabarces et al. 2001: 552). Some of them are knowledgeable on the host's conditions and reproduce popular and scholarly knowledge in equal stead.

When matched with scholarly studies, many of the sources I mobilise produce accurate local mythologies, national tropes and transnational rivalries. Addressed to visitors-pilgrims, the event activates a twin form of 'recreation': as a rebirth of the national community in global cosmic spaces, and as the community's 'experimental travelling', which internalises encounters with visitors-others 'away from the spiritual, cultural, or even religious centre of [its] world, into its periphery, towards the centres of other cultures and societies' (Cohen 1979: 182–3). The dramatisation of the national scene as a transnational or glocal event involves a repertoire of emotional, material and human mobilities – including 'the relational mobilizations of memories and performances, gendered and racialized bodies … and atmospheres' (Sheller and Urry 2004: 1). Yet, by fixating upon Brazil's racist histories, we downplay the frustrating flexibility of the spectrum between 'black' and 'white', which might include phenotype, morality and status as evaluating criteria circumstantially (Stephens 1989; Russell-Wood 2002b: 24–6). By the same token, using 'gender' as our sole criterion provides an incomplete picture. The emotional onus of the story is, I argue, the transformation of the cultural community's 'deferred action' or *Nachträglichkeit* (Laplanche and Pontalis 1973: 111–4, in Aravamudan 1999: 15) into political and cultural motion, enclosed in a series of artistic parables. By deferral I allude to the postponement of expressing direct hostility until a time that favours action. Ceremonial and protesting dramatisations are excellent examples of this deferral, bridging the mega-event's *chronic* and *kairotic* gap.

Ceremonial and activist parables show Brazilian humans in various states of (im)mobility, but always as part of a larger unity that Western modernity rejected centuries ago. This rejection of human holism in mind, body and heart was complemented by early modern resurrections of Aristotelian readings of Plato (Wenning 2009), which divided the soul (*psyche*) into *noetic* (*nous* = reason), *epithymic* (*epithymía* = appetite, desire) and *thymotic* (*thymós* = spiritedness) properties. This compartmentalisation recognises *thymotic* properties as auxiliary to reason, only when the soul is not corrupted by bad upbringing (Plato 1974: 441a) – a condition modern state apparatuses attribute to social rebels (Tzanelli 2011: chapter 5). Though the Brazilian soul rests on emotional expressivity, its performative focus on the body and gestural expressions and the overall emphasis on image making (e.g. honourable self-presentation) suggest an alternative take on modernity or a worldview originating outside such Western cosmological frameworks of 'order and progress' (Gellner 1985), but communicating with them.

I explore these Brazilian performative 'texts' with the help of scene theory. Although the concept of 'scene' is primarily used by academic researchers of music, it is compatible with sociological and anthropological understandings of theatre 'technologies', including staging terrestrial and digital venues for social performances (Bennett 2004: 230; Peterson and Bennett 2004). According to Straw (1991: 379), scenes activate 'a particular state of relations between various populations and social groups as [they] coalesce around specific coalitions of musical style'. As both local and trans-local instances, scenes refer both to musical styles and human interaction in domains in which these styles circulate. The concept has resonance with sub-cultural analysis but also the well-established 'neo-tribal' theory (Maffesoli 1996; Bennett 1999, 2005; Malbon 1999), because both enable us to examine networks of cultural flows. In any case, the Brazilian social scene is heavily influenced by the development of music and dance sub-cultures such as those of samba. The tourist capital of samba music and dance as 'staged' events (MacCannell 1973, 1989) also implicates the mobility of Brazilian *habitus* from the national to international settings (as *dispositif*). Nonetheless, 'staging' presupposes spectatorship and a plot to perform. Contexts of international communication and such as that of the 2014 World Cup are perfect for the activation of national iconicity, the principle of identifying through semblances, which is often reduced to stereotyping others (Herzfeld 2005: 56).

However, iconicity belongs to the workings of national modernisation. The emphasis of this modernisation on image needs complementing by that of musicality and multisensory epistemology. My understanding of iconicity does, however, refer to the multisensory communication of 'archplots' or central artistic-as-social scenarios (on cinematic archplots; see McKee 1999: 3–4, 41–2), which usually centre on images. Throughout this study I abstain from viewing archplots as mere artistic narratives, stating instead that like stage artists and dramatists, whole societies create their dramas with distinctive plots, stages and scenes, but also roles and actors (DaMatta 1991: 200). These socio-cultural archplots also remind us that at the heart of each tale we will find a person (hero, heroine) or object (e.g. magical artefact), whose destiny needs to be decided by cosmic forces (Sklovsky 1990 [1925] in Smith 2008: 173).

If Brazilian epistemologies promote sensory holism, then one cannot study the ceremonies by merely prioritising visuality: although previous takes on the primacy of the 'tourist gaze' (Urry 2002) have been revised, so as to filter other sensory experiences through seeing (Urry and Larsen 2011), the approach can still *only* account for global audience reception of the spectacle. Epistemological critiques of this approach in the field of tourism (Veijola and Jokinen 1994; Perkins and Thorns 2001; Sheller and Urry 2004; Cresswell 2006; Veijola and Valtonen 2007; Hannam 2008; Veijola 2009; Tzanelli 2011, 2013c, 2014) attest to the globality of multisensory apprehending of the world, but their Brazilian particularities have their own experiential and political contexts. We must bear in mind at all times that aesthetic styles are integral to social formation and are 'held by place by the "demands" made by societies to think their key values at a level of abstraction *appropriate to their principles of social formation*' (Witkin 2005: 59, emphasis added). Some indigenous Brazilian contexts, such as that of the Suyá of the Matto Grosso region, prove that emphasis on visuality as a globalised mark of cosmopolitanism is methodologically problematic. The Suyá attribute social significance to speaking and hearing, but link sight with anti-social behaviour such as witchcraft – a phenomenon also present in Mediterranean cultural discourses as the 'evil eye' (Tzanelli 2011: chapter 1). Suyá sensory hierarchies are centred on body ornamentation, especially around the lips and ears – practices concomitant with an emphasis on aurality (Herzfeld 2001: 249). The Suyá live in one of the poorest parts of Brazil, in which Scherper-Hughes studied the (apparently inexplicable) indifference of mothers to new-borns in more urbanised poor areas. The lack of expressivity and affectionate touch is definitely contextual on such occasions, given the fact that young mothers have to compete for scarce resources with their children. Such examples prove that generalisations of sensory engagement are even more precarious when we explore conceptions of beauty and aesthetic preference. Lest we attribute civility to the nationally and globally mixed urban visitors during the 2014 World Cup, examinations of their performative synaesthetics need to be 'exorcised', so to speak, from any notion of advanced (urban) aesthetics.

If synaesthetic performativity provides another epistemological tool, then the idea of thinking and interpreting 'in rhythm' can also be valuable in

Brazilian contexts (in which even foreign visitors are asked to comply with popular rituals they may not fully comprehend). Particular music genres have been the core of Brazilian 'ways of doing things', including narratives of collective movement (migration) and settlement, as well as the cultures of protest produced by these collective mobilities and moorings (Veloso 2003). This phenomenon, which I examine as an artistic datum, is part of what I defined in previous sections as 'articulation'. DeNora (2003: 39) argues that 'music' and the 'social' are co-produced, even though 'new musicology' tends to posit 'social structure' as its backdrop (De la Fuente 2007: 417). She claims that although musicologists 'never [actually] *see music in the act of articulating social structure or as it is mobilized for this articulation*' (DeNora 2003: 37, emphasis added), this is what happens all the time. As already explained, Brazilian musical articulations are supported by native technopoetic assemblages and the respective communities that operate them. I therefore contend that music, as a social event and as technology, allows processes of mobilisation of social forces and of articulation of their interconnectedness (proximity) to combine in the creation of 'surplus value' (Buscema 2011: 43). The *biomechanics* of Brazilian identity communicate with its 'biopolitics', the ways the nation's 'human capital' – a combination of intellectual and embodied capital – supports entrepreneurial business in the mega-event's neoliberal context (Lemke 2001: 198).

Let us not forget that artistic contexts have, or might acquire, a political background – otherwise put, the movement and marketing of their texts is always burdened with situated meaning and value (Cresswell 2006: 1–8; Adey 2010: 34–6). Brazilian music and performance are constitutive of the culture's *eudaimonic* ethic as much as they are a form of intercultural communication. As a form of mobility, musical articulations of *Brasilidade* affect other aspects of human motion (Nederveen Pieterse 2004: 26–8), including people's so-called '*thymotic* properties'. The following chapter's detailed analysis of the ceremonial spectacle certainly proffers such *eudaimonic* versions of *Brasilidade*, but its transnational articulations appear both to reproduce and modify the Brazilian cosmographic template.

4 The ceremonial script

From tropicalism and *Brasilidade* to cosmographic mobilities

The 2014 World Cup opening and the closing ceremonies should be read as bilateral mobility vehicles: while on the one hand they enabled a global trafficking of Brazilian heritage by audiovisual and kinaesthetic means, they also legitimised the articulation of Brazilian desire to claim foreign cosmographic riches. As I will proceed to argue, this utopian exchange of 'magical goods' (Sahlins 1976) or 'cultural capital' (Bourdieu 1984) adumbrates the performance of affective capital in the ceremonies. The bilateral mobility schema is a priori deemed unequal, prompting one side to consume (visitors) and the other to produce (hosts). This allows the hosts to use performative kinaesthetics so as either to issue debt ultimata, or use the very principle of hospitality to enhance their status as global cultural donors. In these ceremonial contexts we observe that even stereotyped conceptions of 'uncouth' Brazilian masculinity are ennobled with technical skills that match feminine artistry's civility. Another prominent feature of ceremonial performance is the practice of strategic code switching from 'individual' to 'person', and filiative to affiliative community, or vice versa, which promotes Brazil itself as a flexible, networked entity. Needless to add that although a federal state is composed of regional histories, the fate of local culture is to be assimilated into the capital-centre's uniform narrative. The idea of a singular Brazilian culture is fiction, ceremonially projected through such powerful state-capitalist technologies that 'it score[s] the retina, leaving a perceptual after-image, which distort[s] subsequent perception' (Archer 1988: 2, in Albrow et al. 1997: 26). I analyse the events in separate sections, beginning with the opening ceremony and proceeding to the closing one. Despite their global hues, both events seem to promote a singular aim: the dissemination of Brazilian 'character' or Brazilianness (*Brasilidade*) as a flexible commodity, a political-cultural good that stands at the heart of the global mobilities enjoyed by the mega-event's visitors.

The opening ceremony: indigenous tropicopolitans as natural goods

Undoubtedly, the opening event set spectacle standards rather high, projecting a feel of natural opulence that can be seen, heard and felt by global synaesthetes as a whole. The transfer of native holism to visitors also revised Western discourses that consider urban strangers (*Fremden*) as subjects separated from their surroundings (Simmel and Wolff 1950), but retained this separation at a moral level. A cast of 660 dancers around a ball on the Arena de São Paulo pitch paid tribute to the country's nature, people and football (BBC Sport 2014c). The ceremony showcased three Brazilian treasures: nature, people and football (World Cup Portal 2014b). Its central element was a so-called 'live ball' with over 90,000 clusters and 7,000 lighting units, which moves around during the show. The show was divided into four acts:

Act one: Nature: mineral and vegetable wonders
Act two: People: happiness for living, diversity and passion for music and dance
Act three: Football: Brazil's true art
Act four: Official song 'We Are One', sung by Jennifer Lopez, rapper Pitbull, Claudia Leite and Olodum

The programme, which provides the first glimpse of filiative-to-affiliative code switching, was choreographed by Paulo Barros, a two-time winner of the samba school title at the Carnival in Rio de Janeiro, who trained circus artists and army soldiers to perform (Associated Press 2014). Moving from the logic of a kinetic 'performative museology' (Kirshenblatt-Gimblett 2002: 59), solely appealing to distant cosmopolitan taste, to more combined synaesthetic narratives of identity and contemporary global consumption practices of cultural specificity, produced a mediatised, global public sphere (Habermas 1989a; Thompson 1995). The fact that before Act one's 'Brazilian nature' parable, a giant LED ball in the centre of the pitch provided insight into the world's fifth largest country (Tyers 2014), suggests a replacement of native orality with virtuality as scripture. Obscuring the particular in favour of the universal, the ceremony prepared us for what figured as a more general mega-event norm: the presentation of the national-allegorical as a universal imperative (Tzanelli 2010, 2013c).

Act one

If the globe places Brazilian socio-cultures at the ceremonial centre, then we may discern in it 'the charismatic nexus' of a culture's 'supreme, ultimate mortality' – what Cohen (1979: 180) terms its 'centre'. The Brazilian centre invites pilgrims-audiences to explore the community's moral values, practices and hierarchies as things to be admired from symbolic distance (Eliade 1989). At the same time, its constant inspection by the indigenous performers, who live in harmony with nature, is more attuned to actual policy discourses. These discourses support cross-scalar interactions in global environmental governance and bottom-up change – once exclusively coordinated by non-governmental organisations (NGOs) in countries such as Brazil. Therefore, the interchange of groups of Amazonian plants with indigenous groups can be read as respect for Brazilian ecosystems that include humans, animals and plants. However, one may also note that from the ceremonial outset, Brazil's symbolic 'globe/centre' is over-determined by 'advanced' forms of technology that Portuguese conquerors first introduced to the country. Indeed, this is the technology on which the ceremony itself depends as a narrative. The globe is, ultimately, an imported world picture that enmeshed local conceptions of time and space into the 'metaphysics of roundness'. This imported notion of the globe/global as geometric roundness turned native cosmology into a 'poetic-scientific bastard heaven, a product of geometry as much as of mythology' (Sloterdijk 2009: 29, 34).

An informed viewer may ever regard ceremonial representations of liquid routes (water, rivers, sea) vis-à-vis Portuguese constructions of the Atlantic and Indian oceans 'as a space supportive of their specific strategies for dominating distant land spaces' (Steinberg 2000: 257), leading to 'a very significant restructuring of time-space relations' (Inglis 2010: 6; Giddens 1990). Attraction to the centre of the ritual entails a certain degree of respect for the exotic by indigenous populations. In this respect, the introductory ceremonial sequence resembles the cosmology of Pan-Amazonians for whom the internal social order 'requires the incorporation of the powers of the society of others … [the stranger as] the culture hero from whom everything was learned' (Erikson 1996: 79, in Sahlins 2013a: 185). The globe as strangeness reminds us once again that especially Amazonian people attribute material and immaterial values (such as shamanistic powers) on things of foreign origins (Descola 1996), just as contemporary humans value touristic goods from faraway lands as symbolic capital. Therefore, the act unfolds as a thanatourist narrative on the Brazilian cosmography of riches, mourned by the performing indigenous community (Stasch 2009) – and by extension, the mega-event's global communities of viewers/'pilgrims' (Coleman and Eade 2004; Tzanelli 2013b).

These pilgrims are given the opportunity to see and hear what remains mostly inaccessible to them due to Brazil's geomorphological idiosyncrasy. One may argue that where lack of accessibility is a given, the picturesque provides in the ceremony snapshots of Amazonian nature for global tourist gazes (Urry and Larsen 2011). However, such representations are not based on European ideas of the picturesque as aesthetic appreciation detached from personal interests and desires (Budd 2003). The ceremony's main concern ramifies on artistic and pragmatic-political objectives: on the one hand, the procession proffers an aesthetically pleasing version of global Amazonian imaginaries as ecologically diverse. On the other, however, in the context of (however elementary, global knowledge on) accelerated climate change, it allows space for the mobilisation of scientific categories to shape aesthetic guidance on how to appreciate natural objects (Carlson 2000 in Todd 2008; 158, 164). Let us not forget that 'tropicalisation' was originally used to describe the acclimatisation of flora, fauna 'and even machinery to warmer habitats' (Aravamudan 1999: 6).

How is this tropicalisation experienced during the ceremony? Priority is given to an 'aesthetics of participation' through the audience's multisensory engagement with the Amazonian environmental panorama that promotes a holistic, perpetual unity of humans with nature (Berleant 1995). The performers literally blend humanity into ideals of healthy biodiversity: dressed as flowers, plants and animals and circling the globe, they issue a reminder on the fragility of nature in rapidly expanding urban enclaves such as those of Brazil.

This embodied performance of the new bio-geographies proffers life scenarios after 'the end of Nature' (McKibben 1990 in Lorimer 2010: 491). The fear that 'nature' as a pure essence and form, and defined in relation to society, is coming to an end (Castree 2005), in combination with critiques of the disembodied human subject (Thrift 2007), prompt explorations of relational models of multi-naturalism. Such hybrid bio-geographies are often placed alongside established multicultural dilemmas in countries such as Brazil, which is plagued by issues of 'environmental racism' (Jamal et al. 2003; Blanton 2011) in urban milieux. Simply put, the ceremony suggests that humans in the flesh and in the spirit are not segregated from nature but accepted as part of humanity without prejudice based on colour, class or origins. If the world is socially constructed, both materially and discursively, then people – with their diversity of cultures, politics and practices – can no longer be set to one side. 'There is a growing but grudging awareness amongst bio-geographers that invoking Nature is a situated and political act; "social values" matter' (Lorimer 2010: 494). One may argue that the ceremonial shift from the tropical to urban spaces later in the ceremony tries to encapsulate the coexistence of this twin discourse of 'nature'. In this respect, the mega-event's spectacle is an ecological one, characterised by interspecies entanglements in indigenous settings and social differentiation in urban cultures – an urban-as-natural ecology. The introduction of people on trampolines performing to ambient music also represents Brazilian love of nature in affective terms of 'play': the serious *jôgo* of life.

Act two

Sporting activities are tied up with everyday activities in this act's utopian representation of Amazonian nature, which opens with a series of indigenous canoes that circumnavigate the globe (Tyers 2014). The section's feminisation of natural beauty concludes with the introduction of an imposing giant female figure that symbolises Brazil's diverse population. This way, the ceremony portrays *Brasilidade* as multicultural and *maravilhosa* – not just a colourful and exotic surface, travelling the world as a marketable good, but a loved entity (*linda*), properly respected at home (*casa*) (DaMatta 1991). A series of groups in different costumes dancing in different rhythms also speaks the language of Brazilian multiculturalism and hybridity. Their circling of the female figure emulates the mind walking of the Yolngu tribes towards the

Figure 4.1 The mega-event's giant female *Brasilidade* 'deconstructed'
Source: Jimmy Balkovicius (Flickr), Creative Commons 2.0. Licence: www.creativecommons.org/licenses/by-sa/2.0/

creative walk of their ancestors, bringing it forward into the present so as to give sense and direction to the living (Morphy 1991: 114). By travelling from place to place in one's imagination, 'one finds in each place, and recalls to memory, particular ancestral beings and their stories' (Ingold 2010: 19).

Many First World mobilities depend on the successful demobilisation of places and human groups (Cresswell 2001; Sheller 2004: 15), so we should approach the segment's indigenous 'dreamscape' with some caution. The routes of the ceremonial canoes (around the globe) figure as nodes of economic activity that simultaneously build up the 'backbones of cultural transformation' (Nederveen Pieterse 2004: 34; Holton 2007). As is the case with other instances of colonisation, colonial values and institutions could not last in an alien context without undergoing processes of translation into 'hospitable traditional analogues' (Nederveen Pieterse and Parekh 1995: 2). The alien technology, which in the ceremony is represented through luminous electronic projections of mathematical schemata on a globe, reminds us that virtuality and virtualisation 'are not necessarily "new" epistemologies but rather more like uncanny and belated recognitions' (Aravamudan 1999: 17) of the ways national archives are interpreted by localities. The ceremonial segment juxtaposes by technological means conceptions of 'digitality' to indigenous 'orality' (Ong 1982), so the Brazilian 'tribes' interpret the encounter into an embodied local idiom of dance and music.

The feeling of fracture or *tempos mixtos* (mixed epochs) dominating Latin American hybridity was introduced by colonisation, after all, a particular movement that stimulated glocal 'temporalizations of space' as well as political re-conceptualisations of individual and collective freedom (Cresswell 2006: 3–4). The ceremonial procession's representation of time provides a prelapsarian momentum of circularity: all tribes-performers circle the globe, as this is what is dictated by the local experience of temporality, but all of them also learn to interpret this alien technology by inspecting alien technology. From a ceremonial point of view, what regionally and nationally functions as immobile indigeneity, externally forms the core of ethno-scapal and ideoscapal movement, ready to be enjoyed by millions of viewers and tourists. The realisation that contemporary Brazilian culture may be carrying an 'invasion trauma' by the Western European Enlightenment, but its *tempos mixtos*, both linear and circular, are Enlightenment's hybridised half-children, suggests a more sensitive, responsible approach to the 'archive' that both sacralises the trauma and contests it (Benjamin 1968: 262; Derrida 1997, 1998).

At the same time, we must consider that what might appear to progressive foreign critics as a primitivist construction of 'aboriginal internal others' (e.g. Thomas 1994), may in fact enclose performative manifestations of resistance to tourist audiovisual exposure (Jamal and Hill 2002: 95–7). In other words, the performance of Amazonian *indigenismo* alongside imageries of tropical ecological harmony might be responding to a longing 'for untouched, primitive and native people who are there to meet the demands of tourists: both in terms of service and as an object to be enjoyed and photographed' (Mowforth and Munt 1998: 69; Mowforth and Munt 2009). In this respect, the mega-event's stage is a 'contact zone' (Pratt 1992) for the European *conquistadores'* Galilean conception of the world with the beginnings of a pluralisation of indigenous subjectivity through intercultural contact (Aparicio and Chávez-Silverman 1997: 2). The globe is a representation of technology in its own right: as a superimposition onto the Amazonian 'landscape', it helps us recall the built environments of American modernity. In the heart of a Brazilian mega-city, it is a 'skywalk structure', completely divorced from social networks that operate beneath its de-hypostasised gaze (Davis 1990). Most of the ceremony's segments are geometrically arranged around the imaginary globe, which promotes a concentric conception of space. What is absent from its utopian indigeneity is equally important as an exclusionary framework of belonging: there are no *favela* representations as such in it, and its successive musical and kinaesthetic repertoire has faint echoes of its samba and no *Umbanda* (a syncretic/hybrid Catholic/folk spiritual religion) or *Candomblé* (an esoteric Yoruban religion) references (Jaguaribe and Hetherington 2004: 161).

The absence of African spirituality is staggering: not only does it push for a simultaneous erasure of its urban geographies of migrant poverty, but it also forbids their 'archaeological' inclusion (*à la* Foucault 1997a) into Brazil's national biography (Freire-Madeiros 2009, 2013). In the comparable Haitian context it was suggested that voodoo practices should be considered as 'ritual re-enactments of Haiti's colonial past even more than as retentions from Africa' (Dayan 1998: xvii). In Brazil's case, African religious rituals play such a pivotal role in national memory, binding rather than fragmenting the imagined community. Peculiarly then, the centrality of Amazonian indigeneity *and* flora in the ceremony projects a 'Brazilian character' firmly grounded in South American soil. This character ceases to be a diachronically mobile value, with multiple migration histories. This migration narrative, which partially guided London's handover to Rio for the next Olympic Games (see Tzanelli 2013c: chapter 4), is probably deemed destabilising.

Aside from the fact that *favela* cultures are iconoclastic vis-à-vis Benjaminian Arcadian images of modernity, their promotion of *bricolage* realities and popular cultures (hip-hop, samba dance and music, capoeira) and their adherence to realist aesthetics, conflicts with the ceremony's romantic synaesthetics (hence with the mega-event's ideal type of the tourist synaesthete). Their 'vertiguous chaos' does not match the rushing order of the modern metropolis, but institutes a different 'socio-scape' (Albrow 1997). This is so, because it promotes in its ordered stead an almost 'mapless', unregulated materiality that is less comprehensible to foreign audiences than the supposed simplicity of Lévi-Strauss's *tristes tropiques* (Jaguaribe and Hetherington 2004: 158). Considering the censorship by previous Brazilian authorities of artistic projects centring on *favela* poverty (Wheeller 1996) as well as violent governmental responses to more recent protests organised by *favela* activists over mega-event expenditure, a dose of political realism is necessary, if undesired. Where the ceremonial 'globe' promotes a European visualisation of Amazonian reality, the *favela* would disclose real power geometries of contemporary policy that superimpose 'civilised progression' onto Brazilian urbanity (Massey 1993, 1994, 2005; Marcuse 1996). The ceremonial segmentation between Amazonian beauty and disorderly urban cultures within the same ceremonial act ameliorates this difference, translating the transition from indigeneity to urbanity in terms of touristification. In other words, it is not that migrant cultures are fully erased, but rather that they are re-packaged as cosmetic tourist goods.

At this point one must reiterate the deep historic entanglement between art and politics in Brazil: abstracting mobility from its contextual meaning-making processes allows viewers to reduce social action to mere behaviour. The introduction of capoeira in the ceremony counteracts this reductionist strategy, suggesting that instead of considering it as an organic (*à la* Durkheim) narrative relegated to biology, we should think of the role of the martial artist's body in terms of mechanical social action. As I proceed to explain, the ceremony's capoeirists enact Brazilian socio-cultural personae in embodied ways and through 'deliberate choreographic accounts' (Farnell 1994: 931). Therefore, we might regard the bodily mobility of performers as the negative image of the immobility of slave labour that originally performed the capoeira (also Sheller 2003: 27–8, on sites and practices of subaltern agency). Temporal distancing from these colonial realities allows the ceremonial viewer to consume embodied symbols of what used to signify resistance, first to colonial and later to native authoritarian regimes. We might consider the spectacle as an officially sanctioned artistic manifestation of social segmentation and re-stratification (e.g. Tomlinson 2005), but this alone would not illuminate the in-between social spaces and 'adjacent border zones' of Brazilian human mobilities; some diachronic, intersectional observations (gender, class, race) in these bodily performances are also necessary for an investigation of racial criss-crossings in South America (see also Nederveen Pieterse 2004: 36–7, on Latin American *criollos*). Post-modern arguments of hybridisation as a 'travelling culture' (Clifford 1988, 1992, 1997), need to be approached with caution, as every movement blocks another one (Sheller and Urry 2006; Uteng and Cresswell 2008). With this in mind, the ceremony blocks and then releases memory: the capoeirists' circular performance around the Brazilian centre globe can support the resurrection of subjugated knowledge or denote utopian unity of centre with periphery as much as it can reinforce past oppressive patterns. Touristic consumption of artstyles such as that of capoeira is supposed to promote the 'universalisation of particularism' (Robertson 1992: 130), after all, which may lead to the global valorisation of local practice under the label of exoticism and with the endorsement of cultural nationalism (Appiah 1992 in Nederveen Pieterse and Parekh 1995: 9).

There are various arguments concerning the original meaning of capoeira. One general observation would be that as they were part of African slave cultures, the performances articulated intercultural encounters (between colonisers or travellers and natives) as an interstitial experience, enabling shifts 'outside the box of Cartesian epistemology' (Nederveen Pieterse 2004: 110). Another would be that with its evolution into a martial art and an artstyle-dance, things came to what one might call a full 'embodied hermeneutic circle'. At the start of the nineteenth century, public officials in Rio de Janeiro considered capoeira a 'game' (*jôgo*) played by black slaves. Indeed, descendants of West African slaves regarded it a 'game of life' even as the ethno-racial background of the capoeirists began to diversify. The style would be performed in military and religious processions and entertainment to deride officials but also interact with other spectators. However, as later in the century severe injuries of spectators and visitors began to be reported and knives were introduced, authorities also began to inflict severe punishments on performers, including incarceration and lashing (Chvaicer 2002: 527–32). The criminalisation of the custom was bound by fears of African gang formation, disruption of public order and the obligatory racist Eurocentrism that found the African continent and its people 'lagging' in the civilisational stages and polluting New World societies with habits of banditry. Detention data prove that the ethnic profile of the capoeirists soon diversified, and participants of mixed ancestry, such as black, *mulatto, fulla* and *pardo* (of skin colour lighter than mulatto but darker than white), or even new immigrants who spoke Portuguese, made a tentative appearance. Many of those were even employed by the government in security organisations (national guard, navy, army) and fought on the Paraguayan Front (1865–70), with the promise of emancipation.

It was after the war that capoeira was recognised as a martial art associated with self-defence and war. Now impoverished, many capoeirists worked as bodyguards of politicians, who used them in newly emerged systems of opponent blackmail, and later came to influence politics directly. In the final years of the old empire, capoeirists figured as a threat to new republican values and were criminalised again as proponents of African 'sexual aberration' and non-European tendencies. These prejudices did not disappear in the first three quarters of the twentieth century, but were blended in new discourses of a violence monopoly by the state (Elias 1982; Tzanelli 2008), which sought to maintain public safety and an impeccable Brazilian image abroad. *Brasilidade* as *linda maravilhosa* would soon be touristified, so the capoeirists also had to be disciplined into the new exotica of tourist mobilities. The movement from Afro-Brazilian heritage to urban tourist legacy was institutionalised under Getúlio Vargas (1930–45), with the calendrical formalisation of relevant art styles (including Carnival's designation to the 'impure' days before Ash Wednesday), but also the regulation of their content (each performance had to include an *enredo*, or plot based on Brazilian history) (Connerton 1989; Tzanelli 2013c). Reflecting post-1940s European institutions of *scholé* as holidays for the working classes (see Dann and Parrinello 2009), these traumatic changes partook in later Brazilian articulations of 'human' as a being in (e)motion. Vargas's policies subdued *capoeiragem* under a surveillance that was lifted only in recent years (for comparison, see Chakrabarty 1991). The end of Vargas's regime in the 1970s brought new possibilities for inclusion of these once African styles. Where the military regime built the *Casas de Cultura Popular* (houses of popular culture) as unifiers in a 'genealogy of the nation that excluded all ruptures and conflicts' (Avelar 1999: 42), contemporary Brazilian cultural policy recognised the socially empowering potential of samba and capoeira (Dimitrova Savova 2009: 562).

To understand fully the cosmological subtext of the ceremonial act, we must consider how capoeira introduced in modern Brazilian societies a more organised approach to violent foreign contact, resistance and democratic inclusion (Lewis 1992). Like *Candomblé*, which forged syncretism between African paganism and Catholic forms of worship as 'colonial mimicry' (Bhabha 1994; Thompson 1984), capoeira is an artform of *mélange* migration that began as African resistance to subjection before evolving into a tourist staple. However, as a social event that included singing and dancing in a circle, but also combat manoeuvres such as jumping and kicking, which complied more or less with the definition of a martial art, capoeira originally confused social outsiders: at least until more recent introductions of ceremonies (art) in football mega-events (in which symbolic wars between nations take place; Garland and Rowe 1999; Tzanelli 2006), dancing was not supposed to go hand in hand with boxing. Capoeira movements presented 'a specific kind of a martial art – without physical contact – thereby lending the entire activity the semblance of a game. The confusing definitions, therefore, stem from the significant differences between the life experiences and epistemology of the observers and the participants' (Chvaicer 2002: 563). The epistemological dilemma was, according to the first Brazilian race relations analyst, Gilberto Freyre (1963), no less one of 'peaceable, bourgeois' nature, hence implicated in multiple Euro-African experiential mobilities.

Sheller (2003: 114–6) notes that the 'social body' of the colonial society used to be conditioned by 'economies of touch' to regulate proximity and distance with slave labour and the native populations. Gazing and touching others allowed colonial masters to 'domesticate' the other and 'consolidate the imperialist self' (Spivak 1999: 130). *Capoeiragem*'s Yoruban origins are bound with ideas of dance as a language subjected to the twin principles of fun and social answerability. Yoruban playing 'involves spending time with people for its own sake, engaging them in a competition of wits verbally and/or physically, and playing it out tactically to disorient and be disoriented, to surprise and be surprised, to shock and be shocked, and to laugh together – to enjoy' (Thompson Drewal 1992: 17). As social expression, capoeira is supposed to strengthen body and soul, like Eastern martial arts (e.g. karate, kick-boxing), but its submergence in Euro-African contact also produced the urgency in slaves to be treated in non-essentialist terms. This reciprocal flow of responsibility and 'accountability' (Landry and MacLean 1996) matches suggestions that 'I for myself' exists in public only as an 'I for others' (Bakhtin 1990: 32) – the very principles of horizontal kinship endorsed by religious processions, in which 'everyone is united by fraternal ties with the saint' (DaMatta 1991: 76–7). Where in old and new religious contexts contact with god(s) would be established through movements, songs and music, in new consumption contexts *capoeiragem* promotes individual *eudaimonía* and the cosmetic principles of self-presentation.

These cosmetic-individualist principles guide the World Cup's ceremonial performance by pragmatic necessity, but whereas the ceremony precludes audiences from touching or moving in capoeira as everyday rhythm (e.g. Edensor 2014), it amplifies the effect of the gaze and the affect of the Brazilian music, modifying the mobility of sound, performance and narrative. Adopting aesthetic reflexivity as an esoteric experience, and 'de-contextualisation' (hooks 1992: 31) as a strategy conducive to stylistic mobility, the ceremony generalises capoeira movement into a consumable practice that builds 'healthy bodies' (Featherstone 1991; Tzanelli 2013a), and promotes touristic pilgrimages without religious depth (Singh 2012). The translation of *capoeiragem* into cultural capital in the global tourism trade (Shaw 1999: 50) replaced informal popular cultures thriving on collaboration 'but governed nonetheless by laws and contracts that have the power to determine one's well-being or position in society' (Davis 2009: 13). Gone are the colourful African costumes, the exclusively black performers say to World Cup audiences: it is our body that traverses millennia of cultural movements from East to West, Africa and Portugal to South America – a ceremonial body dressed now in white from the waist below, so as to challenge Cartesianism's divide between head-torso spirituality (here black) and subliminal-irrational reproductive regions (concealed in white) (Fanon 1970; Tzanelli 2013a). Where working class-ness, abject ethnicity, unlawfulness and 'sin' were placed by the Vargas administration in a continuum to validate the prevalence of the Catholic moral order, like Rio's 2012 Olympic ceremonialism, the World Cup's artwork 'placed dexterity, blackness, ritual bodily dialogue and hybrid music in one emancipatory ludic category' (Tzanelli 2013c: 112).

What had started as a 'streaming off' ritual in north-eastern regions of Brazil plagued by poverty and subjected to authoritarian state violence, would later migrate to *Carnaval* stages as a sort of ritualised venting (see DaMatta's (1991) 'pressure valve' theory and De Certeau's (1984) 'strategy' in social interaction), and even later to domains of cinematic-tourist fandom. The movement from rurality to urbanity is a quintessential characteristic of (post)modern mobilities subjected to *kairotic*, linear imperatives. There is a 'speed hierarchy' (Jensen 2004) enclosed in this performative narrative of Brazilian *tempos mixtos* that corresponds to a spatialised economy of flows: segmented, gated from the dangers of the hoi polloi (Graham and Marvin 2001), the globe/technology allows detached observation of the urban chaos that spreads across the city below (Gwerner 2006: 203–4; Gwerner 2009). The narrative is not disconnected from the real social context of the World Cup, which takes place under rigid surveillance by systems that ensure the safety of global tourists-outsiders (Morgan and Pritchard 2005): the aerial, distant gaze of cosmopolitan tourism partakes in the cultural hierarchies that continue to define Brazil's place in the world as a 'developing nation' (also Szerszynski and Urry 2006; Tzanelli 2013b: chapter 3, on the 'aerial gaze'). Coupling the martial artstyle with music also communicates the (more repressed in the previous act) tonality of the Brazilian city. Loïc Wacquant (2004) suggests that the intensely corporeal practices of boxing communicate a kinetic culture, which is transmitted 'beneath language and consciousness' but projects the participant's socio-cultural biography or *habitus*. Let us not forget (contra Aravamudan 1999: 11) that *habitus'* agential force replies to ideological impositions existing outside colonial situations – including endogenous struggles for recognition that may relate to native structures of thought.

Hence, we may say that in addition to its Euro-African depth, the answerability of 'capoeira struggle' renders the descriptive powers of Brazilian urban materiality with rhythmical expressivity, which is naturally residing in the capoeirist's black body (Hetherington 2003; Highmore 2005). At the same time, the masculinisation of capoeira ritual on the stage bears testimony to a phenomenon conducive to the politics of tourist representations of Brazilian tradition. Like the *Malandro* or the individual of bad mores, who operates outside the confines of a networked society (DaMatta 1991, 1995), it differentiates mobility of character on the basis of gender, reproducing social inequalities within the national space, so as to 'beat' them in the domain of international relations (Uteng and Cresswell 2008: 3–8). This is not unrelated to the fact that *capeiragem* displays are succeeded by Brazil's other 'quintessential' embodied (martial-like) skill: football.

Act three

The third act of the opening event is dominated by representations of football as Brazilian property. Lines of children dressed as referees enter the pitch and others dressed as football players rhythmically kick small balls tied to their feet. The absence of adult players is probably meant to combine narratives of education with the quintessential Brazilian values of family and kinship so as to project football as heritage that originates in the nation's late colonial times. The stage now turns into an articulation of evolutionary nationalism, so as to relate biology to culture (Brooks 2011: 12–3). Children are living testimony to cultural reproduction, so their performance of the game belongs to Brazilian 'character' as a *téchne* from which all contemporary football technologies sprang (Tarde 1903). It is precisely the immanence of football as a *téchne* that suits the Brazilian body that brings the act's synaesthetic performativity close to racist discourse, whereas its designation as an art separates it from racism: like 'character', national football styles are seen as natural to the team. Football styles are constantly related to cultural stereotypes, but they have their own distinct autonomy 'that is always more than reducible to an ethnic/cultural character' (Wren-Lewis and Clarke 1983: 124). The 'football language' with which reporters are equipped to discuss matches is mostly an amalgam of local self-perception and ideoscapal flows, so we may say that it reflects the mega-event's articulation of the game (Tudor 1992: 398–9). All social actors try to assimilate the 'natural character' of themselves and others, 'the ultimate underpinning of the official order of nature and the national spirit' (Herzfeld 1992: 134), but such performative domestications of a British colonial sport amount to the appropriation of foreign cosmographies of riches – a universally accepted discourse in Brazil that transcends elite, folk and pop distinctions (Gellner 1983). The discourse borrows from racist practices of assimilation but relegates those to the domain of 'culture'. As Rousseff noted in her opening ceremonial speech, football might have been invented in England,

> But we like to think that it made Brazil its home. This is where Pelé, Garrincha, Didi and so many other greats were born, who mesmerised millions of people the world over. When the World Cup comes back to Brazil 64 years later it is as if football is coming home. Our people's love for this sport has already become one of our national identity's characteristics. For us, football is a celebration of life. We are the country of football because of the victorious track record, having won the World Cup five times, as well as a consequence of the passion every Brazilian has for their clubs, heroes and their national squad.
>
> (World Cup Portal 2014a)

Giulianotti and Robertson's (2004: 548) comment that 'a nostalgia underlies the transmogrification of old football spaces into "heritage sites"' as much as it guides a post-modern, 'schizophrenic' conflation of past and present football images in broadcast discussions, acquires a new dimension in Rousseff's words. Moreover, again, we stumble upon modified references to a slowly universalised 'sport system', which can be traced to eighteenth- and nineteenth-century Britain (Bottenburg 2001; Elias and Dunning 1986; Holt 1989). This is when newly founded nations in Western Europe first entered transformative processes of urbanisation and industrialisation, which led to the standardisation, codification, and bureaucratisation of many traditional sport forms, first within the British context. Especially Britain's imperial aspirations became intertwined with the diffusion of its popular sport forms such as football, cricket, field hockey and rugby, amongst other sports (Maguire 1999), which helped facilitate new commercial relationships between Britain and the rest of the world. However, Rousseff reminds the world how the post-colonies' trans-modernity also answered to the 'original way of moving the body' – first like an English aristocrat and then like a professional working-class athlete – through the deployment of 'distinctive corporeal techniques, playing styles, aesthetic codes, administrative structures and interpretive vocabularies' (Giulianotti and Robertson 2004: 549).

The declaration of football as a celebration of life, part of the nation's well-being and 'character', introduces strategies of adaptation of foreign code. As an embodied form of mobility, football has been elevated to a product of interactions 'which contribute to the social, civic or economic well-being of a community-of-common purpose' (Falk and Kilpatrick 2000: 103). The ceremony's third act articulates this momentum kinaesthetically also with dancers whose heads are replaced with balls. Their costumes' colours in black and white recall the ways pawns are arranged on a chess board, as well as the game's underlining principles of strategy and composure – values traditionally ascribed to male peers (Driver 2000 in Tzanelli 2012b; Tzanelli 2013b: 133–4). One may also argue that colour binarism is constitutive of the organisation of football cultures, which promotes a sort of social *chromophobia* (colour fear) reflecting 'a much deeper fear of visibility and difference in a society that explicitly cheers for individualism but implicitly applauds standardisation and adherence to norm' (Dimitrova Savova 2009: 558). Conforming to Rousseff's address, the performance's visual aspects also argue against a separation of national habitus from artistic style, 'de-differentiating' low culture (football) and higher, intellectualising cultural forms (the performing arts, literature) (Giulianotti and Robertson 2004: 548–9). Whereas natural expression hinges on meaning making, aesthetic expression prioritises the fact that certain things (artistic embodied performances) have a certain meaning (style) (Chateau and Lefebvre 2014: 107). The analogy is predicated upon an 'authorised' in the Brazilian context discourse, according to which, like cinema's aesthetic expressivity, ceremonial expressivity builds upon (assimilates and exceeds) what it designates (Eco 1987).

The segment's synaesthesia does not preclude the role of iconicity in expressions of identity. Purifying iconic similarities (football like art) allows for felicitous classifications of the sport as a form of artstyle immanent to the national spirit (also Herzfeld 2005). At the same time, we can discern a ceremonial strategy of place branding (Muñiz and O'Guinn 2001) on the basis of football's immanence from the place in which it is hosted (Urry 1995: 22–3; Morgan et al. 2003) – or, perhaps more correctly, processes of production of cultural practices of space ('Brazil, the land of football'). Again, the role of iconicity cannot be side-lined, as Brazilian narratives of football constantly partake in the production of Brazil as a 'space myth' comprising place images (Shields 1991). At the same time, football as a Brazilian brand is better articulated synaesthetically (with music and cinema images) as an urban good (Urquìa 2005; Donald and Gammack 2007; Nagib 2011; Nelson and Deshpande 2013): many famous football players, including Pelé, are a product of '*favela* scapes'. Hence, the act's opening with children playing with small-sized balls communicates both the extension of heritage to younger generations and the idea that *futebolarte* and *jôgo de futebol* are part of the national family's branded style, which purifies disorderly domains (*favelas*) so as to incorporate them into public self-presentations. 'Family' stands here for 'person' as part of a national network. For, if football is artwork ceaselessly in progress, 'improved by and reassembled around a sublime feint here, a pinpoint pass there, a momentary touch of crowning genius', then style matters more than individual victories (Archetti 1994: 42). Here we note convergences of style as form with the ceremonial narrative's content for the production of Brazil's very own aesthetic cosmopolitanism.

The ceremony's focus on the immanence of football style in conjunction with indigenous cosmologies also supplements (missing representations of) magic with widespread connotations 'not only of competition, but also of luck and destiny' (Humphrey 1994: 68). To call football a *jôgo* is to imply the presence of a generous dose of serendipity in its execution, alongside any well-crafted strategy. It has been noted that in Brazil the things that survive are the soccer clubs, the carnival associations and the lottery system, which is known as the 'animal game' (*jôgo do bicho*). Whereas European epistemologies emphasise in the game strategic and tactical calculation, Brazilian takes on football also frame it in terms of the team's magic as destiny/destination. Like *jôgo do bicho, jôgo de futebol* is based on a totemic logic through transformations of the game's geometrical-strategic rules into highly personalised beings (animals) (Lévi-Strauss 1972). Only highly gifted lottery players can turn numbers into highly visible animate beings. There is a great deal of magic involved in a *jôgo* that masters abstract things (the European provenance) into beings endorsed with personhood (winners). Popular description of famous players as 'magicians' or 'tricksters' do enter ceremonial narratives: Pelé's appearance in the 2012 Olympics handover to Rio de Janeiro had such a dose of magic, as he impersonated the notorious *Malandro* or bad man of Brazilian *rua* cultures (Tzanelli 2013b: 115). Connotations of *jôgo* as political (*político*) or illegal betting (*jôgo sujo*: dirty tricks) follow on from the term's connection to versatility (*ter jôgo de cintura*: to be flexible; *fazer o jôgo de alguém*: to go along with somebody), strategy (*seconder o jôgo*: to play one's cards close to the chest) and danger (*estar em jôgo*: to be at stake). Again, we note a ceremonial account of *Spieltrieb* or sporting play as a form of freedom.

Marcuse's (1955, 1964) discussion of the 'play principle' as a key element in human freedom insofar as it constituted a form of pure creativity unbounded by constraints (e.g. the commodity economy's need to 'sell' sports in ever-expanding markets; Inglis and Hughson 2000: 291–2) develops in the contradictory space of the mega-event's ceremony. Other cultures also use the term to describe *malandragem* types of monetary play with grave consequences for personal relations (in Greek *tzogadóros* denotes the illegal or addicted card player, and by extension the shadowy trickster) (DaMatta 1991: 138). All these connotations, which remain gendered in a vocabulary of masculine honour and public performance, neutralise the fear of human freedom's spoliation by resorting to ideas of ludic tourist play (Dann 1989). Though commoditised, ludic play provides escape from everyday routine. It is not coincidental that the ceremony aestheticises childhood play when we know that in reality Brazilian *jôgo* has been ruined by corruption over the last decade and a half. Like the Geertzian cockfighting paradigm, ceremonial representations of *jôgo de futebol* are mere artistic mimesis of social structures, simulations of the Brazilian social matrix and a 'dramatization of status concerns' (Geertz 1973: 436–7) in a society of privileged persons.

In the context of the 2014 World Cup, destiny translates into destination, a teleological movement towards the nation's cosmological centre, the achievement of perfection or completion. Thus, even though children play and chiaroscuro football men dance, the overall discursive composition is one of a very serious post-colonial game. As the nation's globally praised *téchne, jôgo de futebol* (e.g. Archetti 1997) is the *lógos* (reasoning) of creativity, as much as it is elevated to a Brazilian logo (Lury 2004). Here we may consider how the act fits into global political shifts in a recuperative ('healing') fashion: let us not forget that, originally, play as a psychological construct was promoted as an 'outlet for healing the emotions' (Cannella and Viruru 2004: 105). However, the European toy is firmly connected to adult rituals and pleasure (Aries 1962) – a reminder that propels audiovisual participants to ask whether the scene's consumption object is the children. The act's carousel feel ultimately questions Western corporate structures that in post-tourist spaces such as that of Disney World, visually focus on play and fun, while obscuring the football workers' labour (Hunt and Frankenberg 1990; Ritzer and Liska 1997: 99). This essentially Western viewpoint can only be disrupted by outside viewers, as in other cultures and poorer social groups this neat distinction between play and labour does not apply at all (Bloch and Adler 1994).

Significantly, the act matched the craft of football with new technologies granting mobility to paraplegic people. Just before the opening match, a symbolic kick-off took place at the Corinthians Arena: a paraplegic patient, moving around using an exoskeleton (a robot vest that controls brain activity) got up and walked onto the pitch. Undoubtedly a prelude to the 2016 Paralympic spectacle, the demonstration of the 'Walk Again' project was provided by 156 scientists, engineers and university technicians, in addition to research institutes throughout the world (World Cup Portal 2014b). Constructing links between technology, *téchne* and *technicity*, the demonstration reinforced linear conceptions of time in post-colonial space. The demonstration suggested that Western technology is not supposed to be conceptualised as being apart from the human body, but as complementary or even constitutive of it (Stiegler 1998; Clark 2000), hence a component of *eudaimonía*. Standing outside divisive phenotypical discourse, this enabling mobility re-articulates a cosmopolitan ethic through technology (Haraway 1991). There is no better way to carry this message through the following act than by mobilising the most familiar means for a cosmopolitan articulation of belonging: music.

Act four

The ceremonial conclusion with the World Cup's theme song 'We Are One (Ole Ola)' prompts us to investigate how the musical background and lyrics of musical 'texts' become a site of contested meanings and changing community ideals (Mitchell 1996; Malbon 1999; Duffy 2000). Performed by Jennifer Lopez, rapper Pitbull and Claudia Leite under the rhythms of the famous Brazilian band Olodum, it figured the stars (bouncing) around a giant round stage that opened up like a melon (Associated Press 2014). Reminiscent of typical triadic arrangements in *Carnaval* processions (DaMatta 1991), the musical trio updated traditions of ceremony, because its secular composition and transnational identity combined artistic roots with professional routes. Jennifer (Lynn) Lopez (b. 1969, Bronx, New York) is an American actress, author, fashion designer, dancer, producer and singer. Her musical repertoire combined the 'romantic innocence of Latin music' (ranging from salsa to *bachata*) with hip-hop and rap, branding the fusion 'Latin soul' (Morales 2003: 163). Though not Brazilian, Lopez's Puerto Rican roots ensured the presence of Nuyorican African-American influences in her work, especially in the form of lyrics. Nuyorican heritage is a distant relative of the hybrid salsa genre that was born in 1960s migrant Cuban enclaves of Miami and New York, which sought to re-interpret older music and dance styles such as son, *charanga*, rumba, cha cha, mambo, *guaracha* and *guaguancó*. The ballroom, aristocratic setting of some of the genres, whose African origins were sidelined in favour of a more appropriate stylistics for colonial aristocracy, did not speak the social language of working-class migrants, who moved into North America the street cultures of their home(land) (Tzanelli 2007: 130–1; Morales 2003: 58).

Lopez considers herself the transmitter of a double Puerto Rican heritage – incidentally, in competition with the Cuban salsa, even in contemporary club contexts we associate with cosmopolitan cities such as New York or London (Román-Velázquez 1999: 69). Hence, the song's upbeat, singing style, which is frantically performed by the athletic Lopez, kinaesthetically matches what she imagines as her distant heritage. Only this is not the case, as, in reality, her bodily movements suggest an additional performative fusion of horizons, between Latin American and Afro-Brazilian kinaesthetic. It is not coincidental that the 2014 World Cup ceremonies were backed by the famous Olodum band, which was founded in 1979 and went on to pioneer hybrid 'samba-reggae' – yet another stylistic addition to the opening ceremony's anthem. As an artstyle, 'samba-reggae' corresponded to Brazilian social and political discourse, but concealed this under Olodum's *requebra* ('Shake Your Booty') style. Close to Lopez's ceremonial dancing, *requebra* movement only *seemed* to be a version of the stylised, *risqué* dance of *Carnaval* samba. In reality, its 'quick butt moves and sexy grinds replaced the methodical, rhythmic dance steps reminiscent of Africa' (Hinchberger 2014), leading black activist dancers headlong into what would become known as the Brazilian style of *axé*.

Lopez's global networks (she has worked with artists such as Tina Turner) and profile mirrors that of Claudia Leite – more commonly known as 'Claudinha'. Born in 1980 (São Gonçalo, Rio de Janeiro) as Cláudia Cristina Leite Inácio Pedreira, Claudinha is a Brazilian *axé* and pop recording artist, and former vocalist of the group *Babado Novo* (2001–8). She is currently, alongside Ivete Sengalo, who featured in the closing ceremony, one of the most popular female singers in Brazil and Latin America, and her voice has figured in global cinematic hits, such the dubbed Brazilian version of *Cars 2* (dir. John Lasseter). Amongst her global appearances one may include that in September 2011 at the Rock in Rio music festival stage along with Rihanna, Katy Perry and Elton John, and on Puerto Rican Ricky Martin's single 'Samba' for the Brazilian release and worldwide re-release of the album *Música+Alma+Sexo* (2011). Leite's combination of Puerto Rican professional networks and Brazilian *axé* influences is another manifestation of artistic 'routes' in 'roots'. Originally considered a rude word, *axé* developed into a popular music genre. *Axé* emerged in Salvador, Bahia, in around 1986, as a fusion of different Afro-Caribbean genres, such as *marcha*, reggae and calypso, with Brazilian music styles such as *frevo, forró* and *carixada*. The most important creator of this music style was Alfredo Moura, with Carlinhos Brown, Luiz Caldas, Sarajane and others following. The word '*axé*' comes from a Yoruba religious greeting used in the *Candomblé* and *Umbanda* religions to denote 'soul', 'light', 'spirit' or 'good vibration'.

Today considered one of Brazil's most popular music-dance genres, axé's actual social roots can be found in Brazilian inspiration from the US Civil Rights movement. As the story goes, the genre was born by a group of black activists who founded *Ilê Aiyê* in 1974 as an outlet for their militancy during Carnival celebrations. Its president, Antônio Carlos Vovô, wanted to call the group 'Black Power', but the police of the 1964–85 dictatorship 'advised them not to' (Hinchberger 2014). Yet, *axé* survived military rule to influence contemporary pop *samba-arte*, such as that performed in the opening ceremony. Leite's *axé* style was evident in her embodied discourse during the ceremonial performance, but her pop persona was, like Lopez's, more committed to commercialised music styles that can also reach the top of American charts (Morales 2003: 93).

The socio-cultural matrix of the ceremony's musical trio is completed with the appearance of Pitbull. Born Armando Christian Pérez (1981), Pitbull is an American rapper and Latin Grammy Award-winning artist from Miami, Florida. The son of Cuban expatriates, Pitbull moved from his childhood education in the works of Cuba's national hero and poet José Martí, to a drug-dealing spell as a youth, and then to creating the soundtrack for *2 Fast 2 Furious* (dir. John Singleton), which served as his passport to fame. Complementing Lopez and Leite's sexualised femininity, the rapper's rough style was reflected in the reasons why he selected his stage name: 'He dubbed himself "Pitbull" because, he says, "they bite to lock. The dog is too stupid to lose. And they're outlawed in Dade County. They're basically everything that I am. It's been a constant fight' (Wiltz 2004). As the son of a hustler, a Cuban exile who 'made a fast fortune on *la cocaina* during the '80s and lost it just as quickly' (ibid.), Pitbull's appearance injected the song with a much-needed *Malandro*-like feel. His self-professed 'struggle to the top' is replete with references to misrecognition, crime and love for labour ('music is my hustle, my cocaine') (Honneth 2007; Gregg 2009; Hesmondhalgh and Baker 2010). His interstitial identity as a Cuban American who raps in English and Spanish, a blue-eyed Latino ('You can't get much whiter than me'; Wiltz 2004) serves as a tropicopolitan characteristic. Pitbull's on- and offstage self-narration seems to be both about belonging and being on a constant resentful move: borrowing his appearance from a stupid dog akin to the infamous Geertzian cock, tricks others into believing that his 'inside' (soul) is not skilled or clever. Appearances matter, he argues, but only as self-presentational mechanisms, techniques of sociality in a market society.

If only for this artistic temperament, one wonders whether the song's actual 'Muse' is not the social style of Pitbull the 'individual' or Lopez's early ghetto persona. Written by Daniel Murcia, Thomas Troelsen, Jennifer Lopez, Henry Walter, Nadir Khayat, Lukasz Gottwald, Armando Perez, Sia Furler and Claudia Leite, the song is a twin hymn to football and nation. Urging imaginary interlocutors (fans) to 'put their flags up in the sky, and wave them side to side (side to side)', so that they 'show the world' where they are from, is, at best, a way to signpost fan groups in terms of socio-cultural belonging. This is supported by the interlocutor's designation as an abstract Brazil that, when 'the going gets tough', can consider how everything becomes one (love, life, world, fight, night, place and so forth). The lyrics continue by stressing that this world ('your world, my world') is 'our world today', an ethical singularity allowing the singers to 'invite the whole world … to play'. The verse is repeated in Spanish rather than Portuguese, but the use of Latin-based *jugar* as a translation of 'to play' connects to Brazilian understandings of *jôgo*. Possibly with an eye to the final, which is presented as a night we watch the unity of the world in one fight of 'two sides', the lyrics stage a cosmic drama that makes the heart 'work so hard'. However, the repetition of *força* (force) in Brazilian Portuguese outlines a combative cultural politics of encounter, closer to Pitbull's self-narration as the struggling hustler. In fact, the following verses, which are also rendered in Brazilian Portuguese, continue along the same lines of aggressive masculinised self-presentation ('When I call the whole world to play is to show that I can / Cheer, cry, smile, scream / No matter the outcome, let's vent'). The concluding invitation to 'vent' during the game (*vamos extravasar*) is a rendition of DaMatta's (1991: 264–6) 'safety valve', a *cathectic* ritual (Connell 1987, 1995) that we might associate both with football celebration and nationalist mobilisation (Delanty and O'Mahony 2002: 112–3; Giulianotti and Robertson 2007). One wonders, therefore, if the ceremonial pop chorus 'ole, ole, ola' is not the military counterpart of the call to raise the flag. Sitting between Vargas's nationalist authoritarianism and Freyes's confusing racial equality, the song prompts the *synaesthete* to participate, without specifying in what.

It seems then that the opening event oscillates between identity as a naturalised given (especially with regards to the World Cup's hosts) and subjectivity as a formulated ontology (during the ceremony's attendance). Identity narratives and subjectivity formulations purport the movement from what is written in blood (national consanguinity) to what is dictated by law. This complex interplay between heritage and legacy defines Brazilian transmodernity's dilemma as a clash between an unwritten, holistic moral code and an explicit, written constitutional code founded on the principles of equality and individualism (DaMatta 1991: 154). To put this in context, the opening ceremony's kinaesthetic and audiovisual styles prey on both codes so as to articulate a vision of community, which is not only bound by blood but also by de-territorialised emotion and moral reason. The commercialised utopianism of the concluding musical message forms thus an uneasy continuity with the rooted plot of the first three acts. Even the three celebrity singers' cosmography of riches has to retain an anchor to dominions, dress them in class, gendered and racialised colours and evoke affects that may subsequently crystallise to emotions. However, rooting is also epochally driven in human narrative, and legacies tend to appear more often in contemporary environments – though this does not imply a decisive elimination of heritage contestations. The following sections suggest that the closing parable performs such an epochal move, opening up Brazil's cosmic 'map' to the horizon of foreign riches. However, as the shift to football legacies is matched by Brazil's tropicopolitan musical spirit and Carnival performance, these riches are progressively assimilated into a unique narrative of belonging.

The closing ceremony: performative rupture and trans-modern dilemmas of belonging

The closing ceremony's content mirrors social theorists' inclination to compartmentalise time in terms of changing social action. This does not mean that we deal with yet another version of Beck's (2000a) 'second modernity' or with multiple modernities as such, but it seems that its artists (Brazilians and foreign) display second modernity's characteristics: aesthetically reflexivity complete with emotion, sensory holism and spatio-temporal consciousness. 'Time' is a stretchy dimension, and expands, contracts or circumnavigates the desired riches throughout the event, but mostly moves forward in a more recognisable Western motion. The progression of time affects projections of heritage as an immobile property, making space for the presence of legal planning. Succinctly put, the closing event reflects on what happens when the host negotiates its identity and belonging with guests, foreign institutions and transnational regulators with the help of intelligible spatiotemporal narrative and performance. This negotiation may be staged, but stages introduce inquisitive audiences to other possibilities – and above all, the possibility to question the quality of personages, the stability of plots and their moral codes.

We were prepared for this difference by the opening ceremony's closing act, which was dominated by fusion music styles and a transnational community of singers. Truly, unlike the opening event's glorification of *casa*, the closing

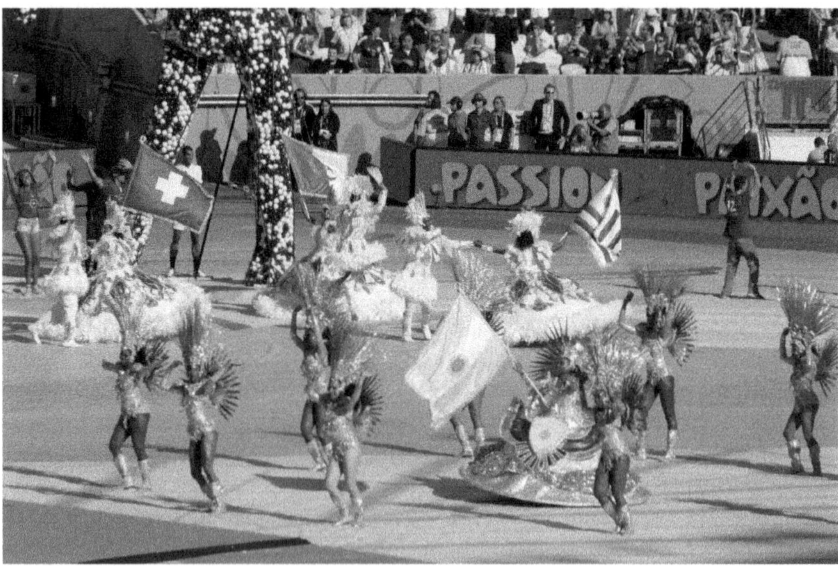

Figure 4.2 The closing ceremony's *Carnaval* atmosphere: samba schools and *foliões*
Source Jimmy Balkovicius (Flickr), Creative Commons 2.0. Licence: www.creativecommons.org/licenses/by-sa/2.0/

ceremony is mostly characterised by a constant movement of people – the equivalent of Carnival's *foliões* (*folie*: madness) (DaMatta 1991: 80) – outside the usual circle of the Carnival. Carnival dresses are called *fantasias*, a term denoting both the festival's fancy costumes or disguises and 'dreams, illusions or idealisations of daily life' (DaMatta 1991: 40). As I explain below, not only is the ceremony's pop *fantasia* a commercialised spectacle 'pleasing to the eye' (Debord 1995), but it is also a gendered narrative of national dream-work (Gourgouris 1992). As is the case with the opening ceremony's tribal formations, the closing event's samba *personae* could be considered as peripheral figures from Brazilian socio-cultures, brought to life as narratives of the country's past. However, given that samba is Brazil's living culture and its gendered exposure speaks the language of touristic romance, it would be better to regard these ornamented female sambistas as equivalent to Carnival's focus on illicit or forbidden exoticism: that which is outside the system or which lies in its interstices (Turner 1969; Geertz 1980).

As is the case with most South and Latin American contexts, samba's half-dressed female dancers can assume the aura of cultural values without losing their materiality as embodied commodities (Sánchez Taylor 2000). Because samba has been earmarked as part of Brazil's heritage kinaesthetics, its mega-event commoditisation in the form of a tourist spectacle allows for the style's global mobility also in legacy domains, where serious national rituals are replaced by liminoid tourist pleasure (Turner 1974b). To throw a provocative suggestion on the table, in this ceremony, female sambistas both disrupt and reinforce the neat Brazilian distinction between doing (an embodied subject's performative privilege, a worker's activity) and seeing (a disembodied gaze(r)'s role, an employer's supervision privilege) through globally intelligible conceptions of sexuality. Like the lucky football player's mastery of *jôgo do bicho*, they are modernity's quintessential fantasies that successfully deceive spectators – in opposition to the Brazilian working animal or *besta*, the fool pretending to be something he is not (DaMatta 1991: 145; Herzfeld 2004: 28).

Attended by former Brazil international Kaka, Brazil legend Pelé and ex-England midfielder David Beckham, amongst other football celebrities (Gill 2014), the closing ceremony was divided into two acts, with the first focusing on harmonisations of Brazilian and global heritage kinaesthetics (national ceremony and football rituals and rules), and the second on transnational musical articulations (hybrid music genres performed by foreign and Brazilian singers and composers). Set to a soundtrack of samba music, incorporating a cast of 400 people and featuring GRES Academicos do Grande Rio, the ceremonial script was intended as a unique tribute to football, as it symbolically brought together the two sides battling to be crowned winners when the full-time whistle was blown in Rio. The second musical act complemented the first because it affectively enhanced the symbolic battle's core with blends of appropriate melody and lyrics.

Act one

The first act opens with an on-pitch expression of the sport's values through four characters – freedom, solidarity, passion and diversity – and subsequently includes representations of all 32 teams (FIFA.com 2014d). FIFA's peaceful message is mediated by eight-metre-high giants with a big red heart in the middle of their lattice sternum, who are accompanied by 22 samba dancers from the Lapa district of Rio. What is hidden from FIFA's cognitive scope connects to the international regulator's current concerns about domestic disorder, which could mar the mega-event's safe delivery. More correctly, one may argue that in calamitous social wars' stead (protests) (Veloso 2003), the ceremonial connoisseurs train body and soul to 'peacefully compensate thymotic urge through the consumption of the arts as well as sports' (Wenning 2009: 93). For this reason, the whole closing ceremony's plot proffers balancing combinations between affect (turned into emotion), reason and bodily desire.

Lapa's embodied appearance is such a civilising experiment for the domestic cosmopolitan tourist gaze: its whitewashed bohemian outpost of Santa Teresa stands apart from Rio's tourist mythology, as it offers to local artists affordable homes with panoramic views, to older, open-minded middle-class flâneurs banal consumption experiences and to younger Brazilian 'darenots' the best alternative to *Zona Sul*'s (South Zone) 'soulless' clubs. *Cariocas* who do not endorse Rio's 'fortress socialising' prefer its clubs, the

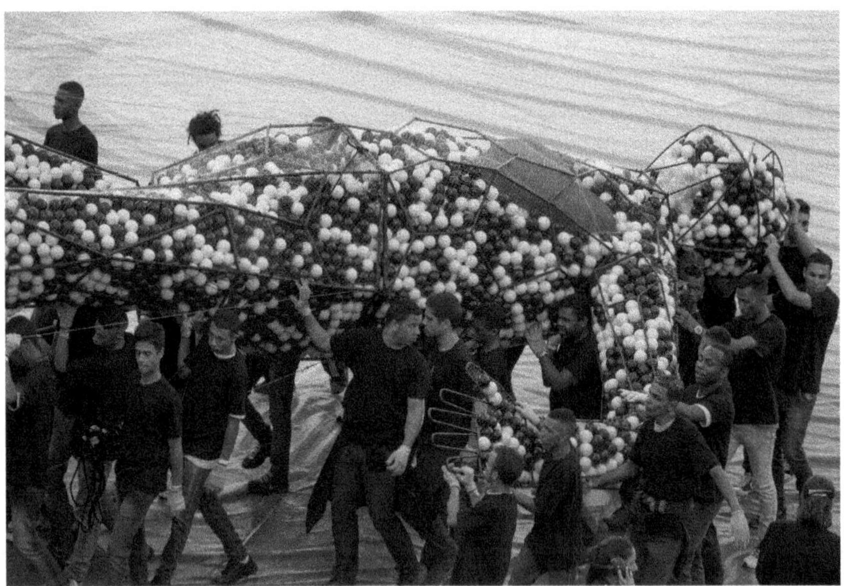

Figure 4.3 Brazil's cosmopolitan statement on peace and solidarity
Source Jimmy Balkovicius (Flickr), Creative Commons 2.0. Licence: www.creativecommons.org/licenses/by-sa/2.0/

Figure 4.4 Articulating FIFA's peaceful message: technology's heart and soul
Source: Jimmy Balkovicius (Flickr), Creative Commons 2.0. Licence: www.creativecommons.org/licenses/by-sa/2.0/

modernist accent of slave-built 1723 Arcos da Lapa aqueduct, the staging of impromptu samba in its cobblestones and sidewalks, and its street musicians' *cavaquinhos*, the diminutive guitars that give samba music its characteristic tink. Such aesthetic preferences come close to foreign tourist consumptions of 'World Music' that took shape in the first half of the century – jazz, tango, samba, son – only to join the realm of tourist commodities (Negus 1999; Connell and Gibson 2004). Though these styles 'became the basis and inspiration for an extraordinary profusion of local musical renaissances ranging from motown to bossa nova to *juju* to reggae' (Denning 2001: 362–3), their origins in deep social divisions persisted. Just like cinematic adaptation, 'World Music' was never accepted as a genre but demoted to a marketing category, distinct only for its blend of multiple genres from the 'developing world' (Frith 2000; Hesmondhalgh 2007: 513–5, for a critique of Frith).

A startling example of Rio's most recent splintering urbanism (Marcuse 1996), Lapa provides a social momentum in the history of Rio samba (Carmon 2006). The neighbourhood's ill repute in the early twentieth century earned it the title of 'South America's Montmartre', due to the cabarets, brothels and casinos that Getúlio Vargas banned in the 1940s. Lapa's original twin self-presentation as the territory of debonair *malandragem* on the one hand, and the tempestuous black bisexual drag queen *Madame Satã* (dir. Karim Aïnouz) – a 2002 Brazilian-French cinematic *persona* – on the other, is reflected in its contemporary alternative gender-bending heritage, which is carried by the transvestites lining Lapa's streets. *Madame Satã* follows the life of the famous transvestite João Francisco dos Santos, a poor black trickster, artist, convict, homosexual father and frequenter of the bohemian neighbourhood of Lapa (IMDB 2002). In *Madame Satã*, Lapa itself develops into a character in 'a drama of marginality, the apotheosis of feverish creativity and full-throttle pageantry' (Carmon 2006). The film's Euro-Brazilian, Christological-Africanist arc is evident in the title (Madame Satã as the hermaphrodite Satan that traffics bodies and souls, a humanised black witch-wizard, confusing human perception), which spatialises Rio's sodomist hell (Lapa's brothel).

We know that 'World Music' and cinematic adaptations of political content stir national consciousness or contribute to transnational political movements (Connell and Gibson 2004: 343; Tzanelli 2013b: 4, 6), so the covert presence of such a cinematic reference is not coincidental in a country constantly torn apart by social clashes. It is not incorrect to argue that musical traffic and its embodied commodities (singers, sambistas) articulate a sort of Brazilian ambivalence towards gentrification and touristification with the help of commoditised Lapa. As much as the area experienced a second 'cultural renaissance' after a brief 1960s beach-going craze that pulled away its clientele, its alternative feel continues to scare the middle classes to date. The ceremonial samba body is the sexual carrier of tropicopolitan aesthetics, which, like Shakira's belly-dancing *téchne*, prioritises the sinful domains of reproduction to seduce the *synaesthete* (Bakhtin 1968: 26; Tzanelli 2013a). The abject properties of the Afro-Brazilian travelling body recycle the archplot of coerced Caribbean and, more generally, Latin American mobilities (Sheller 2003, 2004) – irreparably connected to slavery (abroad and domestically) and feminisation (at home). The closing ceremony thus borrows from Lapa's histories, present and potential futures: literally incorporating its 'camp' marginal artstyles into the bodies of the sambistas, it excludes the excluding upper classes from its affective experiential core. For the foreign *synaesthete*, Lapa's 'back regions' of performance might be 'public' (Goffman 1987) but are not accessible (comprehensible); simultaneously, its synaesthetic specificities (embodied hedonism) exclude those who promulgate social into global cultural distance (Middleton 2000): the native middle classes. This projects a unique local cosmopolitan aesthetic, which turns the movement of surfaces (cinematic mobilities) into an emotional statement with social depth (socio-cultural resentment).

However, if hermaphrodite *linda Lapiana*'s *téchne* of bodily movement is affective, football technology is rational in more pronounced ways. The shift from resentment to civilised assimilation communicates transparently the global consumerist ethos of the mega-event: a giant replica of Brazuca is lowered from the sky to introduce another version of technicity as enabling mobility in global sports. 'Adidas Brazuca' is the new match ball that was supplied by Forward Sports of Sialkot, a company based in Pakistan. The ball has reduced thermally bonded panels but increased consistency and aerodynamics compared to its predecessor. Teams like Bayern Munich and AC Milan and top players such as Argentina's Lionel Messi and Germany's Bastian Schweinsteiger were involved in its perfection for the football pitch. As the ball replaced one that apparently made players look 'like drunken sailors' (Howells 2014), it complied with the 'technologisation' of the event's spatial reconfigurations. More importantly, though, the ball's name, Brazuca, originated from a million-vote Brazilian fan poll, and is a local word that describes the Brazilian way of life (Howells 2014). The presentation of this global piece of technology in the closing event suggests that Brazilian *eudaimonía* is harmonised with the globalised athletic spirit that hones the body so as to educate the soul. Yet, as a pursuit that is not individualist, football's technologisation also has to conform to Brazilian understandings of *personage*. The ceremonial presentation of Brazuca has to transcend the commercial logic of commodity so as to enter the cosmography of riches as a reciprocal gesture (also Appadurai 1986: 33).

This is achieved with the introduction of embodiments of all 32 competing nations in the stage. The 'nations' are represented by women dressed in ballroom costumes in the colours of their respective national flag and carrying this flag, and men dressed accordingly accompanying them. Due to the presence of Lapa samba dancers, each national character couple also symbolises the unity of *mestre de sala* or 'room master', with *e porta bandeiras*, the samba school's flag carrier. The ceremony's couples follow the strict rules of the Brazilian sambadrome as these were developed from the colonial era through the years of authoritarian surveillance: the *porta bandeiras* gyrates while displaying the flag, and the *maestre de sala* dances around her to draw attention to both. During samba festivities and Carnival processions, the moves of these personages are regulated by a set of rules, and during the parade they are evaluated by judges. Hence, these ceremonial couples are simultaneously kinaesthetic assemblages and surveillance survivals, post-colonial nationalist symbols and embodied commodities for the global tourist synaesthete. The primacy of the gaze in this consumption ritual connects to the performance's gendered and racialised principles of self-presentation: whereas originally *portas bandeiras* were male, their transformation into a female spectacle articulated anew the female poetics of womanhood (e.g. Herzfeld 1985 on poetics of manhood).

The equally exhibitionist function of the *mestre de sala* has also been compared to the *Zé Pilintra* of ethnic Afro-Brazilian traditions (Lourenço 2009: 9, 16). An *Umbanda* and *Catimbó* (or *Catimba*) spiritual character, *Zé Pilintra* originally figured as a sort of benevolent patron spirit of bars, gambling dens and gutters, thus coming close to later Brazilian understandings of the *Malandro. Zé Pilintra*'s connection to Bahian backlands and his love for *xaxado* (a Bahian folk dance) connect him to more contemporary representations of *malandragem*. Both in elite and pop registers *Malandro-Zé Pilintra* characters appear in the form of a white suit-clad *negro* or *mulatto*, sporting a Panama hat, a bright red tie and chrome white shoes – component accessories that we encounter in Pelé's appearance at the London 2012 handover ceremony to Rio (see Tzanelli 2013c: 116). Thus, although the national football couples retain in the closing ceremony all the magical properties of embodied performance we associate with ancient Afro-Brazilian cosmologies, they are in fact contemporary articulations of the South American trickster who inhabits the country's inner urban environments of Rio de Janeiro or São Paulo. The closing ceremony's white benevolent national 'spirits' suggest that Afro-Brazilian syncretism and its subsequent Western and European perceptions (as in, for example, Walt Disney's creation of a cartoon character from true *Portela* samba dancers as *Zé Pilintra* composites) are still alive as spectacles. Their phenomenological journey showcases a native hermeneutics, in which moral whiteness coexists with blackness: the ceremony's *mestres de sala* may be dressed in white, but the stage's giant effigies, which belong to the world of spirits, are black.

From the 32 national spirits, two *portas bandeiras* representing the finalists split from the group and proceed, each together with a freestyle footballer, to the centre of the stage. Only the two football national characters – representing Joachim Low's *Nationalmannschaft* and Alejandro Sabella's *Albiceleste* – enter centre pitch. A samba display by dancers from various schools commences around the two finalist *portas bandeiras* – one dressed in gold and representing the Cup, and the other in silver. The golden *porta bandeiras* dances between the two finalists in the ceremonial stage to 'seduce' them in a sexualised fashion, and in response, the global *Carnaval's* two *mulatas passistas* proceed to display their embodied artistry *à la capoeira*. Indeed, the freestyle player's artistry transposes sambistas' exaggerated mobility from the hips to the feet, thus copying closer the capoeirists' prioritisation of the bodily base, which regulates balance and precision. Moving the ceremonial focus away from the head and the waist, the two *mulatas passistas* present athletic competition as a rational dialogue.

Act two

The musical show that follows Shakira's opening performance includes Wyclef Jean, Carlos Santana, Alexandre Pires, Ivete Sangalo and Carlinhos Brown, per NDTV Sports. Nowhere is ceremonial fracture more apparent than in the second act, which develops conceptions of belonging across Brazilian understandings of the isolated individual and the networked person. Whereas despite their general Latin American political positionality and artistic orientation, the first three artists are foreign, the last three performers are Brazilian-born singers who maintain the closing ceremony's strong flavour of the host nation. Perhaps the most established of all six, Carlos Santana (b. 1947, Autlán de Navarro, Jalisco, Mexico), acts as a collective representation of the act's musical feel. From his early ground-breaking Afro-Latin-blues-rock fusion outfit in San Francisco, Santana 'has been the visionary force behind artistry that transcends musical genres and generational, cultural

Figure 4.5 Articulating the beautiful football 'cockfight': international and national singers, Brazilian dancers and the much-desired 'gold' *porta bandeira*
Source: Jimmy Balkovicius (Flickr), Creative Commons 2.0. Licence: www.creativecommons.org/licenses/by-sa/2.0/

and geographical boundaries' (Santana n.d.). Individually, the artist's signature splits them into localised artstyles that mirror Brazilian culture as a misunderstood, individual being, but the group's World Music 'signature' suggests that the mega-event's artworld is a particular version of the social world (DeNora 2003): mobile, hybrid and experimental, like the networked Brazilian person.

Shakira, who has appeared at the last three tournaments ('Hips Don't Lie' was performed with Wyclef Jean in 2006; 'Waka Waka (This Time for Africa)' was performed for the 2010 World Cup and recognised as the top-selling World Cup song), performs 'La, La, La (Brazil 2014)' alongside Carlinhos Brown. Born in 1977 as Shakira Isabel Mebarak Ripoll in Barranquilla, Colombia, to a Lebanese-American father and a Colombian mother, she climbed the ladder of fame in just a few years. Her widely disseminated self-narration presents her as a cosmopolitan with roots and routes. A self-declared soccer enthusiast, she has had little Milan with soccer player Gerard Pique, from Spain. 'I have an intricate relationship with soccer for obvious reasons, and I truly understand what the World Cup means to so many people, myself included', she stated in an interview (Irizarry 2014). The comment attains significance if we consider Shakira's appearance in World Cup ceremonies in relation to her previous associations with national branding. Declared by the Colombian government as 'the country's biggest export'

(Cordey 2011), she has been used to promote domestic tourism, even though her belly-dancing career had cast her as a hybrid artist. Her hybridity was considered a safe way to purify the country's image, which was tainted by decades of cocaine wars and FARC terrorism. With networks covering both literary and pop artworlds (García Márquez 2002), Shakira the professional singer better exemplifies the Western individual who aesthetically reflects on the world around her to interpret it. Her attachment to reflexive modernisation (Giddens 1994; Beck 2002; Lury 2004: 38), which heralds the consolidation of individualism through experiential authenticity, is cleverly manipulated in her public appearances to produce a poetics of womanhood in which femininities and sexualities are understood as 'style' (Attwood 2006: 86; Tzanelli 2013c).

Shakira's public personage is ornamented by modern cabaret costumes, body jewels and other glamorous props that activate a spectacular and excessive audiovisual complex through hybrid choreographies (Keft-Kennedy 2005: 292). Although her ornamentalism is not tropical in the conventional Brazilian sense, her established self-presentation as a post-modern 'orientalist' (replaced in the song's official video clip with an equally hybrid samba costume) is nicely complemented by Carlinhos Brown's Brazilian popular ethos. The Bahian singer's (b. 1962 in Salvador as Antonio Carlos Santos de Freitas) musical style blends *tropicália*, reggae and traditional Brazilian percussion. From his 1990s involvement with Salvador's young percussionists and singers (*timbaleiros*), to his 2007 collaboration with Brazilian poperatist and London 2012 performer Marisa Monte, in the release of *A Gente Ainda Não Sonhou* (People Are Yet to Dream), and the 2011 recording with Los Van Vans of '*Soy Loco Por Tí, América*' for the Red Hot Organization's most recent charitable album *Red Hot+Rio 2*, Brown blended in his work folk, technical (especially percussionist) and mythical elements (legends) with modern appliances and tools (electronic) (Neder n.d.). Both artists exemplify a version of technicity that blends bodily and social capital. Both artists exemplify the capacity of all persons to be 'mobile' through the ways they appropriate what is possible in mobility domains and putting this potential to relevant use (Kaufmann 2002: 37; Kaufmann et al. 2004).

'La, la, la', co-written by Shakira with the collaboration of Jay Singh, Dr. Luke, Mathieu Jomphe-Lepine, Max Martin, Cirkut, Raelene Arreguin, Lisa Lalalila and John J. Conte Jr., was the second song chosen as the World Cup anthem. First recorded as 'Dare (La, La, La)' for Shakira's most recent self-titled album, a couple of months before the tournament it was remixed in its World Cup version, issued with a few changes in lyrics and featured Brown as co-performer. After the latter was recorded in English and in Portuguese, it served as an impulse for the original to head into the Billboard music charts, whereas the World Cup version supported the World Food Programme (Irizarry 2014). It is significant that 'La, La, La's' repurposed version of 'Dare (La, La, La)' for the 2014 World Cup effectively turned a love song into an anthem proclaiming Brazil's greatness, and calling the players to score. The hybrid lyrics introduce a world picture in the form of a green carpet ('*o mundo é um tapete verde*') that merges the experience of hosting the World Cup (in Latin languages, *Mundial*) with celebrity exposure. The aesthetics of football cosmopolitanism seem to follow the movement of the ball (*bola*), placing emotions at the centre of Brazil's anticipated celebrations (*coração fica na rede*: the heart is part of the matrix/plot). Just like any cinematic archplot, the song needs to appeal to emotions through the elevation of everyday events to the cosmic (extraordinary) realm. The following English part complements this statement, prompting the synaesthete to 'feel how the planet' has 'become one' to beat like a drum 'in the same rhythm'. Thus, inner feelings (agony) develop with the sound of cymbals and 'a whistle', which is taken as a signal to 'kick the ball' so that the world 'ascends like an eagle'.

The lyrics suggest that we reconsider Malbon's (1999) *écstasis* as a bifurcated phenomenon of bodily extension (stretching to a physical and emotional limit) and elation (symptomatic of banal conceptions of *eudaimonía* as pleasure). 'In Rio we play like we dance', continues the song, allowing us to make yet another connection between samba and *futebolarte* as embodied arts or artistic crafts. The accompanying resignation ('there's no tomorrow … leave all behind … no space for fear or sorrow') calls into being a pilgrim, a personage who, unlike fateless individuals, belongs to a national-fan community (DaMatta's 1991: 181–2). The musical interlocutor makes sure that Brazilian contenders are determined to pursue the Cup, which is never mentioned as such, leaving open interpretations along the lines of a sexual innuendo ('Is it true that you want it? Then act like you mean it'). Shakira's on-stage performance of this part matches her highly eroticised popular image, which is regulated by commonplace understandings of hyper-femininity. Her imaginary interlocutor is placed in the role of a Brazilian man, who has everything to lose if he does not perform successfully in public ('With everyone watching, it's truth or dare, can you feel it?'). The concluding set of verses invites all strong contenders to take to the stage, as they have arrived at their destination, but notes that the 'drums of destiny' favour Brazil as the land of samba *futebolarte*. With a rhythmic chorus, the anthem 'dares' all to claim the trophy, which may as well be Shakira instead of a Cup. However, musical passion is also articulated by more complex semiotechnological means, which include Brown's career-making drums and other electronic instruments (Hennion and Latour 1993; Langlois 2012). The electronic and percussive beats, which resemble belly-dancing's Andalusian-African routes, are harmonised with the logic of the basic samba step. Accordingly, Shakira and Brown's performance was accompanied by both professional and amateur samba dancers, articulating in an alternative fashion the nature of football as an artistic craft. As a result, the hymn is an accessible product that can speak different 'languages' – Portuguese probably being the most desirable due to the dispirited, by then, Brazilian fans.

The end of the song is followed by another performance by Jean and Pires, who begin proceedings with '(*Dar um Jeito*) We Will Find a Way'. Jean's appearance is enhanced by a Fender guitar, especially manufactured for the occasion. Just like the introductory song's arrangement, Brazilian sambista Alexandro Pires (b. 1976, Uberlândia, Minas Gerais) and Mexican guitarist Carlos Santana's acoustic synergy in 'We Will Find a Way' are kinaesthetically framed by amateur dance groups. The song's title is displayed at the bottom of the stage's podium, providing extra red carpet glamour to the performance that we also tend to associate with MTV music videos. The human-machine assemblage articulates the street and club cultures of Brazil, rather than its historical mysticism, allowing foreign synaesthetes to participate in the event as more literate audiences. Like 'La, la, la (Brazil 2014)', the song works as a metaphor, but instead of speaking about love, it discusses homelessness. The introductory lyrics could easily be considered autobiographical, given that despite his birth in a musical family and his university education, Santana's humble beginnings included hard work in kitchens and dishwashing (Shapiro 2002). However, the song's heartening suggestion that 'all [are] one voice, one heart, one soul / Once we set that Goal / You know we're gonna score', connects Brazilian individualism to football triumph. The song's explosive emotionalism (*Então vamos gritar / Explode emoção*) is also filtered in the Portuguese lyrics through anticipated victory for the 'nation' (*é tão forte a sensação, de vestir uma nação*: the feeling is so strong, dressing a nation) (Metro Lyrics n.d.a). With Santana's emotional electronic guitar and Jean and Pires's multi-scalar performance, the semiotechnological assemblage captures the heart of global audiences. Santana's idiosyncratic dress style also complements the lyrics: not far from *Malandro*'s Latin *jeitinho*, the black-hatted man, who is also covered in black leather and armed with a guitar, literally mediates (*jeito*: way, mediation) between the depths of poverty and the elation of a public spectacle. Again, therefore, art finds a way to turn Brazilian tragic cosmologies and cosmographies of riches into phenomenological discourse.

Then Alexander Pires do Nascimento performs 'Campayo'. Although Pires commenced his career playing *Pagode* or *Pagode Romântico*, a new, more romantic style of samba, he became known for his *samba-canção*, a more realist style with elements of Brazilian country music. He performed within the band *Só Pra Contrariar*, which he joined in the 1980s, and is known for his international collaborations with celebrities such as Gloria Estefan (1999) and Julio Inglesias (2007). His contemporary 'electro-samba' style (also the title of his 2012 studio album, *Eletrosamba*) approximates Santana's electronic compositions while retaining distinctive elements from older affective Brazilian genres. While Pires is singing, Ivete Sangalo (b. 1972, Juazeiro, Bahia) makes an entrance with Fuleco, the 2014 FIFA mascot. The armadillo-like mascot was conceived in 2000 and named using a portmanteau of the words *futebol* and *ecologia* (ecology) (FIFA.com 2012b). It is supposed to be in love with social media, in possession of special dance moves celebrating Brazil's unique rhythm (inspired by samba, *forró, frevo* and *axé*) and the mission to 'encourage kids … all over the world to be part of the FIFA World Cup' (FIFA.com n.d.d). A three-banded armadillo, which is native to Brazil and categorised as a vulnerable species on the International Union for Conservation of Nature (IUCN) Red List, the mascot carries a message of environmental concern, ecology and sport. Again, we note a felicitous blend of human-animal ecologies, which comes close to the *anthropopoetic* (making of the national human) game of nationalism.

In the ceremony, the mascot dances amongst other dancers to Sangalo's rhythm. A veteran of 'wowing the crowds in Rio de Janeiro', Sangalo's presence refocuses the closing event to the host nation's fans, potentially ameliorating tensions brought about by the host team's 'dreadful end to the competition' (Dudko 2014). Her fusion of *axé*, samba-reggae, pop, MPB (*música popular brasileira*) and Latin pop offers an easily translatable 'World Music' of global commercial reach. Her *blocos* appearance in Salvador's Carnival and her other performances at *trio elétrico* (a platform equipped with a high-power sound system and a music group on the roof invented for Carnival performance, akin to the one used in the ceremonies for celebrity singers) in off-season Carnivals have been as lucrative as her commercial deals with companies like Avon, Grendene, Panasonic, Garnier, Danone, Arisco, Bradesco and Nova Schin, among others. Coupling Sangalo with Fuleco is a mythological game in Barthesian terms (it naturalises culture) that is placed in the service of branding (Barthes 1979). A chain of associations is activated to join the Brazilian deep plot: just like Sangalo's and Fuleco's commercial success, national styles are commodities that travel the world as signs of national beauty, greatness or prowess (also Lash and Urry 1994). If the 'nation' is a natural commodity, even global artistic *téchne* can attain the natural properties of togetherness: unsurprisingly, in the ensuing ceremonial *grand finale* all artists are reunited on stage to dance with each other, sing and, in Shakira's case, even introduce her young son dressed in an Argentine football kit. The ambivalence of this act – 'even legacies cast roots along their routes', apropos Clifford – gives way almost immediately to a medley of samba, anthems and fan singing. It is this contemporary hauntological ambiguity that will guide the next chapter's empirical and analytical observations.

5 A defeated people

The loss of riches and the return of debt

Inescapable asymmetries: officialising the cosmography of riches

Despite the fact that football's borrowing from cultures of violence, ritual and discourses of sacrifice allowed anthropologists to monopolise its analysis for a while, the field's broader association with the nexus of (emotional and material) mobilities and immobilities make it suitable for interdisciplinary analysis. Sociologically, football signals the supplanting of the social realm (*Gesellschaftlich*) with cultural life (*Gemeinschaftlich*) (Tönnies 1957) – otherwise put, the replacement of religious belief with the society's self-veneration rituals. Because imagined communities use football to strengthen their bonds, the game might also be implicated in more contentious processes of networking, extortion and familial-racial exclusivity. For reasons I need not mention again, these social realities have to be 'shoved under the carpet' in public, global contexts. Even former FIFA President João Havelange, a Brazilian with first-hand knowledge of the dubious role networking practices play in his country's sports, openly presented football as 'the most democratic of all sports, we all talk to each other in a football stadium; everyone is equal. This feeling of democracy in the game is very important since football belongs to everybody' (*FIFA Magazine* April 1998: 3, in Giulianotti and Robertson 2007: 167). Never mind that this 'feeling' rarely follows citizens out of the stadium, in this or various other national contexts; what matters is how the promise of democracy might linger for a while in the minds of fans, when various other social concerns tend to overshadow their everyday lives. The events following the loss of the Cup to Germany, or ('God forbid') to Argentina, are therefore pivotal factors in the production of dystopian scenarios in Brazil's urban streets.

We may open the narrative by pointing to the clouds that began to gather in Brazil's tropicopolitan skies, long before the country's historic defeat to Germany. These clouds are part of the 'social drama' (Turner 1974a) that would soon unfold, and whose cosmic feel today allows us to consider the defeat as a 'paradigmatic human event' (Geertz 1973: 450). Like its ceremonial equivalent, the 'event's' structural base suggests its reading as an 'art of being Brazilian'. Let us not forget, of course, that as much as its cosmic proportions were based on structured principles, like art, they also allow space for the generation and regeneration of 'the very subjectivity they pretend[ed] only to display' (ibid.: 451). It is reported that at one point, at the end of the opening ceremony, fans chanted and booed against Brazilian President Dilma Rousseff and football's international governing body, FIFA. The reactions could safely be attributed to complaints 'that spending on the World Cup and the 2016 Rio Olympics has diverted cash from the poor and infrastructure improvements' (Associated Press 2014). While many Brazilians took to the streets to celebrate, before the event's official kick-off, police in São Paulo used tear gas to break up one protest and 'striking airport workers in Rio de Janeiro blocked a road outside the airport, demanding a wage increase and a World Cup bonus' (BBC Sport 2014c).

This portmanteau of incidents that celebrate, destroy and regenerate Brazilianness in global domains, pushes us to crack open another door to the politics of mobility. There we enter the salons of 'persons proper' who are, by profession, assigned with various trafficking responsibilities and charged with various shortcomings for their failure to do the job of internationalising Brazilian culture fairly. One may recognise in the mega-event's 'deep play' the transverse 'doubleness of an event which, taken as a fact of nature, is rage untrammelled and, taken as a fact of culture, is form perfected' (Wagner-Pacifici 2011: 96). Weber's contention that the political vocation connects its participants with diabolical powers, making it impossible for them to relate 'good' or 'evil' acts to good or evil means correspondingly (Gerth and Mills 1948: 123), makes eudaimonic pursuits for the collective a risky business. On this, demonic politicians, such as Rousseff, have to perfect their art of communicating futural visions of a healthily functioning polity in ways that parallel and borrow from Brazil's cosmological aesthetics. The 'trick' the Brazilian politician plays balances the doubleness of the mega-event: while acknowledging its representational (hence cultural) basis, it attributes the origins of such representations to *Brasilidade*'s natural potency to civilise globally. Rousseff and her team's public articulation presents the 2014 FIFA World Cup as a project of redistribution (*daíõ* – see also Chapter 2 on *eudaimonía*) to the Brazilian people, who are asked to 'invest' trust in their governors and money in the mega-event for future material and immaterial returns. This essentially 'temporal lending' (see De Certeau 1985: 193, on credit) comes with a clause written in big, block letters for external and internal audiences: the Brazilian people's pursuit of *eudaimonía* was made possible through a double form of lending, which also necessitated a lot of borrowing (ancient *dámimi* corresponds to the modern Greek *daneízomai*: to borrow). This double lending is synchronic, internal and material (for the completion of mega-event works), but also has a diachronic, external and symbolic dimension (an unpaid global debt to Brazilian culture).

Redemption, hospitality and global citizenship

So, the current guardian of order, Dilma Rousseff, stayed attuned to the tempo of embarrassing public incidents, which exposed the hierarchical nature of Brazilian society to the bone. Her speech at the opening ceremony of the 64th FIFA Congress in São Paulo (now posted on the Brazil 2014 official website) marked a special occasion: the celebration of the 110th anniversary of FIFA and the centennial of the Brazilian national team. Not only did Rousseff stress Brazil's 'enormous contribution' to making football the most universal sport on the planet, but she also argued that 'with us it reached the status of art' (World Cup Portal 2014d). Sports such as football have contributed significantly to the transnationalisation of non-European peoples through stronger connectivity within the 'international community' (Holton 2005). Conforming to Brazilian cultural codes, Rousseff's discourse reinforced a 'vertical ethics', linking superior (international organisations) and inferior (the host country) members of the event by sacred patronage ties. It was important to emphasise the complementary aspects of such hierarchical relations, instead of focusing on their antagonistic aspects – a practice also guiding Brazilian moral structures (DaMatta 1991: 184–6). Therefore, Rousseff's argument amounts to claims to Brazil's global citizenship status (Bianchi and Stephenson 2014): if, as she mentioned, Brazilian players have been naturalised by other countries – an issue 'already a concern for President Blatter and FIFA' – then Brazil is ready to host 'the Cup of Cups' (World Cup Portal 2014d). The comment turns football players into world citizens, travellers rather than 'vagabonds' (Bauman 1998), who can nevertheless retain their roots in an expansive homeland vision. Rousseff's vision of modernity has not 'liquidised' (Bauman 2000) all local values on the altar of synchronisation, despite the fact that popular and official discourses alike endorse the country's '*Carioca*' style of play, an essentially multi-racial play, conforming to symbolic appropriations of the European sport by blacks and mulattos (Leite Lopes 1997). Her speech is not just about globalisation processes but about a more 'rudimentary politics of recognition' (Giulianotti and Robertson 2007: 172), involving post-colonial Brazil's onus of maintaining a native cosmopolitan (tropicopolitan) presence (Sheller 2014b).

Consequently, we must place the converging pressures of 'globalization, commercialization and governmentalization ... [on a par with] the significance of national history and the institutional constraints on [football] policy to place the incident in perspective (Houlihan and Green 2008: 9, 13). For Rousseff, the mega-event provided an opportunity to connect celebrations to the humanist Olympics values, as set forth by Pierre de Coubertin: peace, harmony and tolerance (World Cup Portal 2014a). 'Like its Christ the Redeemer', Brazil welcomes all 'with open arms' to a Cup 'for peace ... inclusion, tolerance, dialogue and understanding', she exclaimed. Her Brazilian people were presented as 'cheerful, generous and hospitable', with ample 'capacity for hard work and ... the determination ... [not to] give up' (World Cup Portal 2014c). There is no doubt that with regards to urban development, Rousseff has set herself politically after Lula's 'post-ideological' mix of orthodox market economics and progressive social policy – known today as the 'Brazilian model' (Padgett and Downie 2008 in Andrews and Mower

2012: 5). However, at some point in her speech, the discourse of hard work to complete a project that the 'naysayers' thought beyond the country's capabilities introduces para-theological ideas of redemption. Like a suffering Christ (the Redeemer), Brazil achieved things once thought impossible: to rank as the 'seventh economy in the world, as well as a global leader in various sectors of industrial production and agribusiness', and complete the World Cup preparations, while 'massively reduc[ing] inequality, bringing 42 million Brazilians into the middle class and lifting 36 million out of extreme poverty' (World Cup Portal 2014c).

It is significant that the speech was placed on a global website: its textual nature (Geertz 2000: 17) allowed billions of Internet users to 'read' it as Brazil's cosmological statement. However, as media can also determine the nature of the message that they carry, an electronically mediated statement of this sort purports Brazilian technicity and technique's synchronisation with the West. In short, the discourse of industriousness subsumes Brazilian transmodernity's mobile ethos of migration and travel into the Western vision of industrial modernity (Domingues 2006a). The nation strategically assumes the role of 'carer' in the global service sector, opening its Christian arms to accept all athletic visitors-pilgrims. The strategy responds to pragmatic ends, turning hospitality into an essential tool not only for the maintenance of the host's 'good name' as a 'donor' (Tzanelli 2004), but also for the maintenance of communal solidarity. Yet, leisure economies enable cultural mobilities that ought to be beneficial for cultural givers and native workers (Derrida 1994; Derrida and Dufourmantelle 2000). This is the reason Rousseff does not neglect to clarify that the apparently beneficial conditions under which such mobilities were enacted ultimately determined the venture's positive outcome: investments in modern stadiums, new transport networks, and a modern communication and broadcasting system that uses state-of-the-art technology, including fibre-optic networks and cutting-edge equipment in all 12 host cities (World Cup Portal 2014c). The additions will yield 'benefits for life', for 'all Brazilians', alongside the revenues the mega-event will bring to the country (ibid.).

Evidently, Rousseff tries to offset in her speech accusations of welfare underspending and the fact that infrastructural investment was partly financed from federal banks and state governments and partly from the private sector (at approx. 8 billion reais). There are a number of 'facts' upon which the nation-wide debate on spending was based, and which also supported some pivotal cultural codes of blaming (e.g. Alexander 1989). In Brazilian cosmological registers, Rousseff is the quintessential example of a complete human with power, prestige, beauty and grace due to her connections to powerful people 'at the top' – an *alguém* or 'real person', rather than a *cidadão brasileiro* or *indivíduo* (DaMatta 1991: 167). Hence, her presentation of numbers ought, in a doxic context, go unquestioned by the masses, but whispers of underhand dealings only multiplied with time. The originally estimated costs of US$1.1 billion on stadium works alone, rose to a reported

$3.6 billion that even 'unnamed' government officials blamed on corruption (Panja 2014). Notably, the Brazilian government also earmarked an additional R3 billion ($1.3 billion, £780 million at June 2014 rates) for investment in infrastructure works and projects for use during the 2014 World Cup and beyond, provoking increased discontent among Brazilians, who also criticised Rousseff for the failed completion of many of the proposed works. A rising domestic opposition to hosting the event in 2014 polls followed the largest social unrest in a decade after the 2013 Confederations Cup, prompting the government and police to promise to crack down on demonstrators during this year's games (Moraes 2014).

A concomitant issue has been the rights of those who lived on land that would be repossessed for use. An IPS report suggested that 30,000 families in Rio de Janeiro alone would be forced to move for the competition, whereas the Americas Program of the Center for International Policy placed the overall estimate at 170,000 people countrywide. In particular, *favela* evictions proved that the 'Cup of Cups' did not sit well with the values the government wanted to promote through the mega-event; contrariwise, the major cities' unprecedented 'spatial cleansing' (Herzfeld 2006) granted Brazil the global face of a formalist *bela*, respecting appearances as content. Alongside these issues, the UK-based Latin America Bureau reported that FIFA's threats over the completion dates of projects were used as excuses for ignoring the rights of workers by construction firms. A report entitled 'Mega-Events and Human Rights Violations in Brazil' produced by *A Publica* in late 2012 documented strikes at six of the 12 World Cup stadiums, with demands ranging 'from wage increases and benefits like health insurance, food assistance and transportation, to improved working conditions (in particular, the protesters had complaints regarding the security situation, sanitation, and food), increased overtime payment and the end of "inhumanely long" working hours' (Atkins 2013).

To these, predominantly urban, complaints, one may add other grievances, which blatantly contradict the World Cup opening ceremony's focus on respect for indigenous rights. These grievances concern the construction of the 'Belo Monte Dam' in Amazonia – a long-term corporate plan repeatedly hindered by global and local activists, which provided indigenous Brazilian social movements political direction towards a twin goal: environmental conservation and protection of indigenous life. One may even claim that the Belo Monte project realises Lula's post-dictatorship policy of *abertura*, by interpreting idea(l)s of democratic openness into participation in corporate projects that grant Brazil a globally progressive kudos. As such, it casts the Brazilian federal polity as a network of loosely interconnected societies 'based around intersecting secrecy flows and jurisdictions, often parasitic upon powerful "onshore" societies' (Urry 2014: 10). Needless to add that such undertakings are advertised as 'necessary temporary measures', so that nobody admits that they are integral to, or a permanent feature of, post-colonial modernisation (Faubion 1988; Nederveen Pieterse 1998; James 2006).

However, their ultimate contribution to Brazilian polyphony is to exclude some voices from its orchestration; to let privileged classes articulate for those who 'are destined not to think' (Rancière 2004: xii). Ironically, in the World Cup's ceremonial instance the domain of law, which is supposed to make visible the dispossessed, is turned into a bogus way to divide Brazil's imagined community into social positions and functions: while rendering Amazonian groups visible as ecosystemic guardians, it makes them less articulate, less socially present even in aesthetic terms.

The Belo Monte project is part of the construction of about 70 dams in South America; it binds the governments of weaker regions and nations (such as Bolivia, Peru and Ecuador) into building additional dams, with large social and environmental impacts (Tzanelli 2013b: 181). The dam's construction is already affecting plants and animals and a network of indigenous and conservation areas, as well as indigenous communities living along what is known as the Xingu's 'Big Bend'. The Xingu River, which passes through these areas, is important for the Amazon as it sustains the livelihoods of over 25,000 indigenous people from 18 ethnic groups. The Brazilian government is planning to construct the three largest hydroelectric dams in the world in the heart of this tropical rainforest. The $17 billion project threatens the biodiversity of the area, because it will divert the flow of the Xingu to generate electricity, flooding over 640,000 km, cutting off the flow of the river, and leaving populations without access to water, fish or means of transport and generating unclean energy (biogases). About 1,000 indigenous people from the Xikrín, Juruna, Arara, Xipaia, Kuruaya, Kayapó and other ethnic groups live in this region, so flooding it will wash away centuries of history and particular lifeworlds.

The problem is ethically loaded: not only does it involve effective communication between Brazil's multi-polar, urban power with its peripheries (Shils 1975), it also concerns the nature of new Brazilian socialism as an inclusive, anti-authoritarian ideology. Where *getulismo* demarcated ethnic territories as properties of the 'right', law-abiding and networked persons, socialist *abertura* was supposed to recognise, amongst other things, indigenous definitions of home territory, thus enlarging its imagined community's real citizenry. It is significant that indigenous representations populated the World Cup's ceremonial events. Though sanctioned by the state, their makers could place in discreet but powerful ways in an audiovisual frame, what Herzfeld (2002) has explored as the 'absent presence' of indigenous voices that should claim centrality in scholarly discourses of Western civilisation, and what De Sousa Santos (2000 in Barreira 2011: 154; De Sousa Santos 1999a, 1999b) has described as the 'sociology of absences', the ability of institutional frameworks to erase or amplify disenfranchised voices.

However, if the ceremonies communicated ambivalent messages, other global artistic networks have partaken more openly in activist projects concerning accessible, popular translations of such situational ethics (the meaning of land for the Amazon's people) into morality as propagated by the 1948

Universal Declaration of Human Rights – a 'bible' that influenced contemporary considerations of cultural-as-intellectual property (Eagle Merry 2003; Urry 2014: 36–7). James Cameron's charitable *Avatar* project, 'Amazon Watch', has been collecting global donations in support of the Kayapó demands for demarcation of ancestral territories. Attacks by ranchers and illegal settlers on the Kayapó and Juruna are regular incidents and not properly addressed by the federal government. The support for the demarcation of the Kapot Nhinore ancestral territory of the Kayapó and Juruna indigenous peoples in the upper Xingu in the Brazilian state of Mato Grosso, via the Instituto Raoni, a foundation headed by a chief, is constructed on mergers of heritage and legacy that support biopolitical representations of the land (Tzanelli 2013b: 172–3). Not only does the Belo Monte controversy cast a shadow over Rousseff's digital utopian discourse, but it unveils how in the World Cup context a variety of public performances (corporate, statist, ceremonial, artistic and activist) bring together different, conflicting mobilities in the same spaces of place (Castells 1996; Zukin 2003).

Offsetting her government's policies against European dystopian visions of 'Brazilianization' (Beck 2000b: 161–3) that speak of the dangers of absolute neoliberalism ('a stateless, rigidly stratified society [that] witnesses the elite inhabiting luxurious fortresses, travelling in superlimousines, and recruiting private armies to ward off the desperate dispossessed'; Giulianotti and Robertson 2004: 552) is a necessary move for Rousseff. Her visibility in the global money economy has been enhanced through media and scandal-mongering (e.g. Urry 2014: 11), to such an extent that she has been seen as the cause of every contemporary Brazilian social ailment. Popular discourses of her backing by Lula's political networks constantly paint her initiatives in the colours of 'amoral familism' (Banfield 1958; Coleman 1988; Putnam 1993) as a suspect professional version of 'network capital' (Elliot and Urry 2010). Neutralising transaction secrecy makes space to consider the global cosmography of riches that Brazil can attain. Thus, private 'donations' ('with benefits') are replaced with the ideal of Brazilian giving to world cultures. 'Donations' in mega-events that merely divert resources away from the donor's group destroy the moral basis of communal trust. In this vein, even the recruitment of transnational and native artists with heavy involvement in charity projects rekindled old links between Catholic and Marxist discourses of giving, used both in policy and party planning. Though looking at future legacy pacts with other nations, Rousseff's emphasis on delivering 'the Cup of Cups' is constitutive of Brazilian discourses of *patrimonio*: the county's heritage of accepting and nourishing strangers, like Christ the Redeemer. It is small wonder that her presidential stint was marked by accusations in the press of offshoring national resources. Such practices betray patrimony conventions, just as 'bad football' gives away the nation's characteristic riches to another country (Germany) from which Brazil received numerous migrants.

Patrimony is not merely offset by mega-event legacies in Rousseff's speech: addressing herself to the Brazilian national team, she reminds them that 'underneath the green and yellow uniform, [they] embody a powerful heritage of the Brazilian people ... The Seleção represents our nationality. It stands above governments, parties and interests of any group' (World Cup Portal 2014c). Such heritage conservation is as essential as the country's eventual transcendence of its authoritarian past, its 'absolute freedom' and 'popular demonstrations and demands, which help us continuously improve our democratic institutions' (ibid.). Rousseff's definition of national 'respectability' does what most nationalist discourses achieve on public stages: it converts a temporally bound international contract into a sense of place, exclusive to the Brazilian masses (De Certeau 1984). The strategy resonates with home audiences, as hospitality is supposed to provide 'the poor, the dependent, and the politically disadvantaged with unique opportunities for symbolizing the reversal of their plight ... allow[ing] them to invert their political dependence in the moral sphere' (Herzfeld 1992: 171; Herzfeld 1987). Yet, we must also bear in mind that Rousseff's own policies towards demonstrations, strikes and other public protests have not always matched her left-wing ideals; contrariwise, they reminded everybody that even mega-events can have nefarious outcomes, by way of strengthening authoritarian tendencies (see van der Westhuizen 2004 on the 16th Commonwealth Games; Korstanje and George 2012 on Argentine nationalism after the 1978 Football Championship).

It is perhaps the heritage burden that the Brazilian football team found too heavy to carry during that calamitous quarter final. Though calculative to the last detail, Rousseff's polished speech might inadvertently have further fuelled the 'flashpoint event' (Waddington 2010) that led to public unrest after Brazil's equally blazing defeat on 8 July against Germany. I will revisit its unfortunate consequences only tangentially below, as my interest is not to research further in social protest as such. Rather, I want to examine how, just like the World Cup ceremonies, Brazilian fan reactions to the defeat appealed to a withering national cosmos characterised by perfection, beauty and honour. The appeal mourned the loss of a national image as a gateway to a more private domain, in which a socio-culturally divided Brazil of *gâuchos, cariocas* and *Paulistas* can still magically get together to honour its dead ancestry.

Articulations of resentment and urban pilgrimage

8 July 2014 will probably be penned as one of the grimmest moments of Brazilian history: initially set to expunge the memories of the 1950 'Maracanazo' victory of Uruguayan football over Brazil at Estádio do Maracanã, with fireworks and 'Force Neymar' memorabilia, the hosted 2014 World Cup found the nation unprepared for the 7–1 loss to Germany in Belo Horizonte's Estádio Mineirão. The country's media had a mournful feast over the shattering of national pride in what is already known as the 'Mineiraço'. This defeat was for *GloboEsporte* the 'disgrace of all disgraces', and for *Lance!* 'the biggest shame in history', whereas Belo Horizonte-based *O*

Tempo recognised it as 'the worst in Brazil's history … in Brazil' (McNulty 2014). Even before the appearance of coherent domestic and international report records, the global circulation of the image of a sad old man, clutching a replica of the FIFA World Cup and dreading the next German goal, had encapsulated the atmosphere better than thousands of words (Hooton 2014). Brazilian coach Luiz Felipe Scolari, previously remembered both for his 2002 World Cup victory and a notable Portugal defeat by Greece in Euro 2004, responded to public recriminations with a dignified apology as 'the person who decided the tactics' (BBC Sport 2014d). However, the Brazilian players' confusion and bitter tears were to be met with disbelief, anger and irony by fans, who cheered Germany's seventh goal or successful passes with 'Ole' (Wallace 2014) and turned popular players such as David Luiz into villains overnight.

If this record of unprecedented Brazilian 'humiliation' and 'catastrophe' presents us with the Brazilian worldview's popular foreground, the worldview's recesses hide the story of an uneven 'order and progress'. The story, which was proudly imprinted on the national flag, was reportedly surrendered on Copacabana beach by Brazilian fans to a group of Germans in a symbolic gesture of defeat. It was also burned in the streets of São Paulo by groups of angry fans, who could not process the failure (Watts 2014). The flag belongs to the rule of law, a domain of hope for all the things that are supposed to flourish in a utopian future polity (Frye 1965; Claeys and Sargent 1999; Yar 2014b). The marring of a utopian promise embedded in the domain of law, produces communities of individuals, nomads in one's own home. One may suggest that many of these 'monadic nomads' composed the mass of Brazilian fans that moved physically and symbolically in the cities of the 2014 mega-event towards their home(land)'s vanishing 'centre'. This 'centre' appears in matches played by the national team as a collection of memories about national land, complete with multi-sensory composites or signs of 'home'. Functionally comprising affective, emotional and embodied composites, these physical and symbolic move(ment)s inhabited Brazilian *ruas*, public sites, in which the harsh realities of life are more manifest. The street and the public site are also the locus of multiple mobilities and the domains of public transportation – all intermediaries between 'home' and 'work' that make people more prone to commit acts of violence (DaMatta 1991: 193; Hall et al. 2003; Duval 2007: 212–22; Korstanje et. al. 2014). Incidentally, Cohen (1979) provides another link between the street's 'in-betweenness' and what can be classified as a 'major journey' by means of transportation to national and international shrines.

All these are more than mere 'spaces' or places, as they come into being through social practices, bearing the promise to transform individuals into persons, who can demand compensation by the highest authority. Sallnow's (1981, 1987; Eade and Sallnow 1991) revision of Turner, according to which pilgrimages do not necessarily endorse *communitas* in religious and non-religious contexts, but 'a complex mosaic of egalitarianism, nepotism and factionalism, of brotherhood, competition and conflict' (Sallnow 1981: 176; Eade 1992) certainly enhances the present argument. My argument recognises the divisive and hierarchical nature of fan marches, even when these attain a semi-religious national aura. In addition, Morinis's (1984) reminder that we should not prioritise the experiential and emotional over the intellectual, social and spiritual basis of pilgrimage, can be adapted to enhance the emphasis on the practical-artistic action of these fans. Immediately, we can make a connection to Brazilian kinaesthetic practices of walking, seeing and doing (Ingold 2010, 2011), prompting 'kinaesthetic appropriation of space' (De Certeau 1988: 98) or perhaps a 'chronotope': a space-time formation stimulating the national imagination to dream anew (Gourgouris 1996; Till 2005). As anger, frustration and even grief, performed in front of cameras and broadcast globally, are intermingled affects at the event's emotional core, we may have to tie such mobilities to 'structures of feeling' or the ways individuals constitute their everyday lives or the lived experience of the quality of life at a particular time and place (Williams 1977: 131; Crouch 2009). Such structures do not preclude the imaginative or virtual travel of information but tie those to the world of actual reach – what Schütz (1945: 545) defines as one's 'actual Here' and 'Now', in which all time perspectives originate, and under which events are organised within the world. Like other sports, football uses 'the nation' as its anchor point and rallying cry, making it impossible for sport to be 'reconfigured as postnational and subsequently stripped of its "productive" capacity to promote forms of identity' (Rowe 2003: 281). This performance of feeling within particular structures of space travels today virtually in every possible direction, in videos, photographs and texts (Engelbrekt 2011).

However, the visual attributes of this performance are only part of the story for a home crowd used to relating temporality to sound and melody (see also Chagas 2010: 3). The contextualisation of listening to particular songs could be identified as a post-Husserlian, universal feature of human consciousness for neuro-phenomenologists (Varela 1999), but the ways in which particular songs and rhythms evoke collective memories, hence cultural meaning, are macro-social phenomena. The ironic reversal of the rhythmic samba song's lyrics 'I am Going to Celebrate' ('Cry! I don't care. The hour has come. You are going to pay for me. You can cry, You can cry, You can cry more!') enhanced the carnival(esque) atmosphere of the humiliating aftermath. The music's indisputable historic background of protest and its lyrics produce what DeNora (2003: 49) termed the 'Music Event', a blended social scientific and artistic recognition of the ways music 'is mobilised in action and … associated with social affects'. Notably, in Brazilian Portuguese, *cantar* (to sing) is used metaphorically to describe the act of sexual proposition or seduction – as is the case with the function of Italian *cantadas* or the songs of the Mexican *mariachis,* which would be used by lovers as preludes to a relationship or marriage. However, singing and dancing in public and in football fan groups mediates between the private and the public. Being a Brazilian in this case comes down to 'melting into the anonymous crowd dancing the samba in the streets and savagely beating [the] European mistress' (DaMatta 1991: 63).

Or the mistress who came to one's home and settled comfortably in a corner, as is the case for Brazil's old migrations of German communities in the south. Connotations of a damaged love affair in the lyrics remain significant. There is an obvious (symbolic) reversal of (symbolic) role playing here, as the ornamented Brazil assumes in the song the status of a resentful male lover. Above all, the song speaks the language of a Brazilian psyche, the 'grand' national narrative of a constantly traumatised ethno-scape that travelled the world, hosted *conquistadores*, rose in football glory, and now fell into an inferno of dejection and oblivion. 'We Brazilians don't know how to lose', a fan explained to reporters (Watts 2014). Such celebrations of football victory may proximate nationalist expressivity by anonymous, fluid, mobile and unmediated populations (Gellner 1983: 138) – especially where histories of migration, diaspora and colonialism guide popular knowledge and sentiment (Armstrong and Giulianotti 1997). In any case, their emphasis on imaginary vengeance stands between the fully fledged rebellion of *Malandros* and the passivity of the *caxias*. Eternally deferred, this vengeance characterises the spiritual trepidation of the renouncer, whose mind-walking routes bring her upon the ultimate temptation: to get back the allegedly stolen riches by employing her legendary feminine cunning. Thus, we may say that for a while, dancing and singing's *cathectic* process promises to heal the Brazilian soul, but never manages to do so, as its resentful core simply performs a temporal trick (revenge should come in the *future*). The true function of the Brazilian renouncer in such contexts is, as DaMatta (1991: 211) claims, 'not to offer a higher life by virtue of social and economic ascent', but 'a wholly new social world'.

The Durkheimian observation that religion is society worshipping itself (Durkheim 1969: 20–1) is obviously applicable to footballing nationalism as well as its racist extensions. The incident is significant, like the numerous offensive Twitter jokes (Coscarelli 2014) at the Germans' expense, which appeal to a global war-ridden popular imaginary ('Man the goalie really holocaust them the game, I bet Brazil's coach was like Aw Schwitz', writes someone; 'What Brazil doesn't realize is that if Germany wins it *will* conquer & colonize the good parts of the country', adds another; 'Stop with these nazi jokes, they're not funny. Anne Frankly, they're offensive', concludes a third). The global proclivity to purify collective memory is nicely reflected in the Brazilian national domain through a simple switch from race to gender. In both cases, the imaginary articulates, but in the Brazilian case it articulates through music. Thus, Rousseff's Twitter invitation to Brazilians to 'shake off the dust' and 'rise again' knowingly filtered a political message through the lyrics of a popular samba song, when the national team's ignominious exit matched the 2013 mass summer protests, smothered by police, with new waves of violence in Rio de Janeiro, Recife, Salvador and São Paulo. The doctored picture of a fan depicting the Christ the Redeemer statue with Uzi machine guns in outstretched arms and the slogan 'The Cup Stays' (Gibson 2014) borrowed from military tropes that clashed with Rousseff's more romantic image of resurrection.

Of course, long before the defeat, samba music and kinaesthetics had been placed in the most appropriate social space: the disordered space of rebellious *favelas*. Ridden with poverty and violence, for decades now such social spaces have allowed music and art to become powerful channels of social protest, simultaneously nurturing civilised alternatives to public harm (see Fryer 2000). It has been noted that 'in Brazil there has been a strong move on the part of NGOs and the government to address violence issues through the creation of favela community arts spaces/cultural centers, which in various cases have managed to bring members of feuding groups into a neutral space and transcend conflict through art and play' (Dimitrova Savova 2009: 553). Thus, samba *favelarte* can be part of the national community's centre under certain conditions, complying with the necessary securitisation of public space. In Brazilian urban spaces the 'protesting body' is not disconnected from the artistic body that speaks through rhythms of movement and synchrony, as recent anti-2014 World Cup protests attest (Jensen 2009, 2010; Edensor 2011, 2014).

There is a harsher, realist approach to such complaints in that under certain circumstances, people might mobilise stereotypical expectations of bureaucratic or state unfairness to offset their sense of personal failure. Whereas cultures observing the cult of entrepreneurial individualism view failure as a sort of moral deficiency that needs justification, cultures observing the rules of personhood and familial solidarity explain it on the basis of 'lack of social connectivity' (Herzfeld 1992; DaMatta 1991). The fans' retroactive reaction against public cuts in the aftermath of the 7–1 defeat directed accusations of moral deficiency against a state that operates like a networked family, excluding the poor, 'disconnected individuals'. A solid history of anti-FIFA protest in this context certainly helped the 'cause': prior to the opening ceremony of the 2013 FIFA Confederations Cup staged in Brazil, people unhappy with the amount of public money spent on hosting the 2014 FIFA World Cup demonstrated outside the venue, whereas attendants of the 2013 ceremony booed Rousseff and FIFA President Sepp Blatter. The events escalated, leading to 30 people being injured and 22 arrested 'as police used rubber bullets and tear gas to disperse protestors' (Reuters 2013). This individualised expression of *ressentiment* is inappropriate for official articulations of deferred action. Note that, contrariwise, Scolari's invocation of the discourse of accountability addressed a modern Western individualist ethos at domestic fans, while simultaneously keeping alive the code of personalised duty to restore faith in Brazilian football heritage. The unshakable resemblance of nationalism with religion extends in this non-European context to the transcendentalised status of a game. The unobtrusiveness of profane symbols (e.g. charismatic football players and the popular cultures they sustain in commoditised contexts) that connect ideas about self and body, as well as family and foes, banalises sacralised ideals of nation and heritage (Billig 1995). The failure to articulate unity is thus a malfunction of the social imaginary that is supposed to transcend local differences and unite all citizens in a single identity. Otherwise put, 'symbols of hope may always become instruments of despair' (Herzfeld 1992: 6, 33).

We can make a stop half way to nationalist and racist contexts so as to consider the function and purposiveness of commoditisation in sacralising rituals of the game. The very appropriation of artistic-aesthetic forms in hyper-consumption milieux of sporting cultures involves the creation, reproduction and distribution of football team insignia that, by turns, are reproduced in press domains (magazines, newspapers, Internet fan sites and the like). This circuit of 'signs' (ideas, images and their tangible dimensions), no less significant than straightforward processes of collective worshipping of national heroes, sustains a 'culture industry' that remains dependent upon collective memory (Lash and Urry 1994; Giulianotti 1999; Inglis and Hughson 2000; Tzanelli 2007). Brazilian *futebolarte* presents the practical aspects of such popular cultures as another facet of artistic creativity: the selling of team kits as badges of identity; the adoption of football songs as 'anthems'; and the production of team or charismatic player (auto)biographies channel the football-cultural industries' signs into *lieux de memoire* 'proper' (Nora 1989; DeNora 2000; Giulianotti 2001), where 'art' attains its elite qualities at all times (Leoussi 2004). Notably, contemporary *futebolarte* is close to Becker's (1982: x) conception of an artworld that interprets commonplace understandings of the arts as the social world 'of fashionable people associated with those newsworthy objects and events that command astronomical prices'. Such felicitous blends of pop and elite are also experienced in embodied ways as 'pilgrimages' of the kind preceding or following Brazil's historic defeat (e.g. Connerton 1989).

The observation holds the key to a live sociology of mobility (Sheller 2014b), insofar as it sketches the contours of a cultural political economy of movement: closer to the thanatic rituals of national mobilisation, but distanced from its funereal feel, commoditised football aesthetics sustain nodal synergies between nationalism and capitalism (Tzanelli 2012c, 2013b: 69). Although the 'aesthetic resides in the internal qualities of the game [and] the misnamed "aestheticisation of soccer" [rather than] … the socio-historical organisation of soccer … how audiences relate to the game, not the nature of the game itself' (Inglis and Hughson 2000: 294), its 'proto-aesthetics' always become enmeshed into a secondary 'game' of quotidian creativity, involving reproductive interpretation of football events, characters and sites (Willis 1990). This is so, because temporality (the imagined community's progression in time) is an intrinsic property of the commoditised (tangible and intangible) football 'objects', which will always exist in time, and will potentially signify the amount of time elapsed since their creation. *Futebolarte* resembles, in this respect, the aesthetic regime of the arts proper, which relates to the past, setting up as the 'very principle of "artisticity" the expressive relationship inherent in a time and a state of civilization … previously considered to be the "non-artistic" part of works of art' (Rancière 2004: 20). The historical associations of the work of art that Benjamin (1968) noted, pertain, almost inevitably, to any object passing through ancestral hands (Miller 1987: 124–6). Ancestry might be territorially bound, but people's extended fields of action, usually 'woven around *significant places*' (Dürrschmidt 1997: 64, emphasis in original), may adhere to non-material 'sites'. Football's proto-aesthetics are always experienced in motion (through mobile experiences such as consumption, travel, street marches and celebrations), so there are continuities between living and honouring the past in aesthetic ways.

There is more, too: if, as is the case with Brazil, collectively recognised football styles are national styles, then the neat boundaries between consumption of tangibles (football memorabilia), embodied performances (celebrations of victory or commiserations of defeat) and experiential knowledge of the game's proto-aesthetics might dissolve in practice. Strategically bound to national stylistics, all of them serve the ends of the same nationalist-capitalist nodes. It is not just the performances of fans that 'do the job' of these nodes; the overall public performance of players contributes to felicitous mergers between their style of play and their nation's 'style'.

Brazilian anthropophagy meets the global aesthetic

Mergers of national style and football proto-aesthetics develop into a fully articulated aesthetic discourse with the help of the media. Media conglomerates are, today, national and transnational in nature, and their steering power always connects to financial mobilities (Appadurai 1990; Urry 2014). I evidently draw on Habermas's (1989b) theory, which outlines the increasing rationalisation of the lifeworld with the help of 'systemic steering media', such as money and power (on which see also Luhmann 1999). He understands societies as both systems and lifeworlds but separates lifeworld action, which is based on consensus, from systems activity, which controls the social without consensus (Habermas 1989b: 118–9). I will dilute this rigid verdict through my plural hermeneutics: the media might articulate on behalf of global structures, injecting power into state or multinational apparatuses, but they may also articulate the subaltern ethic and its discourses of the periphery. Oscillating between lifeworld and system, media articulations unveil the local origins of what came to circulate in global channels. Here begins the trans-modern story of (ethno-national) character mobility.

Let us remember the photo of the old man ('The saddest Brazilian'), clutching a replica of the FIFA World Cup: those sympathising with this *triste tropique* would be delighted to know that this man, who dubbed himself '*Gaúcho da Copa*', is a local Brazilian celebrity who perfectly captured the mood of the night. Merging the desired *Copa* with a human character from one of the world's leading football nations reiterates the magic properties of the 'gift' in commercial domains (Bruner 1994). When his photo went viral online and turned into a profitable 'Internet meme' (today sold by photographer Michael Steele on Getty Images for £350–£550), BuzzFeed commentator Ryan Broderick added:

> Except there's more to the story. After the now famous picture was taken, he [Mr da Copa] was surrounded by fans of Brazil and Germany [a photo of da Copa with German fans follows]. And he ended up sharing his World Cup trophy statue with a young Germany fan [a photo of da Copa being photographed handing over his Cup follows]. In fact, he shared the trophy with a bunch of Germany fans [here we have a photo of a content Mr da Copa kissing the Cup while handing it over to a German child held by his mother]. So thankfully, the 'Sad Brazilian' World Cup fan wasn't so sad after all [here Mr da Copa poses all smiles with two female German fans and a Brazilian fan holding the Cup. He is holding with one hand Neymar's picture and with the other the statue of a Magi].
>
> (Broderick 2014)

Much like DaMatta's (1991) and Skouteri-Didaskalou's (1980) anthropological interpretivism, Alexander's (2004) structuralist hermeneutics and Büscher and Urry's (2009) hermeneutics of mobility, Broderick's subtitle announces that 'There are two sides to every photo!' Though still unverified, the meaning of this trophy offer to a German crowd has been consolidated in digital channels as a sign of Brazilian magnanimity. Just like Rousseff's oral discourse on the hospitality of Rio's Christ the Redeemer, *Gaúcho da Copa*'s offering, next to the replica of a magician football player, performs a visual trick of political significance. Hence lowbrow practices acquire a symmetrical power with the help of steering media.

The media's steering power enters the magic field of nationhood, when Internet gossip is further explored. Mr da Copa's real name is Clovis Acosta Fernandes and he is a *Seleção* superfan, who has attended seven consecutive World Cups and more than 150 international matches. After quitting his job as a pizzeria owner, he decided to stop dreaming alone: 'Donning a hat, breeches, and boots as his uniform and dubbing himself "Gaúcho da Copa" – very roughly, the Cup Cowboy – Fernandes started an informal supporters group. With a rotating cast, he has attended every World Cup since, as well as Copas America, Confederation Cups, the Olympics, and various international friendlies' (Petchesky 2014). Soon, Fernandes transformed into a global media sensation, with national and international interviews, photographs with global sports tourists, a FIFA camera presence with his replica trophy, and even recent participation in a small protest against football racism. What is more important for this study is that his trip to the 2009 Confederations Cup in South Africa was paid (at R15,000, or over $6,000) by the state government of Rio Grande do Sul, with the aim 'to promote *gaúcho* culture'. There were also rumours that the following year he attended the 2010 World Cup with the sponsorship of a travel agency. Fernandes later claimed that he is adviser to a committee created by the state government, and 'always travels with partnerships' (ZH 2009). A 2014 photograph even showed him posing with his Cup next to Rousseff, whereas in another recent interview he declared that he 'really likes Germany' and 'feels like a little German', because 'the formation of the *gaúcho* has a lot to do with the culture of the German people' (Petchesky 2014).

The references to 'likeable' Germans and '*gaúcho* culture' dispel *Brasilidade*'s romantic unity, exposing the whole South American continent as a Babelic outpost of the historic European 'civilising mission'. An equivalent to the North American cowboy, *gaúcho* (Portuguese) or *gaucho* (Spanish) is the resident of South American *pampas* or Patagonian grasslands, principally found in Argentina, Uruguay, Paraguay, south-eastern Bolivia, southern Brazil and southern Chile. Nineteenth-century Spencerian positivism contributed to *gaucho* characterisations on phenotypical grounds as an 'inferior subrace' born of Indian and mestizo black miscegenation, but the persona itself retained a positive image in Argentine nationalism (Slatta 1992: 14). In Brazil, however, today *gaúcho* refers to the people from the state of Rio Grande do Sul – one of the main post-colonial destinations for German immigrants, alongside São Paulo. In the Argentine *pampas, gauchos* are the main workers (cattle herders) on an *estancia* or property. Mostly made up of rural populations, Argentine and Uruguayan *gauchos* populated nationalist legends in nineteenth-century literature, and become the equivalent of the heroic, macho bandits of Eurasian national mythologies (Tzanelli 2008: chapter 5). The selfsame *gauchos* in Argentina would join the militia (*caudillos*) against Spanish advances in the country. Their significance in various ethno-regional mythologies was enhanced by their representation as silent, strong and honest men, carrying a *falcón* or large knife, ready to use on challengers (for global comparisons, see Gallant 2000). As real historical personae, their 'Robin Hood' literary qualities integrated them into myths of the 'nation's' post-colonial autonomy and uniqueness (Tzanelli 2002b: 181, 186). Implicated in the institutional politics of human sciences, such as anthropology, this 'mythistorical' discourse would soon reinvent the enemy within the nation, as what is seen as alien to sameness in terms of custom, colour or linguistic idiom (Armstrong 1982; Smith 2006).

Evidence for the resilience of the myth is provided by the mascot of the 1978 FIFA World Cup: a *gauchito*, or little boy dressed in Argentine colours and wearing a *gaucho* hat, echoed in the uniform in which Shakira's son appeared in the 2014 closing ceremony. The potency of such symbolism – luckily, in Shakira's case, unnoticed or otherwise uncommented – is manifest in promised apologies by Wolfgang Niersbach, president of Germany's (DBF) National Football Association, to Argentine Football Association President Julio Grodona, for the 'disrespectful' mimicking of *gaucho* dance routines and walking in Berlin by the victorious national team's players (Reuters 2014). The phenomenon is global, rather than symptomatic of Southern and Central American 'idiosyncrasies' (Gallant 1999; Tzanelli 2002a), but regionally, it doubled national pursuits for the cosmography of riches: the civilisational game was now split into an intimate and a global discourse. The former recognised the riches as an ancestral property, whereas the latter continued to associate this with Western European civilisational invasion. Especially post-liberation (1816) Argentine *gauchos* were used as a symbol of the fight against corruption originating in Europeanising tendencies – hence as fighters against symbolic 'cultural pollution' by Europeans.

However, Brazilian images of *gaúchos* as free men were often contrasted to the slaves who worked the northern lands. The concentration of German migrant populations to southern provinces, such as those of the state of Rio Grande do Sul, must have triggered a connection in Fernandes's mind. Brazilian nation building's decentralised logic of authority between north, centre and south (Domingues 2006a), pluralised mythistories of heroic violence, connecting them to riches and memories regions shared with neighbours. This sharing extends beyond Brazilian dominions: originally, the *gauchos/gaúchos* were linked to *Virreinato del Rio de la Plata*, the most short-lived Spanish viceroyalty covering parts of what we know today as Argentina, Bolivia, Paraguay and Uruguay (Lynch 1958). In fact, *gaucho* etymologies tend to connect the word to Arabic (*chauia*) and Moorish (*hawsh*) renditions of herdsmen and nomadic cultures, orientalising their histories. However, Brazilian attributions of *gaúcho* heritage to the south were matched by other mythological mobilities within the 'nation': São Paulo's tale of indigeneity gave birth to the *Paulista* (the native resident of a colonial outpost founded by Jesuit missionaries), and Rio de Janeiro to *Cariocas* (an indigenous Tupi word designating the white man's house). Although Brazil's regional cosmographies were evidently over-determined by borrowings from Europe's colonial heritage (of racism, Catholicism and technology), all its regions chose to forget colonial violence to develop their own articulations (see Domingues 2006b: 547, on mixed articulations in democratic South America; see also Kohn 1945; and Greenfeld 1990 on competitive nationalisms).

So, Fernandes's self-presentation as a caricature of Brazilian football culture (akin to the 1942 cartoon character *El Gaucho Goofy* from Disney's animated film *Saludos Amigos* – dirs. N. Ferguson, W. Jackson, J. Kinney, H. Luske and W. Roberts) might have externally superseded his localised identity. Various global media complexes also articulate national cosmological centres from vague stereotypes that circulate globally (Couldry 2003a, 2003b), but on this occasion, Fernandes's self-understanding as Rio Grande's glorified folk-cum-pop descendant must have spoken the 'right language' to both regional government and the people. The regionalised link between *gaúcho* culture and football acts as a symbolic reversal in Brazil's cosmographic game, where football's civilising tendencies might be claimed by more well-known urban centres, such as the upcoming Olympics host city, Rio de Janeiro, or the celebrated FIFA host city, São Paulo. Just as Rio's intellectuals saw in French civilisation their principal European link, Fernandes saw in the World Cup's abstract 'Germans' Rio Grande's connection to European romanticism. Are the uncouth but strong and hard-working Saxon *Bauern* not the origins of German *Volksgeist* or national spirit, after all (Arnason 2006)? Old and more recent Germanic articulations are also partly defined by the mastery of technology, just like the Portuguese myth of the native world traveller, discoverer and innovator. The opening ceremony's *gaúcho*-costumed dance routines – incomprehensible to the mega-event's foreign visitors – are the equivalent of Rio Grande's *Volksgeist* articulation. In this respect, *Gaúcho da Copa*'s global function conforms to the mega-event's principles of 'doubleness' (Wagner-Pacifici 2011), as a fact of naturalised emotion (the masculine honour attributed to the football as a national game) and cultural form perfected (the visual magic of fandom). The outcome of this mediated 'play' is the withdrawal of Brazilian performative synaesthetics in favour of ocular technologies. 'Doubleness' activates simultaneously a regional nationalist and a global tourist 'eye' which conform to the cosmetic principles of European romanticism (Urry and Larsen 2011: 203) – or the kind of beauty that 'look[s] well in a picture' (Ousby 1990: 154).

Such performances are part of the 'game of life': not a superficial play for public amusement, but a Brazilian *jôgo* of globalised 'appearances'. Their propensity toward *ressentiment* that represses internal otherness to adopt external riches one moment, and rejects these riches as corrupt to glorify internal difference as collective origins the next, is part of Brazil's self-civilising mission, as offshoot of its very own polyphonic trans-modernity (Wade 2001 on race and nation in South America; see for European analogies, Greenfeld 1992). In this context, emotion is consigned to natural expressivity: take for example the numbness or tearfulness of Brazilian players during and after the defeat. The embodiment of emotion was real, but its performativity might also be considered an inculcated reality, no less real than Western connections between truthfulness and responsibility. Apparent resignation is often actual social practice, and the invocation of fate can serve calculative ends (Merton and Barber 2004), as it minimises the effect of social damage at home, while ensuring the compassion of external audiences. As celebrities, members of the Brazilian team are supposed to be 'loved' by fans (unsurprisingly, Getty Images prices for photos of a crying David Luiz are steep); as representatives of the Brazilian imaginary ('*futebolarte* characters'), they are expected to communicate *pathos*, when *eudaimonic* pursuits fail. Only this way, the expressivity of Brazilian players, who demonstrably did not succeed in their craft on the global stage, can be recast as 'national character' and circulated in various mega-library channels as a discourse of responsibility (another facet of Brazilian style). As is the case with most national contexts, the idea that fate subsumes character is elevated to conceptions of destiny as predestination – for, in contemporary Brazil the concept refers to a clearly marked path upward or downward, 'a journey in which one can discern a goal, a direction, or a dominant thread' (DaMatta 1991: 205). Let us not forget that the routinisation of expressive form plays a key role in the consolidation of power (Bauman 1983). Ironically, this formalism ultimately draws on Indo-European and Judeo-Christian understandings of the 'superiority of mind over matter, of thinkers over actors', placing 'rationality above and beyond experience' (Herzfeld 1992: 19).

Coincidentally (not), on 13 July, before the final, BBC journalists opted to interview a selection of German, Argentine and domestic fans, only to stress that on the day, Brazilians had wilfully 'forgotten' their team's defeat by Germany to support its players. The journalists' geopolitical knowledge was accurate: Brazil's historic foe, Argentina, was not supposed to lift the 'Cup of Cups' when the host had suffered such an ignominious defeat and was excluded from the global social drama. Here the cosmography of riches was mapped onto regional cosmological scenarios (Campbell 1964; Herzfeld 2008; Tzanelli 2012c) – scenarios comprehensible even to German fans spotted carrying a placard stating, 'We won't let Argentinia [sic] win in your HOME!' (Gill 2014). These scenarios are constitutive of proximity politics and bring to the stage forced relational closeness 'both "structurally" via the complex institutional interconnections of globalization, and "phenomenologically" via the sort of *experienced* proximity that is provided in time-space bridging technologies – particularly communications and media technologies' (Tomlinson 2000: 403, emphasis in original; Pellegrino 2011: 3–4). Brazil's immediate neighbours provide a ready-made mirror image both to incorporate and destroy so as both to consolidate the country's place in world hierarchies and to restore collective dignity within the nation (Evans-Pritchard 1940, 1956).

Shared borders lead to shared emotions and desires about joining the league of civilised nations, so to speak, so Argentine values and habitus can only be simultaneously despised while pursued. In Brazil, anecdotal stories of the Argentine belief that the country was somehow misplaced amongst America's 'barbarous' hordes, when in reality it belongs to Europe, swap space for time, while simultaneously attributing forgetting of the colonial trauma to the other enemy. In the final, Estádio do Maracanã was swamped by mixed German and South American – especially yellow and green tee-shirted fans – crowds who concertedly booed the Argentine players throughout the game. If the term 'soundscapes' considers sound as a publicly circulated entity, reflecting social practices and the material spaces of performance (Schafer 1994), the fans' orchestrated reactions should not be considered mere noise, but the equivalent of the mega-event's ceremonial sounds. Just like landscape, soundscape encloses the 'contradictory forces of the natural and the cultural, the fortuitous and the composed, the improvised and the deliberately produced' (Samuels et al. 2010: 330) that coexisted more harmoniously in the ceremony. Even as aggressive noise, the voiced indignation appealed to nationally calibrated understandings of cosmographic mobility: what belongs (the global gift of the Cup) to whom (the Brazilians, of course).

Stereotyping circulates in regional national channels, the same way imaginaries of sedentary identities flow globally (e.g. Engelbrekt 2011: 35). It is worth noting that Brazilian BBC journalism acknowledged a difference between the hostility of Brazilians against Argentinians and the romantic appreciation of Argentinians for Brazil as an earthly paradise (Korstanje 2011: 284), a 'place dominated not only by natural beauty but also people who live a good life' (Carmo 2014b). Surely at least Brazilians with pre-booked seats before their team's historic loss turned up on the day. Their 'noise' was responding to 'common knowledge' that the Argentinian boasts he is someone 'who speaks Spanish and thinks he is an Englishman' – the very style that, according to Argentinians, is displayed by Brazilians (after all, Britain became the real Argentine enemy after the Falklands War of 1982). Inversely, it is not coincidental that groups of Argentine fans reportedly sang *Brazil decime qué se siente* (Brazil, tell me how you feel) to rival groups, adding as chorus/refrain, 'Maradona is better than Pelé' (Carmo 2014b). The song was meant as a popular-artistic narrative on style – of paramount importance in Argentine discourses of modernisation, whereby subaltern 'pupils' eventually beat their colonial 'teachers' in the football field. Though principally differentiated as a 'style of play' from that of the English team's by sports journalists in the 1920s, when debates on Argentine identity were buoyant, the 1958 Wold Cup defeat of Argentina by Czechoslovakia (the so-called 'Malmö Disaster') questioned Argentine stylistic agility, giving birth to attempts at 'tactical modernisation' across South America. In this conjunction, European styles of play were placed even higher on football civilisational hierarchies than Pelé's quintessentially 'Brazilian finesse' (Alabarces et al. 2001: 552).

The melody and rhythm of the song was based on *Bad Moon Rising*, by the American group Creedence Clearwater Revival, 'which was already widely used by supporters of local clubs' (Carmo 2014a). It was claimed by its creators that the provocative lyrics were mainly addressed to Argentina's colonial archenemy; the chorus in particular was allegedly selected because it made a good rhyme. The song's creators, ex-students of the college Manuel Belgrano in Buenos Aires – business managers, lawyers and financial experts – were keen to disseminate their creation to other fans within and without the country. Though based on a journalistic anecdote, alleged mobilisations of English habitus by both sides betray true regional propensity to involve cosmographies of riches in ethnic rivalries (Sahlins 2013a, 2013b). As Brazilian contempt during the final referred both to symbolic mobilities of alleged civilised custom (the movement of football from England to South America) and real professional mobilities of football talent (the movement of players from South America to Europe), the 'Maradona joke' became threatening: popular rhetoric involving the figure of Maradona in Argentina emphasises his '*Criollo* style of play', which is used in the construction of an Argentine national identity (Archetti 1994: 42–3; Archetti 1997) – the very style Brazilians recognise in their own multi-racially inspired play.

Maradona's association with Argentine masculine culture (e.g. ideas of hedonism, spontaneity, irresponsibility) (Archetti 1999: 46) match Pelé's black masculine ethos of creative play, but Pelé's individualistic style of play also seems to embody an open and egalitarian society, far removed from the fossilised order of Brazil's former football master: post-war Britain (Levine 1980a: 458). As the son of an itinerant semi-professional from rural central-southern Brazil, Pelé managed to rise from poverty in Tres Corações, Minas Gerais, to multicultural Brazil's symbol of mobile professionalism. Not only did his much-advertised marriage to a white woman of German origins (Rosemeri Cholbi) come to signify Brazil's multi-racial democracy, but it proved that the country functioned on athletic meritocracy without racial prejudice. Declared a 'non-exportable national treasure', with private sponsors (Murray 1996: 120), as a retired player Pelé would proceed to collaborate with multinational corporations on technology and even receive the honours of the Knight Commander of the Order of the British Empire from Queen Elizabeth II (Tzanelli 2013c: 116). There is of course another discourse that overlays such national differences with that of a more generalised 'Latin temperament', often reconstructed to encompass 'both "cynicism" and "artistry" in individual performances'. Invocations of 'roots', 'natural instincts' and temperament were mobilised before to describe Italians, Argentinians and Brazilians alike (see Tudor 1992: 399, on the 1990 World Cup).

Losing the final after such boasts turned the samba lyrics that Brazilians sang before their team's historic loss into reality for Argentine fans. Brazilian *Schadenfreude* must have been ubiquitous and the Brazilian fans' booing of the Argentinians must have been deemed 'well deserved'. Evidently, this particular encounter between Argentine guest-fans and Brazilian host-fans deepened particular hostile scripts of history, reactivating dormant prejudices (Deichmann 2007: 14; Korstanje 2011: 283). The crowds thus displayed this sort of agency via practices (noise and music), once reverberated as private, non-state-sanctioned, 'corporealised' techniques one would expect from concerted national self-presentations organised by the state (Geertz 1980; Herzfeld 2005; Collins 2007). Just like their seemingly disorganised responses to Brazil's exclusion from the final, these practices appealed to ritual and popular ceremony to thwart a crisis and restore 'an impression of certainty, community and comfort, despite overwhelming contextual evidence to the contrary' (Cannadine 1993: 105).

6 The script of post-colonial desire

Positive excess, negative reciprocities

The magic of football mobility

Football is characterised by magical movement, which, in critical realist terms, cannot be contained within the perceptual spectrum of zone 14 – a European phenomenological 'miracle' requiring extensive translation in exogenous cultural domains. Magic requires elaboration on context, so as to make its occurrence socially relevant – a task requiring that we uncover the cosmological universe in which its causes and effects are structured around ideas of benevolent or evil metaphysical intervention (Evans-Pritchard 1937). Truly, magic's structural causality remains a constant feature in its social scientific analysis to the date, even in urban milieux of the 'developed' world (Luhrmann 1991). As the Brazilian case attests, a social presentation of its metaphysics of evil touches upon more familiar fields of social power, cosmological self-narration and hermeneutic predictability (Merton and Barber 2004: chapter 2). 'Magic' is, in other words, a discourse on appearances, perceptions and collective or individual destinies – the themes the present study explored under the rubric of the 'cosmography of riches' in the context of the Brazilian 2014 World Cup. The book's focus on the mega-event's ceremonies and urban fan milieux aspired to cover both ends of Brazil's socio-cultural spectrum, the elite and the popular, while acknowledging the limitations of such research that looks for the particular within the universal in an increasingly globalised world. As this conclusion purports, sketching Brazilian perceptions of the cosmography of riches in pop and elite frameworks leads us to deeper understandings of the country's post-colonial desire for recognition in global domains. Far from being unified, the struggle to acquire citizenship rights in global domains (e.g. Stevenson 2002) uncovers the plurality of interests and needs of different centres, peripheries, classes and other social identities in the country (Walby 1994; Yuval-Davis and Webner 1999; Delanty 2000; Sheller 2000, 2012; Skidmore 2003; Telles 2006; Tate 2011).

On 11 June 2014 it was reported on a website that in the match between England and Italy, the former would lose thanks to Balotelli's 'magic'. The person who predicted the '*Azzurri*'s' victory was witch doctor Jaraquii of Santarem, a town in the Amazon, which lies about 500 miles from Manaus.

Jaraquii, who acts as delegate for FUNAI, Brazil's National Indian Foundation, a government body that oversees the country's indigenous tribes, also declared his preference for Balotelli 'because he's coloured, like us. He's not like Messi and those other white players'; besides that, the witch doctor added, 'I haven't liked the British (or the Americans, to me it's the same thing), ever since one of them asked me if there were still Indians who were cannibals' (Squires 2014). There re-emerges an early colonial phantom of self-consumption; an historical zombie everyone thought was exorcised a long time ago. This was not an isolated incident: other declarations of witchcraft during World Cup matches also stood for an attempt to articulate the unspoken 'evil' of colonial genocide, akin to the European Holocaust specific constituencies continue to deny (Bauman 1989). This 'deferred' exorcism of colonial evil in favour of retrieving revered national ghosts is convolutedly implicated in the Brazilian team's decision to employ Daddy Guarantã, a revered *Umbanda* witch doctor, believed by many to possess the power to swing games, defeat opponents and even strike down players (Roper 2014). The global rumour holding that 2014 World Cup winner Germany broke 'the centuries-old curse of a Ghanaian witch doctor and defeat[ed] Generalissimo Leonard Messi' (ABC News 2014) dates back to the digital circulation of a video showing Nana Kwaku Bonsam, a Ghanaian witch doctor, who allegedly put a curse on Ronaldo's knee (Barrabi 2014). There is no better way to put *Nachträglichkeit* in motion than by crippling the offspring of your old colonial masters when he is entrusted with their honour in a global contest.

Such incidents reveal that the workings of a different kind of anthropophagy from that which Jaraquii found so offensive (Argentinians versus Brazilians) are blended into colonialism's historical complexity, which is also rife with magic (the Portuguese colonisers, the evil English, who once possessed football's secrets). This complexity is a hermeneutic one. It is not of a Habermassian political struggle for multiple interests, however, but of a struggle of one's voice to be heard and recognised as the voice of a legitimate partner in the debate over Brazilian political recognition. By protesting the wrong his ancestry suffered, Jaraquii presented himself as 'the immediate embodiment of [Brazilian] society as such, as the stand-in for the Whole of Society in its universality, against the particular power-interests of the aristocracy or the oligarchy' (Rancière 2004: 66). It is not clear who owns and regulates the Brazilian cosmography of riches in the present, but the polyphonic nation's memory vault looms open and is available to use for the creation of an inclusive future by anyone. Such 'magical articulations' from one of the Brazilian peripheries are built on further exclusions – for even the things that natives of all regions consume are 'known' products marked as intimate memory, rather than of designated foreign provenience (Spivak 1999). Alien quantities, whose status is never properly regulated, become the indivisible remainder of democratic struggle, which is constantly subjected to national and international policing. The revealed 'crime' tends to be attributed to external (f)actors only, in this way leaving internal mishaps unanswered on the global scene – for the pursuit of foreign riches, by means of their recognition as native, demands the public display of cohesion.

What happens with the rest – the protests about expenditure, the poverty of *favela* life and the intensification of 'governmobilities' (Bærenholdt 2013) within and without the country? Again, when placed alongside these national movements and global flows, the domain of witchcraft reveals itself as another facet of the discourse of 'unspoken evil', today sustained by new, Western-born technologies that Brazil accommodated into its own discourse of riches. The declaration of 'technology' as one of the 2014 mega-event's values certainly aimed to harmonise the cosmographic imaginary of Brazil's political centre (in Brasília and the forthcoming Olympic host city, Rio de Janeiro) with external expectations. As we saw in Chapters 2 and 3, the appropriation of European technicity introduced the ultimate hermeneutic game in the country, but as the 'game's' goalposts seem to move with every global techo-financial development, the risk and its dangers never cease. When coupled, surveillance and magic suggest that what exists as Brazil's legitimate property is not only at risk, but exudes danger, spreading it on the country's 'healthy body' and corrupting its heroes. Witchcraft is, after all, Brazil's quintessential African property – both a product of colonial oppression and genocide and a radical otherness that especially the country's urbanity never managed to accommodate, opting to consign it instead to the mediascapes of Internet and ceremonial entertainment.

What is lost in the movement is gained in profit, for in cyber magic and the ceremonial spectacle there is money to be made. Comaroff and Comaroff (2001), who are more interested in the contemporary fortunes of dispossessed immigrants in Africa, make an observation that applies to Brazilian socio-cultural transformations. They commence their analysis with musings over the changing fortunes of gambling, which transformed in today's neoliberal environments from immoral accumulation into financial investment. The 'opaque, even occult, relation between means and ends' of wealth without work, they argue, has enhanced an ubiquitous experiential contradiction at the core of neoliberal capitalism: 'the fact that it appears to offer vast, almost simultaneous riches to those who control its technologies, and, simultaneously, to threaten the very livelihood of those who do not' (ibid.: 782). In South Africa's case, this was accompanied by a twin proliferation of stories about zombies and immigrants who 'steal' local jobs, inducing hate crime, organised mainly by young unemployed men in rural areas (Comaroff and Comaroff 1999). Representations of proletarian pariahs as useless 'part-time zombies', flexible workers in night-time economies who snatch jobs away from family breadwinners, matches Africa's stereotype of magical evil – the 'old woman', or the sexually perverted non-hu*man*, whose deformed genitalia and poisonous secretions make him unsuitable to reproduce (White in Comaroff and Comaroff 2001: 802n.). Zombie stories find an interesting narrative closure in ritual exorcisms that involve 'bringing' them 'back home' – a discourse that parallels the proletarian (black) immigrant's homecoming desire.

Gender order as cultural allegory: cultural intimacy's 'homecoming'

As I explained, 'magic' is a question of fortuitous interpretation. Chapters 1 and 2 explained that Brazilian cultural hermeneutics is gendered racialised and sexualised, providing ready-made ways to approach the country's intimate spaces. Despite its ability to preserve its synaesthetic heritage, Brazil accommodated its global profile into a European primacy of vision (Gregory 1994: 246–62; Jay 1994; Sandywell 2011: 591) from the moment it became a nation. The space of cultural intimacy is, Herzfeld (2005) warns us, rife with practices of 'iconicity' or imagological semblance as stereotyping. In Brazil's post-colonial spaces and multiple lifeworlds, the game of semblance served – as it still serves – a double function that corresponds to Geertz's 'doubleness' of human performance between nature and culture (see Chapter 4 on its ceremonial application). This reassuring play is challenged by globalisation, which questions publicly the most intimate connections between gender, sexuality, race, class and self-identity (Giddens 1994: 106), while simultaneously trying to fit world polities into a singular Western version of such identities (e.g. Sheller 2012a). Whereas these connections persist, the pursuit of foreign riches sets the wheels of production and consumption in fierce motion, turning common workers into technical automata, along the lines of the European revolution in technicity. In a country with a history of labour oppression by colonial and dictatorial 'masters' alike, the need to achieve recognition of a mixed, Afro-Brazilian ancestry *qua* contemporary citizenry over-determines public discourses of cultural 'debt' and heritage. The debt ensures that the Afro-Brazilian worker remains a domesticated spectre – as opposed to the unwanted migrations from former colonial centres and, even more, from poor internal and foreign peripheries. As we saw in Chapter 5, regional articulations of Brazilian cosmology recognised in such human flows variations of the 'usurper', who becomes 'native' only when (s)he becomes appealing to the romantic gaze. The 'literalisation' of such 'zombies' in national arts – non-beings, traditionally considered in Africa as devoid of speech and who will, hence, be subjected to the commands of others (Comaroff and Comaroff 2001: 790) – is achieved in Brazil by means of articulation, by artistic, national and transnational communities.

One may rightly argue that the recognition of regional heroes as examples of Brazil's global migration heritage, an Amazonian witch doctor's spell and a black worker's plea for recognition differ significantly. Yet, a running theme in Brazil's remarkably diverse ethno-cultural mosaic is the external projection of desire for an ontological wholeness, stolen from the country that now has to retrieve it through legalised discourses of citizenship. The stolen ontology is turned into retrieved identity at great cost: for the protesting Brazilian masses in 2013 and 2014, the transformation of 'zombie' strangerhood's fearful spectre into an urban spectacle reflects the fear of 'heritage theft', for who is put in charge of its articulation, and who reaps the fruits of its success, if not the global elites (Urry 2014)? The debate upon mega-event management as a prestige-building mechanism in Brazil (Chapter 1) is part of this interpretative conundrum, which guises itself as macho and feminine, cosmetic iconicity. The exacerbated sense of threatened masculinity in South African societies, leading to accusations of older and/or female subjects of witchcraft and zombie making, seems to match the gendered subtext of contemporary Brazilian protests, as much as it defines Brazilian fan rituals after the national team's defeat. Interpretation is activated by means of a deliberate obscuring of analytical and historical difference in popular domains. As the story goes, when the spectacle's riches (the Cup) are 'stolen' by corporations, foreign teams and privileged professional artists, its essence (encapsulated in football's technical human) reverts into that of an unwanted spectre: a state-controlled, post-colonial and, above all, capitalist 'zombie', more beautiful than one can bear to look at and more able to devour the community's riches, to the point of inducing its collective annihilation (also Davis 1988: 75). The 2014 World Cup's predicament is that its societal spectacle's (e.g. Debord 1995) magical properties are only meant to enrich the Brazilian nation-family; shifting neoliberal capitalism's means and aims outside familial domains leads to Brazil's cosmetic 'clamouring' and collective ontological death. In this respect, Brazil 2014's thanatourist celebrations took place both in state-sanctioned mega-event and unsanctioned or criminogenic popular contexts with the same aim: to avert the imagined, polyphonic community's ultimate destruction. DaMatta's (1991) observation (paraphrased here) that, for Brazilians, the withering of colonial memory is equated with the loss of ontological meaning as well as the destruction of the community's epistemic coordinates, is as accurate as ever.

Equating a cultural and political debt with monetary compensation is, at best, part of *Malandro*'s artistry, to which no global business will respond well. Conflations of this debt with political responsibility towards the masses can also activate the worst of governmobilities, which the 2014 World Cup generally assuaged, without avoiding them altogether (Chapter 5). However, here I am not interested in public protest in particular, but only its cosmological flair, which I explore mostly under public reactions to Brazil's exclusion from the final. Conclusively, I argue that as a socio-cultural context, the mega-event allowed space for the emergence of a particular public 'style' – neither solely peaceful and deferent, nor always openly violent, but resentful. This moderation, which conforms to the consumerist ideology of the spectacle, is Brazil's own understanding of civility. The propensity to demand compensation without reciprocating is a pervasive characteristic of resentful indignation and corresponds to what is known as 'negative reciprocity' (Herzfeld 1985; Ardener 1989). The term's multi-scalar application allows us to accommodate it in the mega-event's political-moral economy to appreciate the damage to which misunderstandings over exchange and reciprocity can lead, for 'the promise of a reciprocation that may never actually occur, or that may be understood to have happened even though it has no obvious realization in the movement of concrete goods' (Herzfeld 2001: 104) can make or break good relations(hips). Negative reciprocities are implicated in the 'administration' of various colonial and national debts by privileged and underprivileged groups in Brazil, which prefer to invoke memory in confrontations with a highest authority instead, or in addition to violence. One may argue that there is historical precedent: just as Brazilian peripheries sought 'rights' in indirect ways, developing socio-cultural skills of networking and 'reaching out' to the powerful metropoles, the former colonised satellites sought to exploit fissures and weaknesses in the system to achieve their goals without risking confrontation by directly challenging the metropolitan authority (Russell-Wood 2002a: 138).

However, the development of kinship and kinship-like networks into a socio-political mechanism is definitely better grounded in twentieth-century post-colonial structures in the country. Indeed, the split between person and individual was solidified from the 1920s and during the years of the dictatorship blossomed into an invisible institution. The shift from foreign to domestic surveillance refocused the national programme to cosmetic pursuits, so as to bolster development in emerging global markets that necessitated contact with foreign consumers (e.g. tourists). It seems that in this context the development of 'indirect' (strategic, covert, therefore 'professional') claims to recognition as prestige became a more permanent interpretative mechanism of conduct in public. Note, for example, how in the 2014 mega-event, the Brazilian repertoire of civilised skills foregrounded programmatic statements on global cosmographies of riches even by President Rousseff (Chapters 4 and 5). The Brazilian social experience taught that in a hostile socio-cultural universe, where 'individuals' had no good 'fate' and 'persons' entertained happy endings because of familial support, one had to network and respect some variation of authority (DaMatta 1991: 9). The global experience, with which domestic cosmologies communicated, suggested a similar inclination to demand with measure, resent in silence and remind of any outstanding debts, so that Brazil can clear its books with its 'defaulters'.

Because dialogue and violence apply as communicative conditions both individually and globally, if done with caution, the transposition of personages (DaMatta's 'individuals' and 'persons') to polities may promote a healthier functioning of global democracy (see also Eade 1997: 8–9). Yet, as this 'transposition' does not equate to mere 'role-playing' – a trick often mobilised in political rhetoric – but true change of deeply ingrained dispositions, the regional and global rules of law need to adopt trans-modernity's core ethics of critically reflexive care. Critical reflexivity is, in Brazil's polyphonic case, a de facto aesthetic process of historic depth. Unfortunately, not only does this political formalism over-determine the country's post-colonial aesthetic (*Brasilidade* as *linda maravilhosa* in all her local hues), but it also, contradictorily, dictates social-as-cultural orders, via individual-as-transpersonal hierarchies. This is why the regional performative competitions of the mega-event are nothing other than struggles for recognition – as better than and different from neighbouring regional and national states. Perhaps the observation that modernity is dominated by a mutual effort of sameness and difference 'to cannibalize one another and thus to proclaim their successful hijacking of the twin Enlightenment ideas of the triumphantly universal and the resiliently particular' (Robertson 1992: 308), is a pronounced characteristic of the 'Brazilian dilemma' – hence, a condition of its own trans-modernity. However, when resentment clouds regional nationalisms and urban protests alike, the country's heritage grows staler and less useful as a tool for international dialogue. Thereafter, it is almost unavoidable for the rebellious 'indignant' to turn their rage against peaceful projects, such as those of mega-events. The 'inessential' nature of artistic and athletic movements will, understandably, overwhelm emotions and subsequent actions in underprivileged spaces, especially in urban social milieux that articulate *Brasilidade*. Internal socio-cultural inequalities set regional social movements against global cultural movements, prioritising the debt to ancestry over responsibility to maintain intercultural dialogue, and flooding the public sphere with phantoms.

What is forgotten in the mayhem is that such global cultural movements are preconditions for the renewal of national discourses and the emergence of hybrid identities. The articulation of Brazilian trans-modernity, in particular, is 'a new articulation between "the global" and "the local"' (Hall 1992), through bilateral, multiple mobilities (Sheller 2014b), and not a solipsistic process. It is one thing to fight injustice with protest, and another to reject and destroy any possibility for collaborative renewal. The movement to conflate the aesthetics of politics with the politics of aesthetics in art is partly responsible for this aggression. In this respect, some of the 2014 World Cup's fan reactions, mostly orientated towards 'style', came closer to the possibility to articulate through practical action, without irreversible damage and violence. For Brazil's social protests proper, however, only a combined rebalancing of power that addresses unequal socio-economic distribution and unequal mobility can produce a progressive politics of place as a collection of socio-cultural relations, experiences and emotions (Massey 1993: 67).

The study's focus on cosmetic phenomenology borrowed heavily from interdisciplinary academic debates on gender politics, but this propensity should not allow scholars to define it as a contribution to the study of gender more so than of the phenomenological development of cosmopolitanism (Brazilian 'tropicopolitanism') as part of the mobilities paradigm. One reason for this qualification is that Brazil's internal and global dialogue between centres and peripheries remains dependent upon rebalancing the relations between its transcontinental, migrant ethos as an established form of otherness, and its collective symbolisations of cultural intimacy, political secrecy and corruption as black, working class and male, or beautiful, mobile and female. This potentially hybrid symbolisation allegorises the nation's deep social crisis and cultural indeterminacy, guising it in the clothes of instantly recognisable social identities. The postponement of the decision to recognise itself as hermaphrodite, truly to come to terms with its symbolic hybridisation, the obduracy of complementarity (male/female, black/white, civil/

uncivil), corresponds to the pervasiveness of a gender-class-race order in Brazilian society (Silva 2014).

More succinctly, however, the gender order's national allegorisation in Brazil 2014's social scenes articulates the fear that any association of the indigenous industry with Western sites of production and consumption is bound to transmogrify or 'miscegenate' it – change both its surface and its depth (Herzfeld 2004: 21; Johnson 1997; Kulick 1998; Parker 2009). Again, we may see in this propensity to allegory Brazil's colonial past: Frederic Jameson's claim that 'all third-world cultural productions … are necessarily allegorical, and in a very specific way: they are to be read as … national allegories, even when … their forms develop out of predominantly western machineries of representation' (Jameson 1986: 67), is contentious. The thesis fails to examine how any national worldview is relational and hybridised at both ends – that of the recipient and the 'maker' (Ahmad 1992) – and rejects the role of industrial (media and tourist) exchange as de facto damaging. Of course, one must account for the ways various interest groups and agencies, including cultural corporations, may 'manipulate, channel (close or open) the cultural boundaries of others to the flows with varying degrees of success in relation to their … power resources' (Featherstone 1990: 7). Although market imperatives in cultural industries may exercise pressures in self-presentational terms, cultural markets also provide a safe(r) space for the articulations of values held dear by indigenous industries. These days imagined communities may choose to communicate, 'orate' (*agorá* from *agorévō*) about their culture elsewhere (*alloú*), in open global markets (*agorá*) (Tzanelli 2013c: chapter 1). Therefore, more correctly, the suspicion towards alien industries falls between a problematic neoliberalisation of Brazilian economy and a domestic habitus favouring personal networking. In this regard, the hybrid profile and global outlook of the mega-event's transnational epistemic communities comes in direct conflict with the cohesive, purist aims of filiative, ethno-national communities.

The prevalence of heritage politics over legacy is assisted by the digital and imagological-auditory nature of Brazilian heritage. Heritage kinaesthetics endorses naturalisations of the country's filiative communities, technologising their merit so as to present them as 'civilised'. However, as kinship is a near-universal constant, its discursive support even by transnational, affiliative groups can be taken advantage of in policy planning. The result is, in both cases, the inducement of affective nationalist labour through scopic, imagological practices, such as those proffered by cinema, which, as the ceremonies proved (Chapter 4), are supported by various constituencies for their commercial value. Setting aside, once more, Brazilian performative synaesthetics, ceremonies based on polished cinematic images set out to represent the nation, its landscapes and histories in mythical forms, inducing emotions that strengthen the viewer's bond to the post-colonial, national cause (Graml 2004; Tzanelli 2013b: 25; Hochschild 1983; Thrift 2007). As a result, the glamorisation of a once vilified, Western European technicity is achieved at the expense of another polyphonic system of perception. Not only does this switch explain how situational ethics became intertwined with Brazilian aesthetics in the 2014 World Cup, but it also reframes the book's 'apparent' gender and racial politics in terms of a broader suggestion on aesthetic cosmopolitan practice and epistemology.

To recapitulate, then, we may say that an apparently dangerous practice of gendering and racialising human diversity, even in artistic domains, becomes recycled by various representational centres or 'machines' that constantly project capital, expertise and dreams onto a once colonised space (Greenblatt 1991; Salvatore 1998: 71). The aim is to manage diversity with the help of 'innocuous' but socio-culturally potent typification that tells a more unified story about Brazil's multicultural histories and experiences. The 2014 World Cup provided an opportunity to recycle Brazilian cosmologies of desire for recognition, which always preserved their memory vault with the help of gendered, classed and racialised self-characterisations. Such characterisations permeated performances staged both in elite and popular domains, allowing an indiscriminate mobility of heritage with the help of one of humanity's most recognised, and now commercialised, 'legal contracts': the hosting of a World Cup. The implosion of colonial and post-colonial memory in the country due to contingent economic and political complications further ensured the crystallisation of such collective self-presentations. The compartmentalisation of the *Malandro* human, who takes from the powerful without giving, and of a *linda maravilhosa*, who offers to humanity to the point of self-sacrifice, certainly resembles the defensive stereotypes of post-colonial nationalisms (see Tzanelli 2008: chapters 6 and 7). Today's mergers of national and commercial projects ironically also provide the opportunity to 'repackage' such remains of traumatic memories into cosmetic thanatourist products, which can now travel the world. Yet, within its land of origins, they can continue to haunt the living, demanding debts their debtors often transfer to other contexts and past culprits. The question is, how, in a globalised world of unrestricted mobilities, which is governed by the secrecy of plutocratic centres, can we ensure that such memorial implosions are treated in caring, yet critical ways? But this is the subject of another study.

References

ABC News (2014) 'Germany wins World Cup, defeats Argentina 1–0 in extra time', 13 July, abcnews.go.com/Sports/germany-argentina-2014-fifa-world-cup-final-live/story?id=24534252 (accessed 2 October 2014).

Adey, P. (2006) 'If mobility is everything then it is nothing: Towards a relational politics of (im)mobilities', *Mobilities*, 1(1): 75–94.

Adey, P. (2010) *Mobility*. London: Routledge.

Adler, J. (1992) 'Mobility and the creation of the subject: Theorizing movement and the self in early Christian monasticism', International Tourism: Between Tradition and Modernity Colloquium, Nice, France, 407–415.

Adorno, T. and Horkheimer, M. (1991) *The Dialectic of Enlightenment: Philosophical Fragments*. New York: Continuum.

Ahmad, A. (1992) *In Theory*. London: Verso.

Ahmed, S. (2004) *The Cultural Politics of Emotion*. Edinburgh: Edinburgh University Press.

Alabarces, P., Tomlinson, A. and Young, C. (2001) 'Argentina versus England at the France '98 World Cup: Narratives of nation and the mythologizing of the popular', *Media, Culture & Society*, 23(5): 547–566.

Albertsen, N. and Diken, B. (2003) '"Artworks" networks – Field, system or mediators?', Department of Sociology, Lancaster University Online Papers. www.comp.lancs.ac.uk/sociology.soc105bd.html (accessed 30 March 2012).

Albrow, M. (1997) 'Travelling beyond local cultures: Socioscapes in a global city', in J. Eade (ed.) *Living the Global City: Globalization as Local Process*. London: Routledge, 37–55.

Albrow, M., Eade, J., Dürrschmidt, J. and Washbourne, N. (1997) 'The impact of globalization on sociological concepts: Community, culture and milieu', in J. Eade (ed.) *Living the Global City: Globalization as Local Process*. London: Routledge, 20–36.

Alexander, J.C. (1987) *Twenty Lectures: Sociological Theory since World War II*. New York: Columbia University Press.

Alexander, J.C. (1989) 'Culture and political crisis: Watergate and Durkheimian sociology', in J. Alexander (eds) *Structure and Meaning*. New York: Columbia University Press, 174–216.

Alexander, J.C. (2004) 'The strong program in cultural sociology: Elements of a structural hermeneutics', in J.C. Alexander (ed.) *The Meaning of Social Life*. New York: Oxford University Press, 11–26.

Alexander, J.C. (2006) 'Cultural pragmatics: Social performance between ritual and strategy', in J.C. Alexander, B. Giesen and J.L. Mast (eds) *Social Performance,*

Symbolic Action, Cultural Pragmatics and Ritual. Cambridge: Cambridge University Press, 29–90.

Alexander, J.C. (2011) 'Clifford Geertz and the strong program: Human sciences and cultural sociology', in J.C. Alexander, P. Smith and M. Norton (eds) *Interpreting Clifford Geertz: Cultural Investigation in the Social Sciences*. New York: Palgrave Macmillan, 55–64.

Alexander, J.C., Eyerman, R., Giesen, B., Smelser, N.J. and Sztompka, P. (2004) *Cultural Trauma and Collective Identity*. California: University of California Press.

Alexander, J.C. and Smith, P. (2001) 'The strong program in cultural theory: Elements of structural hermeneutics', in J. Turner (ed.) *The Handbook of Sociological Theory*. New York: Kluwer, 135–150.

Anastasiou, D. and Schäler, R. (2010) 'Translating vital information: Localisation, internationalisation and globalisation', *Syn-Thèses*, 3: 11–25.

Anderson, B. (2006) *Imagined Communities: Reflection on the Origin and Spread of Nationalism*, revised edn. London and New York: Verso.

André, S. (1985) *Gobineau et la Féminité*. Pisa: Libreria Colliardica.

Andrews, D.L. and Clift, B.C. (2012) 'Olympic Games', in G. Ritzer (ed.) *The Wiley-Blackwell Encyclopedia of Globalization*, first edn. Oxford: Wiley Blackwell, 1576–1580.

Andrews, D.L. and Mower, R.L. (2012) 'Sport', in G. Ritzer (ed.) *The Wiley-Blackwell Encyclopedia of Globalization*, first edn. Oxford: Wiley Blackwell, 1914–1922.

Andrews, D.L. and Ritzer, G. (2007) 'The grobal in the sporting glocal', *Global Networks*, 7(2): 113–153.

Aparicio, F.R. and Chávez-Silverman, S. (eds) (1997) *Tropicalizations: Transcultural Representations of Latinidad*. Dartmouth, NH: University of New England.

Appadurai, A. (1981) 'The past as a scarce resource', *Man N.S.*, 16(2): 201–219.

Appadurai, A. (1986) 'Towards an anthropology of things', in A. Appadurai (ed.) *The Social Life of Things: Commodities in Cultural Perspective*. Cambridge: Cambridge University Press, 3–63.

Appadurai, A. (1990) 'Disjuncture and difference in the global cultural economy', *Public Culture*, 2(2): 1–24.

Appadurai, A. (1996) *Modernity at Large*. Minneapolis, MN: University of Minnesota Press.

Aravamudan, S. (1999) *Tropicopolitans: Colonialism and Agency, 1688–1804*. Durham, NC: Duke University Press.

Archer, M. (1995) *Realist Social Theory*. Cambridge: Cambridge University Press.

Archer, M. (1996) *Culture and Agency*, second edn. Cambridge: Cambridge University Press.

Archer, M. (2000) *Being Human*. Cambridge: Cambridge University Press.

Archer, M. (2003) *Structure, Agency and the Internal Conversation*. Cambridge: Cambridge University Press.

Archetti, E. (1994) 'Argentina and the World Cup: In search of national identity', in J. Sudgen and P. Tomlinson (eds) *Hosts and Champions: Soccer Cultures, National Identities and the USA World Cup*. Aldershot: Ashgate, 37–63.

Archetti, E. (1997) '"And give joy to my heart": Ideology and emotions in the Argentinian cult of Maradona', in G. Armstrong and R. Giulianotti (eds) *Entering the Field: New Perspectives on World Football*. Oxford: Berg, 31–51.

Archetti, E. (1999) *Masculinities: Football, Polo and the Tango in Argentina*. Oxford: Berg.

Ardener, E. (1989) *The Voice of Prophecy and Other Essays*. Oxford: Basil Blackwell.

Argyrou, V. (2013) *The Gift of European Thought and the Cost of Living*. Oxford: Berghahn.

Aries, P. (1962) *Centuries of Childhood*, translated by R. Baldick. New York: Alfred A. Knopf.

Aristotle (1924) *Metaphysics*, translated by W.D. Ross. Oxford: Clarendon.

Aristotle (1946) *Politics*, translated by E. Barker. Oxford: Clarendon.

Aristotle (1984) *The Complete Works*. Princeton, NJ: Princeton University Press.

Armstrong, D. (1982) *Nations before Nationalism*. Chapel Hill, NC: University of North Carolina Press.

Armstrong, G. and Giulianotti, R. (eds) (1997) *Entering the Field: New Perspectives on World Football*. Oxford: Berg.

Arnason, J.P. (2006) 'Nations and nationalisms: Between general theory and comparative history', in G. Delanty and K. Kumar (eds) *The SAGE Handbook of Nations and Nationalism*. London: Sage, 44–56.

Ashcroft, B. (2012) 'Postcolonialism', in G. Ritzer (ed.) *The Wiley-Blackwell Encyclopedia of Globalization*, first edn. Oxford: Wiley Blackwell.

Ashworth, G.J. and Voogd, H. (1994) 'Marketing and place promotion', in J.R. Gold and S. Ward (eds) *Place Promotion: The Use of Publicity and Marketing to Sell Towns and Regions*. Chichester: Wiley, 39–52.

Associated Press (2014) 'A glittering opening ceremony kicks-off FIFA World Cup 2014', IBN Live, 13 June. www.ibnlive.in.com/news/a-glittering-opening-ceremony-kicksoff-fifa-world-cup-2014/478694-5-21.html (accessed 19 July 2014).

Ateljevic, I. (2008) 'Transmodernity: Remaking our (tourism) world?', in J. Tribe (ed.) *Philosophical Issues in Tourism*. Bristol and Toronto: Channel View Publications, 278–300.

Ateljevic, I. and Hall, D. (2007) 'Tourism embodiment of the macho gaze in the South Eastern Europe: Performing masculinity and femininity in Albania and Croatia', in A. Pritchard, N. Morgan and I. Ateljevic (eds) *Tourism and Gender: Essays on Embodiment, Sensuality and Experience*. Wallingford: CABI, 138–157.

Ateljevic, I., Pritchard, A. and Morgan, N. (eds) (2007) *The Critical Turn in Tourism Studies: Innovative Research Methodologies*. Oxford: Elsevier.

Atkins, C. (2013) 'The social cost of Brazil hosting World Cup 2014', *Bleacher Report*. 6 June. www.bleacherreport.com/articles/1663701-the-social-cost-of-brazil-hosting-world-cup-2014 (accessed 27 July 2014).

Attwood, F. (2006) 'Sexed up: Theorizing the sexualisation of culture', *Sexualities*, 9(1): 77–94.

Augé, M. (1982) 'Football. De l'histoire sociale à l'anthropologie religieuse', *Le Débat*, 19(1): 59–67.

Augé, M. (1995) *Non-Places: Introduction of an Anthropology of Supermodernity*. London: Verso.

Avelar, I. (1999) *The Untimely Present: Postdictatorial Latin American Fiction and the Task of Mourning*. Durham, NC: Duke University Press.

Averill, G. (1996) 'Global imaginings', in R. Ohmann (ed.) *Making and Selling Culture*. Hannover: Wesleyan University Press, 203–223.

Ayikoru, M. (2008) 'Epistemology, ontology and tourism', in J. Tribe (ed.) *Philosophical Issues in Tourism*. Bristol and Toronto: Channel View Publications, 62–79.

Bærenholdt, J.E. (2013) 'Governmobility: The powers of mobility', *Mobilities*, 8(1): 20–34.

Bærenholdt, J.E. and Granås, B. (eds) (2008) *Mobility and Place: Enacting Northern European Peripheries*. Aldershot: Ashgate.

Bærenholdt, O., Haldrup, M., Larsen, J. and Urry, J. (2004) *Performing Tourist Places.* Aldershot: Ashgate.

Bajc, V., Coleman, S. and Eade, J. (2007) 'Mobility and centering in pilgrimage', *Mobilities*, 2(3): 321–329.

Bakhtin, M.M. (1968) *Rabelais and his World.* Cambridge: MIT Press.

Bakhtin, M.M. (1990) *Art and Answerability*, edited by M. Holquist, translated by V. Liapunov. Austin, TX: University of Texas Press.

Baldacchino, G. (2010) *Island Enclaves: Offshoring Strategies, Creative Governance, and Subnational Island Jurisdictions.* Montreal: McGill-Queen's University Press.

Bales, K. (2004) *Disposable People: New Slavery in the Global Economy.* London: University of California Press.

Banfield, E. (1958) *The Moral Basis of a Backward Society.* New York: Free Press.

Barbosa, L.N. (1995) 'The Brazilian jeitinho: An exercise in national identity', in D.J. Hess and R. DaMatta (eds) *The Brazilian Puzzle: Culture on the Borderlands of the Western World.* New York: Columbia University Press, 35–48.

Barrabi, T. (2014) 'World Cup 2014: 8 Weirdest Pregame Rituals and Superstitions', *International Business Times*, 17 June, www.ibtimes.com/world-cup-2014-8-weirdest-pregame-rituals-superstitions-1603838 (accessed 2 October 2014).

Barreira, I.A.F. (2011) 'Social movements, culture and politics in the work of Brazilian sociologists', *Latin American Perspectives*, 38(3): 150–168.

Barth, F. (ed.) (1969) *Ethnic Groups and Boundaries.* Boston: Little, Brown & Co.

Barthes, R. (1979) *The Eiffel Tower and Other Mythologies.* New York: Hill and Wang.

Bauman, R. (1983) *Let Your Words Be Few: Symbolism of Speaking and Silence in Seventeenth-Century Quakers.* Cambridge: Cambridge University Press.

Bauman, Z. (1987) *Legislators and Interpreters.* Ithaca, NY: Cornell University Press.

Bauman, Z. (1989) *Modernity and the Holocaust.* Cambridge: Polity.

Bauman, Z. (1991) *Modernity and Ambivalence.* Cambridge: Polity.

Bauman, Z. (1998) *Globalization.* New York: Columbia University Press.

Bauman, Z. (2000) *Liquid Modernity.* Cambridge: Polity.

Bauman, Z. (2007a) 'Collateral casualties of consumerism', *Journal of Consumer Culture*, 7(1): 25–56.

Bauman, Z. (2007b) *Liquid Times: Living in an Age of Uncertainty.* Cambridge: Polity.

BBC Sport (2014a) '2014 FIFA World Cup: Most teams pick bases in south east Brazil', 1 February, www.bbc.co.uk/sport/0/football/25998576 (accessed 25 July 2014).

BBC Sport (2014b) 'Brazil's Soccer Cities: from Rio to Brasilia', 29 May, www.bbc.co.uk/sport/0/football/27618836 (accessed 23 July 2014).

BBC Sport (2014c) 'World Cup 2014 kicks off with colourful ceremony', 12 June, www.bbc.co.uk/sport/0/football/27779059 (accessed 19 July 2014).

BBC Sport (2014d) 'World Cup 2014: Brazil boss Luiz Felipe Scolari on "worst day"', 9 July, www.bbc.co.uk/sport/0/football/28222899 (accessed 9 July 2014).

Beck, U. (1992) *Risk Society.* London: Sage.

Beck, U. (1999) *World Risk Society.* Cambridge: Polity.

Beck, U. (2000a) 'The Cosmopolitan perspective: Sociology of the second age of modernity', *British Journal of Sociology*, 51(1): 79–105.

Beck, U. (2000b) *What is Globalization?* Cambridge: Polity.

Beck, U. (2002) *Individualization.* London: Sage.

Beck, U., Giddens, A. and Lash, S. (1994) *Reflexive Modernization: Politics, Tradition and Aesthetics in the Modern Social Order.* Cambridge: Polity.

Becker, H.S. (1982) *Art Worlds.* Berkeley and Los Angeles: University of California Press.

Bendix, R. (2002) 'Capitalising on memories past, present and future', *Theoretical Anthropology*, 2(4): 469–487.

Benjamin, T. (2009) *The Atlantic World*. Cambridge: Cambridge University Press.

Benjamin, W. (1968) *Illuminations*. London: Fontana Press.

Benjamin, W. (2002) *The Arcades Project*. Cambridge: Harvard University Press.

Bennett, A. (1999) 'Subcultures or neotribes? Rethinking the relationship between youth style and musical taste', *Sociology* 33(3): 599–617.

Bennett, A. (2004) 'Consolidating the music scenes perspective', *Poetics*, 32: 223–234.

Bennett, A. (2005) *Culture and Everyday Life*. London: Sage.

Berleant, A. (1995) 'The aesthetics of art and nature', in S. Kemall and I. Gaskell (eds) *Landscape, Natural Beauty and the Arts*. Cambridge: Cambridge University Press, 228–243.

Best, D. (1995) 'The aesthetic in sport', in W.J. Morgan and K.V. Meier (eds) *Philosophic Inquiry into Sport*. Champaign, IL: Human Kinetics, 377–389.

Bhabha, H.K. (1994) *The Location of Culture*. London and New York: Routledge.

Bhatt, C. (2000) 'Primordial being: Enlightenment, Schopenhauer and the Indian subject of postcolonial theory', *Radical Philosophy*, 100: 28–41.

Bianchi, R. and Stephenson, M. (2014) *Tourism and Citizenship: Rights, Freedoms and Responsibilities in the Global Order*. London: Routledge.

Billig, M. (1995) *Banal Nationalism*. London: Sage.

Blanton, R. (2011) 'Chronotopic landscapes and environmental racism', *Linguistic Anthropology*, 21(1): 76–93.

Bloch, M. and Adler, S.A. (1994) 'African children's play and the emergence of the sexual division of labour', in J.L. Roopnarine. J.E. Jonson and F.H. Hooper (eds) *Children's Play in Diverse Cultures*. Albany: SUNY, 148–178.

Born, G. and Hesmondhalgh, D. (2000) *Western Music and its Others*. Chicago: University of California Press.

Bottenburg, M.V. (2001) *Global Games*. Urbana, IL: University of Illinois Press.

Bourdieu, P. (1977) *Outline of a Theory of Practice*, translated by Richard Nice. Cambridge: Cambridge University Press.

Bourdieu, P. (1984) *Distinction*. Cambridge: Harvard University Press.

Bourdieu, P. (1993) *The Field of Cultural Production*. Cambridge: Polity.

Bourdieu, P. (1998) *Practical Reason*. Cambridge: Polity.

Bowman, G. (1996) 'Passion, power and politics in a Palestinian tourist market', in T. Selwyn (ed.) *The Tourist Image: Myths and Myth Making in Tourism*. New York: John Wiley & Sons, 83–103.

Brazil World Cup Fan Camp 2014 (2012) 'World Cup 2014 Brazil Fanfests', 2 July, www.worldcupfancamp.com/viewtopic.php?f=118&t=10273 (accessed 27 July 2014).

Brecht, B. (1964 [1936]) *Brecht on Theatre*. London: Shevan Press.

Brennan, T. (2003) *The Transmission of Affect*. Ithaca, NY: Cornell University Press.

Broderick, R. (2014) 'Amazing photo of the iconic "Sad Brazilian" World Cup fan sharing his trophy with a young Germany fan', 9 July, Buzzfeed, www.buzzfeed.com/ryanhatesthis/iconic-sad-brazilian-world-cup-fan-shares-trophy#16eh5rk (accessed 21 August 2014).

Brooks, P. (2011) 'Semiotics and thick description (Barthes and Geertz)', in J.C. Alexander, P. Smith and M. Norton (eds) *Interpreting Clifford Geertz: Cultural Investigation in the Social Sciences*. New York: Palgrave Macmillan, 9–16.

Bruner, E. (1994) 'Abraham Lincoln as authentic reproduction: A critique of post-modernism', *American Anthropologist*, 96(2): 397–415.

Bruno, G. (2002) *Atlas of Emotion: Journeys in Art, Architecture and Film*. New York: Verso.

Budd, M. (2003) *Aesthetic Appreciation of Nature: Essays on the Aesthetics of Nature*. Oxford: Clarendon Press.

Buscema, C. (2011) 'The harvest of Dionysus: Mobility/proximity, indigenous migrants and relational machines', in G. Pellegrino (ed.) *The Politics of Proximity: Mobility and Immobility in Practice*. Aldershot: Ashgate, 43–60.

Büscher, M. and Urry, J. (2009) 'Mobile methods and the empirical', *European Journal of Social Theory*, 12(1): 99–116.

Büscher, M., Urry, J. and Witchger, K. (2011) *Mobile Methods*. London: Routledge.

Butler, B. (2006) 'Heritage and the present past', in C. Tilley and S. Keuchler (eds) *The Handbook of Material Culture*. London: Sage, 463–479.

Butler, J. (1993) *Bodies that Matter: On the Discursive Limits of 'Sex'*. London: Routledge.

Butler, J. (1997) *The Psychic Life of Power: Theories in Subjection*. Stanford, CA: Stanford University Press.

Campbell, J. (1964) *Honour, Family and Patronage: A Study of Institutions and Moral Values in a Greek Mountain Community*. Oxford: Oxford University Press.

Campbell, J. (2008) *The Hero with a Thousand Faces*. California: New World.

Cannadine, D. (1993) 'The context, performance and meaning of ritual: The British monarchy and the "invention of tradition", c.1820–1977', in E. Hobsbawm and T. Ranger (eds) *The Invention of Tradition*. Cambridge: Cambridge University Press, 101–164.

Cannadine, D. (2002) *Ornamentalism: How the British Saw their Empire*. New York: Oxford University Press.

Cannella, G. and Viruru, R. (2004) *Childhood and Postcolonization*. New York: Routledge.

Carmo, M. (2014a) 'Canção de "Maradona maior que Pelé" foi "ensinada" a argentinos um dia antes da estreia na Copa', BBC Brasil, 7 July, www.bbc.co.uk/portuguese/noticias/2014/07/140707_argentina_musica_wc2014_hb_mc.shtml (accessed 18 July 2014).

Carmo, M. (2014b) 'Afinal, o que os argentinos acham da gente?', BBC Brasil, 10 July, www.bbc.co.uk/portuguese/noticias/2014/07/140707_wc2014_brasil_argentina_mdb_mc.shtml (accessed 18 July 2014).

Carmon, I. (2006) 'In Lapa, Rio de Janeiro, the Samba Never Stopped', *The New York Times*, 26 November, www.nytimes.com/2006/11/26/travel/26next.html?pagewanted=all&_r=0 (accessed 24 August 2014).

Carr, N. (2010) *The Shallows*. London: Atlantic.

Castells, M. (1996) *The Rise of the Network Society*. Oxford: Blackwell.

Castells, M. (2000) *End of Millennium*. Oxford: Blackwell.

Castells, M. (2004) 'Informationalism, networks and the network society: A theoretical blueprint', in M. Castells (ed.) *The Network Society*. Cheltenham: Edward Elgar, 3–45.

Castoriadis, C. (1987) *The Imaginary Institution of Society*, translated by K. Blamey. Cambridge, MA: Cambridge University Press.

Castree, N. (2005) *Nature*. London: Routledge.

Cavanaugh, W. (2008) 'Migrant, tourist, pilgrim, monk: Mobility and identity in a global age', *Theological Studies*, 69(2): 340–356.

Chagas, P. (2010) 'Spectral semiotics: Sound as enacted experience – A phenomenological approach to temporality in sound and music', www.paulocchagas.com/2010_Spectral_Semiotics.pdf (accessed 19 September 2014).

Chakrabarty, D. (1991) ‘Open space/public space: Garbage, modernity and India’, *South Asia*, 14(1): 15–31.

Chateau, D. and Lefebvre, M. (2014) ‘Dance and fetish: Phenomenology and Metz’s epistemological shift’, *October* 148: 103–132.

Chatterjee, P. (1993) *The Nation and its Fragments: Colonial and Post-Colonial Histories.* Princeton, NJ: Princeton University Press.

Chia-Ling, L. (2004) ‘Art exhibitions travel the world’, in M. Sheller and J. Urry (eds) *Tourism Mobilities: Places to Play, Places in Play.* London: Routledge, 90–102.

Chowdry, G. (2007) ‘Edward Said and contrapuntal reading: Implications for critical interventions in international relations’, *Millennium*, 36(1): 101–116.

Chvaicer, M.T. (2002) ‘The criminalization of capoeira in nineteenth-century Brazil’, *Hispanic American Historical Review*, 82(3): 525–547.

Claeys, G. and Sargent, L. (eds) (1999) *The Utopia Reader.* New York: SUNY.

Clark, T. (2000) ‘Deconstruction and technology’, in N. Royle (ed.) *Deconstructions: A User’s Guide.* Basingstoke: Palgrave, 238–257.

Clifford, J. (1988) *The Predicament of Culture.* Cambridge, MA: Harvard University Press.

Clifford, J. (1992) ‘Travelling cultures’, in L. Grossberg, C. Nelson and P. Treichler (eds) *Cultural Studies.* New York: Routledge, 96–116.

Clifford, J. (1997) *Routes.* Cambridge: Harvard University Press.

Coghlan, A. (1990) ‘How to score goals and influence people’, *The New Scientist*, 126 (1719): 54–59.

Cohen, E. (1979) ‘A phenomenology of tourist experiences’, *Sociology*, 13(2): 179–201.

Cole, M. (2005) ‘Transmodernism, Marxism and social change: Some implications for teacher education’, *Policy Futures in Education*, 3(1): 90–105.

Coleman, J. (1988) ‘Social capital in the creation of human capital’, *American Journal of Sociology*, 94(S1): 95–120.

Coleman, S. and Eade, J. (2004), ‘Reframing pilgrimage’, in S. Coleman and J. Eade (eds) *Reframing Pilgrimage.* London: Routledge, 1–26.

Collins, J. (2007) ‘The sounds of tradition: Arbitrariness and agency in a Brazilian heritage center’, *Ethnos*, 72(3): 383–407.

Comaroff, J. and Comaroff, J. (1999) ‘Occult economies and the violence of abstraction: Notes on the South African postcolony’, *American Ethnologist*, 26: 279–301.

Comaroff, J. and Comaroff, J. (2001) ‘Alien-nation: Zombies, immigrants and millennial capitalism’, *South Atlantic Quarterly*, 101(4): 779–805.

Connell, J. and Gibson, C. (2004) ‘World music: Deterritorialising place and identity’, *Progress in Human Geography*, 28(3): 342–361.

Connell, R.W. (1987) *Gender and Power.* Stanford, CA: Stanford University Press.

Connell, R.W. (1995) *Masculinities.* Berkeley, CA: University of California Press.

Connerton, P. (1989) *How Societies Remember.* Cambridge: Cambridge University Press.

Cordey, H. (2011) ‘Colombia seeks a new, clean image’, *BBC News Magazine*, 10 November, www.bbc.co.uk/news/magazine-15659912 (accessed 7 September 2014).

Coscarelli, J. (2014) ‘Twitter sure does have a lot of Nazi and Holocaust jokes for the Germany-Brazil game!’, The Daily Intelligencer, 8 July, www.nymag.com/daily/intelligencer/2014/07/nazi-holocaust-jokes-during-germany-brazil-world-cup.html?mid=facebook_nymag (accessed 24 August 2014).

Cosgrove, D. (2003) ‘Globalism and tolerance in early modern geography’, *Annals of the Association of American Geographers*, 93(4): 852–870.

Couldry, N. (2003a) 'Media meta-capital: Extending the range of Bourdieu's field theory', *Theory and Society*, 32(5/6): 653–677.

Couldry, N. (2003b) *Media Rituals*. New York: Routledge.

Couldry, N. (2006) 'In place of a common culture, what?', in N. Couldry (ed.) *Listening Beyond the Echoes*. Boulder: Paradigm, 63–82.

Crang, M. and Franklin, A. (2001) 'The trouble with tourism and travel theory', *Tourist Studies*, 1(1): 5–22.

Cresswell, T. (1999) 'Falling down: Resistance as diagnostic', in J. Sharp (ed.) *Entanglements of Power: Geographies of Domination/Resistance*. London: Routledge, 256–268.

Cresswell, T. (2001) 'The production of mobilities', *New Formations*, 43(1): 11–25.

Cresswell, T. (2004) *Place: A Short Introduction*. Oxford: Blackwell.

Cresswell, T. (2006) *On the Move*. London: Routledge.

Cresswell, T. (2010) 'Towards a politics of mobility', *Environment and Planning D*, 28 (1): 17–31.

Crompton, J. (1995) 'Factors that have stimulated the growth of sponsorship of major events', *Festival Management and Event Tourism*, 3(2): 97–101.

Cronin, M. (2013) *Translation in the Digital Age*. London: Routledge.

Crouch, D. (2009) 'The diverse dynamics of cultural studies and tourism', in T. Jamal and M. Robinson (eds) *The SAGE Handbook of Tourism Studies*. London: Sage, 82–98.

Crouch, G.I. and Ritchie, B.J.R. (1999) 'Tourism, competitiveness, and societal prosperity', *Journal of Business Research*, 44(3): 137–152.

Czeglédy, A.P. (2003) 'The words and things of Ernest Gellner', *Social Evolution & History*, 2(2): 6–33.

DaMatta, R. (ed.) (1982) *Universo do Futebol: Esporte e Sociedade Brasileira*. Rio de Janeiro: Pinakothelke.

DaMatta, R. (1991) *Carnivals, Rogues, and Heroes: An Interpretation of the Brazilian Dilemma*, translated by J. Drury. Notre Dame, IN: University of Notre Dame Press.

DaMatta, R. (1995) 'For an anthropology of the Brazilian tradition – or "A virtude esta no Meio"', in D.J. Hess and R. DaMatta (eds) *The Brazilian Puzzle: Culture on the Borderlands of the Western World*. New York: Columbia University Press, 270–291.

D'Andrea, A. (2006) 'Neo-nomadism: a theory of post-identarian mobility in the global age', *Mobilities*, 1(1): 95–119.

Dann, G.M.S. (1989) 'The tourist as a child: Some reflections', *Cahiers du Tourisme, Série C*, 135.

Dann, G.M.S. (2002) 'The tourist as a metaphor of the social world', in G.M.S. Dann (ed.) *The Tourist as a Metaphor of the Social World*. Wallingford: CABI, 1–18.

Dann, G.M.S. and Liebman Parrinello, G. (2009) 'Setting the scene', in G.M.S. Dann and G. Parrinello (eds) *The Sociology of Tourism: European Origins and Developments*. UK: Emerald, 1–63.

Dann, G.M.S. and Seaton, A.V. (2001) 'Slavery, contested heritage and thanatourism', in G.M.S. Dann and A.V. Seaton (eds) *Slavery, Contested Heritage and Thanatourism*. New York: Haworth Hospitality Press, 1–30.

Davis, D.J. (2009) *White Face, Black Mask*. Michigan: Michigan State University Press.

Davis, M. (1990) *City of Quartz: Excavating the Future in Los Angeles*. London: Vintage.

Davis, W. (1988) *Passage of Darkness: The Ethnobiology of the Haitian Zombie*. Chapel Hill: University of North Carolina Press.

Dayan, J. (1998) *Haiti, History and the Gods*. Berkeley, CA: University of California Press.

Dean, J. (2007) 'The net and multiple realities', in S. During (ed.) *The Cultural Studies Reader*, third edn. London: Routledge, 520–534.
Debord, G. (1995) *Society and the Spectacle*. New York: Zone.
De Certeau, M. (1984) *The Practice of Everyday Life*. Berkeley: University of California Press.
De Certeau, M. (1985) 'What we do when we believe', in M. Blonsky (ed.) *On Signs: A Semiotic Reader*. Baltimore: Johns Hopkins University Press, 192–202.
De Certeau, M. (1988) *The Practice of Everyday Life*. Berkeley: University of California Press.
Deichmann, J. (2007) 'International tourism from the perspective of Czech hospitality professionals: A pilot study of exploring origin-specific stereotypes', *E-Review of Tourism Research*, 5(1): 1–13.
De Kadt, E.J. (1984) *Tourism: Passport to Development?: Perspectives on the Social and Cultural Effects of Tourism in Developing Countries*. Oxford: Oxford University Press.
De la Fuente, E. (2007) 'The "new sociology of art": Putting art back into social science', *Cultural Sociology*, 1(3): 409–425.
Delanty, G. (2000) *Citizenship in a Global Age*. Buckingham: Open University Press.
Delanty, G. (2006) 'The cosmopolitan imagination: Critical cosmopolitanism and social theory', *The British Journal of Sociology*, 57(1): 25–47.
Delanty, G. and O'Mahony, P. (2002) *Nationalism and Social Theory: Modernity and the Recalcitrance of the Nation*. London: Sage.
Deleuze, G. and Guattari, F. (1988) *A Thousand Plateaus*. London: Athlone.
Denning, M. (2001) 'Globalization in cultural studies: Process and epoch', *European Journal of Cultural Studies*, 4(3): 351–364.
DeNora, T. (2000) *Music and Everyday Life*. Cambridge: Cambridge University Press.
DeNora, T. (2003) *After Adorno: Rethinking Music Sociology*. Cambridge: Cambridge University Press.
Denzin, N. (2002) *Reading Race*. London: Sage.
De Pina-Cabral, J. (2008) 'Sarakatsani reflections on the Brazilian Devil', in M. Mazower (ed.) *Networks of Power in Greece*. London: Hurst, 231–254.
Derrida, J. (1976) *Of Grammatology*. Baltimore: Johns Hopkins University Press.
Derrida, J. (1981) *Dissemination*. Chicago, IL: University of Chicago Press.
Derrida, J. (1986) *Mémoires – for Paul de Mann*. New York: Columbia University Press.
Derrida, J. (1994) *Spectres of Marx*. New York: Routledge.
Derrida, J. (1997) *Writing and Difference*. London: Routledge.
Derrida, J. (1998) *Archive Fever*. Chicago: University of Chicago Press.
Derrida, J. (2001) *Acts of Religion*. New York: Routledge.
Derrida, J. (2002) *On Cosmopolitanism and Forgiveness*. New York: Routledge.
Derrida, J. and Dufourmantelle, A. (2000) *Of Hospitality*. Stanford: Stanford University Press.
Descola, P. (1996) *The Spears of Twilight: Life and Death with the Last Free Tribe of the Amazon*, translated by J. Lloyd. New York: The New Press.
De Sousa Santos, B. (1999a) 'Towards a multicultural conception of human rights', in M. Featherstone and S. Lash (eds) *Spaces of Culture*. London: Sage, 214–229.
De Sousa Santos, B. (1999b) *Towards a New Common Sense*. New York: Routledge.
De Souza e Silva, A. and Frith, J. (2011) *Net-Locality: Why Location Matters in a Networked World*. Malden, MA and Oxford: Wiley-Blackwell.

De Souza e Silva, A. and Sheller, M. (2014) *Mobility and Locative Media: Mobile Communication in Hybrid Spaces*. London: Routledge.

De Souza e Silva, A. and Sutko, D. (eds) (2010) *Digital Cityscapes: Merging Digital and Urban Playspaces*. New York: Peter Lang.

Devezas, T. and Modelski, G. (2006) 'The Portuguese as system-builders in the fifteenth and sixteenth centuries: A case study on the role of technology in the evolution of the world system', *Globalizations*, 3(4): 507–523.

Dewsbury, J.D. (2011) 'Dancing: The secret slowness of the fast', in T. Cresswell and P. Merriman (eds) *Geographies of Mobilities: Practices, Spaces, Subjects*. Farnham and Burlington, VT: Ashgate, 51–68.

Dikötter, F. (2008) 'The racialization of the globe: An interactive interpretation', *Ethnic and Racial Studies*, 31(8): 1478–1496.

Dimitrova Savova, N. (2009) 'Heritage kinaesthetics: Local constructivism and UNESCO's intangible-tangible politics at a favela museum', *Anthropological Quarterly*, 82(2): 547–585.

Domingues, J.M. (2006a) *Modernity Reconstructed*. Cardiff: University of Wales Press.

Domingues, J.M. (2006b) 'Nationalism in South and Central America', in G. Delanty and K. Kumar (eds) *The SAGE Handbook of Nations and Nationalism*. London: Sage, 541–554.

Donald, S.H. and Gammack, J.G. (2007) *Tourism and the Branded City*. Farnham: Ashgate.

Douglas, M. (1966) *Purity and Danger: An Analysis of the Concepts of Pollution and Taboo*. London: Routledge and Kegan Paul.

Dredge, D. (2010) 'Place change and tourism development conflict: Evaluating public interest', *Tourism Management*, 31(1): 104–112.

Dredge, D. and Jamal, T. (2013) 'Mobilities on the Gold Coast, Australia: Implications for destination governance and sustainable tourism', *Journal of Sustainable Tourism* 21(4): 557–579.

Dudko, J. (2014) 'World Cup 2014 Closing Ceremony performers: Latest names, details and gossip', *Bleacher Report*, 13 July, www.bleacherreport.com/articles/2127942-world-cup-2014-closing-ceremony-performers-latest-names-details-and-gossip (accessed 24 August 2014).

Duffy, M. (2000) 'Lines of drift: Festival participation and performing a sense of place', *Popular Music*, 19(1): 51–64.

Dumont, L. (1975) 'On the comparative understanding of non-modern civilisations', *Daedalus*, 104(2): 153–172.

Duncan, J. (1999) 'Dis-orientation: On the shock of the familiar in a far-away place', in J. Duncan and D. Gregory (eds) *Writes of Passage: Reading Travel Writing*. London: Routledge, 161–179.

Durkheim, E. (1960) *The Rules of Sociological Method*. New York: Free Press.

Durkheim, E. (1969 [1898]) 'Individualism and the intellectuals', translated by J. Lukes, *Political Studies*, 17(1): 19–30.

Durkheim, E. (1992) *Professional Ethics and Civic Morals*. London: Routledge.

Durkheim, E. (1997 [1893]) *The Division of Labour in Society*. New York: Free Press.

Dürrschmidt, J. (1997) 'The delinking of locale and milieu', in J. Eade (ed.) *Living the Global City: Globalization as Local Process*. London: Routledge, 56–72.

Dussel, E. (1985) *Philosophy of Liberation*. New York: Orbis.

Dussel, E. (1995) *The Invention of the Americas: Eclipse of 'Other' and the Myth of Modernity*. New York: Continuum.

Duval, D.T. (2007) *Tourism and Transport: Modes, Networks and Flows.* Toronto: Channel View.

Eade, J. (1992) 'Pilgrimage and tourism at Lourdes, France', *Annals of Tourism Research*, 19(1): 18–32.

Eade, J. (1997) 'Introduction', in J. Eade (ed.) *Living the Global City: Globalization as Local Process.* London: Routledge, 1–19.

Eade, J. and Sallnow, M.J. (eds) (1991) *Contesting the Sacred: The Anthropology of Christian Pilgrimage.* London: Routledge.

Eagle Merry, S. (2003) 'Human rights law and the demonization of culture (and anthropology along the way)', *Political and Legal Anthropology Review*, 26(1): 55–76.

Eco, U. (1987) *Travels in Hyperreality.* London: Picador.

Edensor, T. (2011) 'Commuter: Mobility, rhythm, commuting', in T. Cresswell and P. Merriman (eds) *Geographies of Mobilities: Practices, Spaces, Subjects.* Farnham: Ashgate, 189–204.

Edensor, T. (2014) 'Rhythm and arrhythmia', in P. Adey (ed.) *The Routledge Handbook of Mobilities.* London and New York: Routledge, 163–171.

Ehrenfreund, M. (2014) 'Cheer up, Brazil. Your epic World Cup loss could bode well for your economy', *The Washington Post* (Wonkblog), 8 July, www.washingtonpost.com/blogs/wonkblog/wp/2014/07/08/cheer-up-brazil-your-epic-world-cup-loss-could-bode-well-for-your-economy/?Post+generic=?tid%3Dsm_twitter_washingtonpost (accessed 24 August 2014).

Eisenstadt, S.N. (2001) 'The civilizational dimension of modernity: Modernity as a distinct civilization', *International Sociology*, 16(3): 320–340.

Eliade, M. (1989) *The Myth of the Eternal Return, or Cosmos and History.* London: Arkana.

Elias, N. (1982) *The Civilising Process: State Formation and Civilisation*, vol. II. Oxford: Blackwell.

Elias, N. and Dunning, E. (1986) *Quest for Excitement: Sport and Leisure in the Civilizing Process.* Oxford: Basil Blackwell.

Elliot, A. and Urry, J. (2010) *Mobile Lives.* London: Routledge.

Ellul, J. (1964) *The Technological Society.* Toronto: Random House.

Engelbrekt, K. (2011) 'Mobility and the notion of attainable reach', in G. Pellegrino (ed.) *The Politics of Proximity: Mobility and Immobility in Practice.* Aldershot: Ashgate, 31–42.

Enloe, C. (1990) *Bananas, Beaches and Bases: Making Feminist Sense of International Politics.* Berkeley: University of California Press.

Erlmann, V. (1999) *Music, Modernity and the Global Imagination.* Oxford: Oxford University Press.

Errington, J. (2011) 'On not doing social systems', in J. Alexander, S. Smith and M. Norton (eds) *Interpreting Clifford Geertz: Cultural Investigation in the Social Sciences.* New York: Palgrave Macmillan, 33–44.

Evans-Pritchard, E.E. (1937) *Witchcraft, Oracles and Magic among the Azande.* Oxford: Oxford University Press.

Evans-Pritchard, E.E. (1940) *The Nuer.* Oxford: Clarendon.

Evans-Pritchard, E.E. (1956) *Nuer Religion.* Oxford: Clarendon.

Fabian, J. (1983) *Time and the Other: How Anthropology Makes its Object.* New York: Columbia University Press.

Falk, I. and Kilpatrick, S. (2000) 'What is social capital? A study of rural communities', *Sociologica Ruralis*, 40(1): 87–110.

Fanon, F. (1970) *Black Skins, White Masks.* London: Paladin.

Farnell, B. (1994) 'Ethno-graphics and the moving body', *Man*, 29(4): 929–974.

Farnell, B. (1999) 'Moving bodies, acting selves', *Annual Review of Anthropology*, 28: 341–373.

Faubion, J. (1988) 'Possible modernities', *Cultural Anthropology*, 3(4): 365–378.

Featherstone, M. (1990) *Global Culture.* London: Sage.

Featherstone, M. (1991) 'The body in consumer culture', in M. Featherstone, M. Hepworth and B.S. Turner (eds) *The Body: Social Process and Cultural Theory.* London: Sage.

Feixa, C. and Juris, J.S. (2000) 'Review article: Football cultures', *Social Anthropology*, 8(2): 203–211.

Fennell, D. (2008) 'Ethics and tourism', in J. Tribe (ed.) *Philosophical Issues in Tourism.* Bristol and Toronto: Channel View Publications, 211–226.

FIFA.com (2007) 'Brazil confirmed as 2014 hosts', 30 October, www.fifa.com/worldcup/news/y=2007/m=10/news=brazil-confirmed-2014-hosts-625695.html (accessed 25 July 2014).

FIFA.com (2012a) '2014 FIFA World Cup Brazil: FIFA Fan Fest locations confirmed', 13 April, www.fifa.com/worldcup/news/y=2012/m=4/news=fifa-fan-fest-locations-confirmed-1614471.html (accessed 27 July 2014).

FIFA.com (2012b) 'Fuleco wins name game', 26 November, www.fifa.com/worldcup/news/y=2012/m=11/news=fuleco-wins-name-game-1944138.html (accessed 28 August 2014).

FIFA.com (2014a) 'Team base camps for Brazil 2014 announced', 21 January, www.fifa.com/worldcup/news/y=2014/m=1/news=team-base-camps-for-brazil-2014-announced-2267880.html (accessed 25 July 2014).

FIFA.com (2014b) 'Nerve centre for World Cup TV production opens in Rio', 2 June, www.fifa.com/worldcup/news/y=2014/m=6/news=nerve-centre-for-world-cup-tv-production-opens-in-rio-2353342.html (accessed 28 July 2014).

FIFA.com (2014c) 'Dvorak : "Le profil biologique, une approche complètement nouvelle"', 5 June, www.fr.m.fifa.com/worldcup/news/y=2014/m=6/news=dvorak-le-profil-biologique-une-approche-completement-nouvelle-2354963.html (accessed 27 July 2014).

FIFA.com (2014d) 'Closing ceremony to celebrate Brazil 2014 in style', 12 July, www.fifa.com/worldcup/news/y=2014/m=7/news=closing-ceremony-to-celebrate-brazil-2014-in-style-2404018.html (accessed 24 August 2014).

FIFA.com (n.d.a) 'Host broadcasting', www.fifa.com/aboutfifa/organisation/tv/hostbroadcasting.html (accessed 28 July 2014).

FIFA.com (n.d.b) 'Official [2014] emblem', www.fifa.com/worldcup/officialemblem/ (accessed 25 July 2014).

FIFA.com (n.d.c) '2014 FIFA World Cup Brazil media rights licensees', www.fifa.com/mm/document/affederation/tv/01/47/76/00/2014fifaworldcupbrazil%28tm%29mediarightslicenseelist110414_neutral.pdf (accessed 28 July 2014).

FIFA.com (n.d.d) 'Official mascot', www.en.mascot.fifa.com/about.php?page=routine (accessed 28 August 2014).

FIFA Quality Programme (2014) 'News', 16 June, www.quality.fifa.com/en/News/ (accessed 25 July 2014).

Firth, R. (1961) *History and Traditions of Tikopia.* Wellington: The Poynesian Society.

Foster, K. (2003) 'Dreaming of Pelé: Football and society in England and Brazil in the 1950s and 1960s', *Football Studies*, 6(1): 70–86.

Foucault, M. (1979) *Discipline and Punish: The Birth of the Prison*. New York: Vintage.

Foucault, M. (1980) *Power/Knowledge*, edited by G. Colin. New York: Harvester Press.

Foucault, M. (1984) 'Nietzsche, history, genealogy', in P. Rabinow (ed.) *The Foucault Reader*. New York: Pantheon, 76–100.

Foucault, M. (1989) *The Order of Things: An Archaeology of Human Sciences*. London: Routledge.

Foucault, M. (1997a) *The Archaeology of Knowledge*. London: Routledge.

Foucault, M. (1997b) 'The birth of biopolitics', in P. Rabinow (ed.) *Michel Foucault: Ethics*, vol. I. New York: New Press, 73–79.

Foucault, M. (2007) *Security, Territory and Population*, translated by G. Burchell. Basingstoke: Palgrave Macmillan.

Frabetti, F. (2011) 'Rethinking the digital humanities in the context of originary technicity', *Culture Machine*, 12: unpaginated. www.culturemachine.net/index.php/cm/article/download/431/461 (accessed 12 September 2014).

Franko Aas, K. (2007) 'Analysing a world in motion: Global flows meet criminology of the other', *Theoretical Criminology*, 11(2): 283–303.

Freire-Madeiros, B. (2009) 'The favela and its touristic transits', *Geoforum*, 40(4): 280–288.

Freire-Madeiros, B. (2013) *Touring Poverty*. London: Routledge.

Freud, S. (1965) *The Psychopathology of Everyday Life*. New York: Norton.

Freud, S. (1982) 'The development of the libido and the sexual organisations', in *Sigmund Freud: Introductory Lectures of Psychoanalysis*. London: Penguin.

Freyre, G. (1963) *The Mansions and the Shanties: The Making of Modern Brazil*, translated by H. de Onis. New York: Knopf.

Frisby, D. (1992) *Simmel and Since: Essays on Georg Simmel's Social Theory*. London: Routledge.

Frith, S. (2000) 'The discourse of world music', in G. Born and D. Hesmondhalgh (eds) *Western Music and its Others*. Berkeley: University of California Press, 305–322.

Frye, N. (1965) 'Varieties of literary utopias', *Daedalus*, 94(2): 323–347.

Fryer, P. (2000) *Rhythms of Resistance: African Musical Heritage in Brazil*. Hanover, NH: University Press of New England.

Gallant, T.W. (1999) 'Brigandage, piracy, capitalism, and state-formation: Transnational crime from a historical world-systems perspective', in J. McC. Heyman (ed.) *States and Illegal Practices*. Oxford and New York: Oxford Berg, 25–61.

Gallant, T.W. (2000) 'Honor, masculinity, and ritual knife-fighting in nineteenth century Greece', *American Historical Review*, 105(2): 359–382.

Gallant, T.W. (2002) *Experiencing Dominion: Culture, Identity and Power in the British Mediterranean*. Notre Dame, IN: University of Notre Dame Press.

Gallope, M. (2011) 'Technicity, consciousness and musical objects', in M. Clarke and D. Clarke (eds) *Music and Consciousness: Philosophical, Psychological, and Cultural Perspectives*. Oxford: Oxford University Press, 47–64.

García Márquez, G. (2002) 'The poet and the princess', *The Guardian*, 8 June, www.theguardian.com/lifeandstyle/2002/jun/08/shopping.colombia (accessed 26 August 2014).

Gardiner, M. (1992) *The Dialogics of Critique*. London: Routledge.

Garland, J. and Rowe, M. (1999) 'War minus the shooting? Jingoism, the English press, and Euro '96', *Journal of Sport and Social Issues*, 23(1): 80–95.

Garrison, J.W. (1996) 'Practical notes: Brazilian NGOs from grassroots to national civic leadership', *Development and Practice*, 6: 250–254.

Gauntlett, D. (2011) *Making is Connecting*. Cambridge: Polity.

Geertz, C. (1973) *The Interpretation of Cultures*. New York: Basic Books.
Geertz, C. (1980) *Negara: The Theatre-State in Nineteenth-Century Bali*. Princeton, NJ: Princeton University Press.
Geertz, C. (1983) *Local Knowledge: Further Essays in Interpretive Anthropology*. New York: Basic Books.
Geertz, C. (2000) *Available Light: Anthropological Reflections on Philosophical Topics*. Princeton, NJ: Princeton University Press.
Gellner, E. (1959) *Words and Things*. London: Gollancz.
Gellner, E. (1969) *The Saints of Atlas*. Chicago: University of Chicago Press.
Gellner, E. (1983) *Nations and Nationalism*. Oxford: Blackwell.
Gellner, E. (1985) *The Psychoanalytic Movement, or the Cunning of Unreason*. Oxford: Wiley Blackwell.
Gellner, E. (1998) *Nationalism*. London: Phoenix.
Genius (2014) 'La, la, la (World Cup 2014)', *Lyrics and Music*, www.pop.genius.com/Shakira-la-la-la-world-cup-2014-lyrics (accessed 24 August 2014).
Germann Molz, J. (2004) 'Playing online and between the lines: Round-the-world websites as virtual places to play', in M. Sheller and J. Urry (eds) *Tourism Mobilities: Places to Play, Places in Play*. London: Routledge, 167–180.
Germann Molz, J. (2008) 'Global abode: Home and mobility in narratives of round-the-world travel', *Space and Culture*, 11(4): 325–342.
Germann Molz, J. (2009) 'Representing pace in tourism mobilities: Staycations, slow travel and The Amazing Race', *Journal of Tourism and Cultural Change*, 7(4): 270–286.
Germann Molz, J. (2012) *Travel Connections*. London: Routledge.
Gerth, H.H. and Mills, W. (1948) *From Max Weber: Essays in Sociology*. London: Routledge and Kegan Paul.
Gibson, O. (2014) 'Brazil a mix of mutiny and mourning after "biggest shame in history"', *The Guardian*, 9 July, www.theguardian.com/football/blog/2014/jul/09/brazil-mutiny-mourning-germany-world-cup-2014 (accessed 9 July 2014).
Giddens, A. (1987) *Social Theory and Modern Sociology*. Cambridge: Polity.
Giddens, A. (1990) *The Consequences of Modernity*. Cambridge: Polity.
Giddens, A. (1994) 'Living in a post-traditional society', in U. Beck, A. Giddens and S. Lash (eds) *Reflexive Modernization: Politics, Tradition and Aesthetics in the Modern Social Order*. Cambridge: Polity, 56–109.
Giddens, A. (2009) *The Politics of Climate Change*. Cambridge: Polity.
Giesen, B. (2011) 'Ritual, power, and style: The implications of Negara for the sociology of power', in J.C. Alexander, P. Smith and M. Norton (eds) *Interpreting Clifford Geertz: Cultural Investigation in the Social Sciences*. New York: Palgrave Macmillan, 167–177.
Gikandi, S. (2002) 'Globalization and the claims of postcoloniality', *The South Atlantic Quarterly*, 100(3): 627–658.
Gill, K. (2014) 'World Cup closing ceremony 2014 sees Shakira, Rihanna, David Beckham, Pele, Tom Brady, Vladimir Putin and more in the crowd as celebrities spotted at Maracana in Rio de Janeiro for final', *Daily Mail*, 13 July, www.dailymail.co.uk/sport/worldcup2014/article-2690684/World-Cup-2014-closing-ceremony-Shakira-headlining-Maracana-Rio-Janeiro.html (accessed 25 August 2014).
Giulianotti, R. (1999) *Football: A Sociology of the Global Game*. Cambridge: Polity.
Giulianotti, R. (2001) 'Playing an aerial game: The new political economy of soccer', in J. Naurigh and K. Schimmel (eds) *Sport and Political Economy*. London: Macmillan, 19–37.

Giulianotti, R. (2005) *Sport: A Critical Sociology.* Cambridge: Polity.

Giulianotti, R. (2012) 'Football', in G. Ritzer (ed.) *The Wiley-Blackwell Encyclopedia of Globalization*, first edn. Oxford: Wiley Blackwell.

Giulianotti, R. and Robertson, R. (2004) 'The globalization of football: A study in the globalization of "serious life"', *The British Journal of Sociology*, 55(4): 545–568.

Giulianotti, R. and Robertson, R. (2007) 'Recovering the social: Globalization, football and transnationalism', *Global Networks*, 7(2): 144–186.

Gluckman, M. (1963) 'Gossip and scandal' , *Current Anthropology*, 4(3): 307–316.

Goffman, E. (1987) *The Presentation of Self in Everyday Life.* Harmondsworth: Penguin.

Goldmann, L. (1964) *The Hidden God.* London: Routledge.

Goldmann, L. (1980) *Method in the Sociology of Literature.* Oxford: Basil Blackwell.

Goldschmidt, E.M.R. (1998) *Convivendo com o Pecado na Sociedade Colonila Paulista, 1719–1822.* São Paulo: Annablume.

Goodman, N. (1976) *The Languages of Art.* Indianapolis, IN: Bobbs-Merill.

Gordon, C. and Helal, R. (2001) 'The crisis of Brazilian football: Perspectives for the twenty-first century', *The International Journal of the History of Sport*, 18(3): 139–158.

Gourgouris, S. (1992) 'Nationalism and oneirocentrism: Of modern Hellenes in Europe', *Diaspora*, 2(1): 43–71.

Gourgouris, S. (1996) *Dream Nation: Enlightenment, Colonisation and the Institution of Modern Greece.* Stanford, CA: Stanford University Press.

Graburn, N.H.H. (1977) 'Tourism: The sacred journey', in V. Smith (ed.) *Hosts and Guests: An Anthropology of Tourism.* Philadelphia: University of Pennsylvania Press, 17–32.

Graburn, N.N.H. (1983) *To Pray, Pay and Play.* Aix-en-Provence: Centre des Hautes Etudes Touristiques.

Graburn, N.H.H. (2004) 'The Kyoto tax strike: Buddhism, Shinto and tourism in Japan', in E. Badone and S.R. Roseman (eds) *Intersecting Journeys: The Anthropology of Pilgrimage and Tourism.* Chicago, IL: University of Illinois, 125–139.

Graham, S. and Marvin, S. (2001) *Splintering Urbanism.* London: Routledge.

Graml, R. (2004) '(Re)mapping the nation: Sound of Music tourism and national identity in Austria, ca 2000', *Tourist Studies*, 4(2): 137–159.

Gray, L.E. (2007) 'Memories of the empire, mythologies of the soul: Fado performance and the shaping of saudade', *Ethnomusicology*, 53(1): 106–130.

Greenberg, K. (1996) *Honour and Slavery: Lies, Duels, Noses, Masks, Dressing as Women, Gifts, Strangers, Humanitarianism, Death, Slave Rebellions…* Princeton, NJ: Princeton University Press.

Greenblatt, S. (1991) *Marvellous Possessions: The Wonder of the New World.* Oxford: Clarendon.

Greene, R. (2000) *Unrequited Conquest: Love and Empire in the Colonial Americas.* Chicago: University of Chicago Press.

Greenfeld, L. (1990) 'The formation of the Russian national identity: The role of status insecurity and ressentiment', *Comparative Studies in Society and History*, 32 (3): 549–591.

Greenfeld, L. (1992) *Nationalism: Five Roads to Modernity.* Cambridge, MA: Harvard University Press.

Gregg, M. (2009) 'Learning to (love) labour: Production cultures and the affective turn', *Communication and Critical/Cultural Studies*, 6(2): 209–214.

Gregory, R. (1994) *Even Odder Perceptions.* London: Routledge and Kegan Paul.

Grugulis, I. and Stoyanova, D. (2011) 'The missing middle: Communities of practice in a freelance labour market', *Work, Employment & Society*, 25(2): 342–351.

Gudeman, S. (1986) *Economics as Culture: Models and Metaphors of Livelihood*. London: Routledge and Kegan Paul.

Gudeman, S. (2009) 'Necessity and contingency: Mutuality and market', in C. Hann and K. Hart (eds) *Market and Society: The Great Transformation Today*. Cambridge: Cambridge University Press, 17–27.

Gunder Frank, A. (1966) *Latin America: Underdevelopment or Revolution? Essays on the Development of Underdevelopment and the Immediate Enemy*. New York and London: MR.

Gunn, G.C. (2003) *First Globalization: The Eurasian Exchange 1500–1800*. Lanham: Rowman and Littlefield.

Gutman, H.G. (1976) *The Black Family in Slavery and Freedom, 1750–1925*. New York.

Gwerner, S. (2006) 'Vertical flight and urban mobilities: The promise and reality of helicopter travel', *Mobilities*, 1(1): 191–215.

Gwerner, S. (2009) 'Introducing aeromobilities', in S. Gwerner, S. Kesserling and J. Urry (eds) *Aeromobilities*. Abingdon: Routledge.

Haas, P. (1992) 'Knowledge, power and international policy coordination', *International Organization*, 46(1): 1–35.

Habermas, J. (1989a) *The Structural Transformation of the Public Sphere*. Cambridge: Polity.

Habermas, J. (1989b) *The Theory of Communicative Action, vol. II: Lifeworld and System*. Boston, MA: Beacon Press.

Habermas, J. (1996) *Between Facts and Norms*. Cambridge: Polity.

Hajer, M.A. (1995) *The Politics of Environmental Discourse: Ecological Modernization and the Policy Process*. Oxford: Clarendon Press.

Hall, C.M., Timothy, D.J. and Duval, D.T. (2003) *Safety and Security in Tourism: Relationships, Management and Marketing*. Binghampton, NY: Haworth Hospitality Press.

Hall, S. (1992) 'The question of cultural identity', in S. Hall, D. Held and A. MacGrew (eds) *Modernity and its Futures*. Cambridge and Milton Keynes: Polity and Open University Press.

Hand, M. and Sandywell, B. (2002) 'E-topia as cosmopolis or citadel', *Theory, Culture & Society*, 19(1–2): 197–225.

Handleman, D. (1990) *Models and Mirrors: Towards an Anthropology of Public Events*. Cambridge: Cambridge University Press.

Hannam, K. (2008) 'The end of tourism? Nomadology and the mobilities paradigm', in J. Tribe (ed.) *Philosophical Issues in Tourism*. Bristol and Toronto: Channel View Publications, 101–116.

Hannam, K., Sheller, M. and Urry, J. (2006) 'Editorial: Mobilities, immobilities and moorings', *Mobilities*, 1(1): 1–22.

Hannerz, U. (1990) 'Cosmopolitans and locals in world culture', *Theory, Culture & Society*, 7(2): 237–251.

Hannerz, U. (1996) *Transnational Connections*. London: Routledge.

Haraway, D. (1991) *Simians, Cyborgs and Women: The Reinvention of Nature*. London: Free Press.

Hardt, M. and Negri, A. (1994) *The Labour of Dionysus: A Critique of the State-Form*. Minneapolis, MN: University of Minnesota Press.

Hardt, M. and Negri, A. (2000) *Empire*. Cambridge: Harvard University Press.

Hardt, M. and Negri, A. (2004) *Multitude: War and Democracy in the Age of Empire*. New York: Penguin.

Harrison, D. (2005) 'Contested narratives in the domain of world heritage', in D. Harrison and M. Hitchcock (eds) *The Politics of World Heritage*. Clevedon: Channel View, 1–10.

Harrison, S. (1990) *Stealing Other People's Names: History and Politics in a Sepik River Cosmology*. Cambridge: Cambridge University Press.

Harrison, S. (1993) 'The commerce of culture in Melanesia', *Man*, 28(1): 139–158.

Hart, K. (2009) 'Money in the making of world society', in C. Hann and K. Hart (eds) *Market and Society: The Great Transformation Today*. Cambridge: Cambridge University Press, 1–16.

Harvey, D. (1989) *The Condition of Postmodernity: An Enquiry into the Conditions of Cultural Change*. Cambridge, MA: Blackwell.

Haybron, D.M. (2005) 'On being happy or unhappy', *Philosophy and Phenomenological Research*, 71(2): 287–317.

Haybron, D.M. (2008) 'Philosophy and the science of subjective well-being', in M. Eid and R.J. Larsen (eds) *The Science of Subjective Well-being*. New York: Guilford Press, 17–43.

Heidegger, M. (1967) *Being and Time*. Oxford: Blackwell.

Heidegger, M. (1975) 'The origin of the work of art', in *Poetry, Language, Thought*, translated by A. Hofstadter. New York: Harper Colophon.

Henning, C. (2002), 'Tourism: Enacting modern myths', in G.M.S. Dann (ed.) *The Tourist as a Metaphor of the Social World*. Wallingford: CABI, 169–188.

Hennion, A. and Latour, B. (1993) *La Passion Musicale*. Paris: Editions Métalié.

Herzfeld, M. (1985) *The Poetics of Manhood: Contest and Identity in a Cretan Mountain Village*. Princeton, NJ: Princeton University Press.

Herzfeld, M. (1987) '"As in your own house": Hospitality, ethnography and the stereotype of the Mediterranean society', in D.D. Gilmore (ed.) *Honor and Shame and the Unity in the Mediterranean*. Washington, DC: American Anthropological Association, 75–89.

Herzfeld, M. (1992) *The Social Production of Indifference: Exploring the Symbolic Roots of Western Democracy*. Oxford: Berg.

Herzfeld, M. (2001) *Anthropology: Theoretical Practice in Culture and Society*. Oxford: Blackwell.

Herzfeld, M. (2002) 'The absent presence: Discourses of crypto-colonialism', *South Atlantic Quarterly*, 101(4): 899–926.

Herzfeld, M. (2004) *The Body Impolitic: Artisans and Artifice in the Global Hierarchy of Value*. Chicago: University of Chicago Press.

Herzfeld, M. (2005) *Cultural Intimacy: Structural Poetics in the Nation-State*, second edn. New York and London: Routledge.

Herzfeld, M. (2006) 'Spatial cleansing: Monumental vacuity and the idea of the West', *Journal of Material Culture*, 11(1/2): 127–149.

Herzfeld, M. (2007) 'Global kinship: Anthropology and the politics of knowing', *Anthropological Quarterly*, 80(2): 313–323.

Herzfeld, M. (2008) 'The ethnographer as theorist', in M. Mazower (ed.) *Networks of Power in Modern Greece*. London: Hurst, 147–168.

Hesmondhalgh, D. (2007) 'Aesthetics and everyday aesthetics: Talking about good and bad music', *European Journal of Cultural Studies*, 10(4): 507–527.

Hesmondhalgh, D. and Baker, S. (2010) *Creative Labour*. London: Routledge.

Hetherington, K. (2003) 'Spatial textures: Place, touch and praesentia', *Environment and Planning A*, 35(11): 1933–1944.

Hewison, R. (1987) *Heritage Industry*. London: Methuen.

Hewison, R. (1989) 'Heritage: An interpretation', in D. Uzzel (ed.) *Heritage Interpretation, vol. I: The Natural and Built Environment*. London: Belhaven, 15–23.

Highmore, B. (2005) *Cityscapes: Cultural Readings in the Material and Symbolic City*. Basingstoke: Palgrave Macmillan.

Hinchberger, B. (2014) 'A short history axé music in Salvador, Bahia', Brazilmax.com, 15 August, www.brazilmax.com/news1.cfm/tborigem/pl_northeast/id/1 (accessed 27 August 2014).

Hochschild, A. (1983) *The Managed Heart*. Berkeley, CA: University of California Press.

Hogan, J. (2003) 'Staging the nation: Gendered and ethnicized discourses of national identity in Olympic Opening ceremonies', *Journal of Sport and Social Issues*, 27(2): 100–123.

Hollinshead, K. (2004) 'A primer in ontological craft: The creative capture of people and places through qualitative research', in J. Phillimore and L. Goodson (eds) *Qualitative Research in Tourism: Ontologies, Epistemologies and Methodologies*. London: Routledge, 63–82.

Holt, R.J. (1989) 'Empire and nation', in R.J. Holt (ed.) *Sport and the British: A Modern History*. Oxford: Clarendon Press, 203–226.

Holton, R. (2005) 'The inclusion of the non-European world in international society, 1870–1920: Evidence from global networks', *Global Networks*, 5(3): 239–259.

Holton, R. (2007) *Making Globalization*. Basingstoke: Palgrave.

Honneth, A. (2007) *Disrespect*. Cambridge: Polity.

hooks, b. (1992) 'Eating the other: Desire and resistance', in b. hooks (eds) *Black Looks: Race and Representation*. Boston: South End Press, 21–40.

Hooton, C. (2014) 'The saddest man in Brazil: Germany defeat leaves fan mournfully embracing World Cup trophy', *The Independent*, 9 July, www.independent.co.uk/sport/football/worldcup/the-saddest-man-in-brazil-germany-defeat-leaves-fan-mournfully-embracing-jules-rimet-9593705.html (accessed 9 July 2014).

Horne, D. (1984) *The Great Museum: The Re-Presentation of History*. London: Pluto.

Horne, J. and Manzenreiter, W. (2006) 'An introduction to the sociology of sport mega-events', in J. Horne and W. Manzenreiter (eds) *Sports Mega-Events: Social Scientific Analyses of a Global Phenomenon*. Malden: Wiley Blackwell, 1–25.

Houlihan, B. and Green, M. (2008) 'Comparative elite sport development', in B. Houlihan and M. Green (eds) *Comparative Elite Sport Development: Systems, Structures and Public Policy*. Oxford: Butterworth-Heinemann, 53–82.

Howells, R. (2014) 'World Cup 2014: Adidas "Brazuca" ball scores with fans', *Forbes*, 11 Junc, www.forbcs.com/sitcs/sap/2014/06/11/world-cup-2014-adidas-brazuca-ball-scores-with-fans/ (accessed 27 July 2014).

Hugh-Jones, S. (1992) 'Yesterday's luxuries, tomorrow's necessities: Business and barter in Northwest Amazonia', in C. Humphrey and S. Hugh-Jones (eds) *Barter, Exchange and Value: An Anthropological Approach*. Cambridge: Cambridge University Press, 42–74.

Humphrey, J. (1994) 'Brazil and the World Cup: Triumph and despair', in J. Sudgen and A. Tomlinson (eds) *Hosts and Champions: Soccer Cultures, National Identities and the USA World Cup*. Aldershot: Ashgate, 65–76.

Humphreys, B.R. and Prokopowizc, S. (2007) 'Assessing the impact of sports mega-events in transition economies: EURO 2012 in Poland and Ukraine', *International Journal of Sport Management and Marketing*, 2(5): 496–509.

Hunt, P. and Frankenberg, R. (1990) 'It's a small world: Disneyland, the family and the multiple re-presentations of the American child', in A. James and A. Pout (eds) *Constructing and Reconstructing Childhood*. Sussex: Falmer Press, 99–117.

IMDB (2002) *Madame Satã*, dir. Karim Aïnouz, www.imdb.com/title/tt0317887/ (accessed 25 August 2014).

Inglis, D. (2005) 'The sociology of art: Between cynicism and reflexivity', in D. Inglis and J. Hughson (eds) *The Sociology of Art: Ways of Seeing*. London: Palgrave, 98–109.

Inglis, D. (2010) 'Mapping global consciousness: Portuguese imperialism and the forging of modern global sensibilities', *Globalizations*, 8(5): 1–20.

Inglis, D. and Hughson, J. (2000) 'The beautiful game and the proto aesthetics of the everyday', *Cultural Values*, 4(3): 279–297.

Inglis, D. and Hughson, J. (2005) '"Art" and Sociology', in D. Inglis and J. Hughson (eds) *The Sociology of Art: Ways of Seeing*. London: Palgrave, 1–7.

Inglis, D. and Robertson, R. (2005) 'The ecumenical analytic: "Globalization", reflexivity and the revolution in Greek historiography', *European Journal of Social Theory*, 8(2): 99–122.

Ingold, T. (1996) *Key Debates in Anthropology*. London: Routledge.

Ingold, T. (2000) *The Perception of the Environment*. London: Routledge.

Ingold, T. (2010) 'Ways of mind-walking: Reading, writing, painting', *Visual Studies*, 25(1): 15–23.

Ingold, T. (2011) *Being Alive: Essays on Movement, Knowledge and Description*. London: Routledge.

Irizarry, D. (2014) 'Shakira to perform at 2014 FIFA World Cup closing ceremony', Axs.com, 6 July, www.axs.com/uk/shakira-to-perform-at-2014-fifa-world-cup-closing-ceremony-13941 (accessed 24 August 2014).

Ivy, M. (1995) *Discourses of the Vanishing: Modernity, Phantasm. Japan*. Chicago: University of Chicago Press.

Jaguaribe, B. and Hetherington, K. (2004) '*Favela* tours: Indistinct and maples representations', in M. Sheller and J. Urry (eds) *Tourism Mobilities: Places to Play, Places in Play*. London: Routledge, 155–166.

Jamal, T. and Hill, S. (2002) 'The home and the world: (Post)touristic spaces of (in) authenticity?', in G.M.S. Dann (ed.) *The Tourist as a Metaphor of the Social World*. Wallingford: CABI, 77–108.

Jamal, T., Everett, J. and Dann, G.M.S. (2003) 'Ecological rationalization and performance resistances in natural area destinations', *Tourist Studies*, 3(2): 143–169.

James, P. (2006) 'Theorizing nation formation in the context of imperialism and globalism', in G. Delanty and K. Kumar (ed.) *The Sage Handbook of Nations and Nationalism*. London: Sage, 369–381.

Jameson, F. (1986) 'Third-world literature in the era of multinational capitalism', *Social Text*, 15 (Fall): 65–88.

Jardine, L. (1997) *Worldly Goods: A New History of the Renaissance*. Basingstoke: Macmillan.

Jardine, L. and Brotton, J. (2000) *Global Interests: Renaissance Art Between East and West*. London: Reaktion.

Jay, M. (1994) *Downcast Eyes: The Denigration of Vision in Twentieth-Century French Thought*. Berkeley: University of California Press.

Jennings, W. (2005) 'London 2012 and the risk management of everything Olympic', *Risk & Regulation*, 10: 7–9.

Jensen, B.B. (2004) 'Case study Sukhumvit Line – or learning from Bangkok', in T. Nielsen, N. Albertsen and P. Hemmersam (eds) *Urban Mutations: Periodization, Scale, Mobility*. Aarhus: Forlag, 184–218.

Jensen, O.B. (2009) 'Flows of meaning, cultures of movements: Urban mobility as meaningful everyday life practice', *Mobilities*, 4(1): 139–158.

Jensen, O.B. (2010) 'Negotiation in motion: Unpacking a geography of mobility', *Space and Culture*, 13(4): 389–402.

Jensen, O.B. (2013) *Staging Mobilities*. London: Routledge.

Jensen, O.B. (2014) *Designing Mobilities*. London: Routledge.

Jensen, O.B. and Richardson, T.D. (2004) *Making European Space: Mobility, Power and Territorial Identity*. London: Routledge.

Johnson, M. (1997) *Beauty and Power: Transgendering and Cultural Transformation in the Southern Philippines*. Oxford: Berg.

Kaplan, A. (2003) 'Transporting the subject: Technologies of mobility and location in the era of globalization', in S. Ahmed, C. Castaneda, A.M. Fortier and M. Sheller (eds) *Uprootings/Regroundings: Questions of Home and Migration*. Oxford: Berg.

Kaufmann, V. (2002) *Rethinking Mobility: Contemporary Sociology*. Aldershot: Ashgate.

Kaufmann, V. (2011) *Rethinking the City: Urban Dynamics and Motility*. Oxford and New York: Routledge.

Kaufmann, V., Bergman, M. and Joye, D. (2004) 'Motility: Mobility as capital', *International Journal of Urban and Regional Research*, 28(4): 745–756.

Kaufmann, V. and Mantulet, B. (2008) 'Between social and spatial mobilities', in W. Ganzler, V. Kaufmann and S. Kesserling (eds) *Tracing Mobilities: Towards a Cosmopolitan Perspective*. Aldershot: Ashgate, 37–56.

Keft-Kennedy, V. (2005) '"How does she do that?" Belly dancing and the horror of a flexible woman', *Women's Studies*, 34(3): 279–300.

Kiddy, E.W. (2000) 'Congrados, clunga, candomble: Our Lady of the Rosary in Minas Gerais, Brazil', *Luso-Brazilian Review*, 37(1): 47–61.

Kirshenblatt-Gimblett, B. (1997) *Destination Cultures*. Berkeley: University of California Press.

Kirshenblatt-Gimblett, B. (2002) 'The de-materialization of culture and the de-acces sing of museum collections', *Museum International*, 54(4): 58–63.

Köbben, A.J.F. (1979) 'Unity and Disunity: Cottica Djuka society as a kinship system', in R. Price (ed.) *Maroon Societies: Rebel Slave Communities in the Americas*, second edn. Baltimore: Johns Hopkins University Press, 320–369.

Kohn, H. (1945) *The Idea of Nationalism: A Study in its Origin and Background*. New York: Macmillan.

Korstanje, M. (2011) 'Influence of history in the encounter of guests and hosts', *Anatolia – An International Journal of Tourism and Hospitality Research*, 22(2): 282–285.

Korstanje, M. (2012) 'South Africa 2010: The sociology of soccer', *Revista de Investigación en Turismo y Desarrollo Local*, 13(5): unpaginated. www.eumed.net/rev/tur ydes/13/southafrica_2010.pdf (accessed 7 August 2014).

Korstanje, M. (2013) 'The sense, landscape and image: How the tourist destination is replicated in postmodernist times', *Pasos: Revista de Turismo y Patrimonio Cultural*, 11(3): 55–65.

Korstanje, M. (2014) 'Conceptual discussion of dark tourism: Suffering, egoism and the depersonalisation of death', www.repotur.gov.ar/handle/123456789/3911?show=full (accessed 26 June 2014).
Korstanje, M. and George, B. (2012) 'Falklands/Malvinas: A re-examination of the relationship between sacralisation and tourism development', *Current Issues in Tourism*, 15(3): 153–165.
Korstanje, M.E., Tzanelli, R., and Clayton, A. (2014) 'Brazilian World Cup 2014, terrorism, tourism and social conflict', *Event Management*, 18(4): 487–491.
Kulick, D. (1998) *Travesti: Sex, Gender, and Culture among Brazilian Transgendered Prostitutes.* Chicago, IL: University of Chicago Press.
Landry, D. and MacLean, G. (1996) 'Introduction', in D. Landry and G. MacLean (eds) *The Spivak Reader.* London: Routledge.
Langlois, G. (2012) 'Meaning, semiotechnologies and participatory media', *Culture Machine,* 12: unpaginated. www.culturemachine.net/index.php/cm/article/view DownloadInterstitial/437/467 (accessed 10 February 2013).
Lash, S. and Urry, J. (1994) *Economies of Signs and Space.* London: Sage.
Law, I. (2010) *Racism and Ethnicity.* London: Pearson Education.
Law, J. (1986) 'On the methods of long distance control: Vessels, navigation, and the Portuguese route to India', in J. Law (ed.) *Power, Action and Belief: A New Sociology of Knowledge?* London: Routledge, 234–263.
Lee, C. and Taylor, T. (2005) 'Critical reflections on the economic impact assessment of a mega-event: The case of 2012 FIFA World Cup', *Tourism Management*, 26(4): 595–603.
Leite Lopes, J.S. (1997) 'Successes and contradictions in "multiracial" Brazilian football', in G. Armstrong and R. Giulianotti (eds) *Entering the Field: New Perspectives on World Football.* Oxford: Berg, 53–86.
Lemke, T. (2001) '"The birth of bio-politics": Michel Foucault's lecture at the Collège de France on neo-liberal governmentality', *Economy and Society*, 30(2): 190–207.
Lennon, J. and Foley, M. (2000) *Dark Tourism.* London: Continuum.
Leoussi, A. (2004) 'The ethno-cultural roots of national art', in M. Guibernaeu and J. Hutchinson (eds) *History and National Destiny.* Oxford: Blackwell, 143–159.
Lessnoff, M. (2002) *Ernest Gellner and Modernity.* Cardiff: University of Wales Press.
Lever, J. (1983) *Soccer Madness.* Chicago: University of Chicago Press.
Levine, R. (1980a) 'The burden of success: Futebol and Brazilian society through the 1970s', *Journal of Popular Culture*, 14(3): 453–464.
Levine, R. (1980b) 'Sport and society: The case of Brazilian futebol', *Luso-Brazilian Review*, 17(2): 233–252.
Lévi-Strauss, C. (1972 [1962]) *The Savage Mind.* London: Weidenfeld and Nicolson.
Lévi-Strauss, C. (1974 [1955]) *Tristes Tropiques*, translated by J. Weightman and D. Weightman. London and New York: Penguin.
Lewis, L.J. (1992) *Ring of Liberation: Deceptive Discourse in Brazilian Capoeira.* Chicago, CA: University of Chicago Press.
Lichrou, M., O'Malley, L. and Patterson, M. (2008) 'Place-product or place narrative (s)? Perspectives in the marketing of tourism destinations', *Journal of Strategic Marketing*, 16(1): 27–39.
Lichterman, P. (2011) 'Thick description as a cosmopolitan practice: A pragmatic reading', in J.C. Alexander, P. Smith and M. Norton (eds) *Interpreting Clifford Geertz: Cultural Investigation in the Social Sciences.* New York: Palgrave Macmillan, 77–92.

Linke, U. (1985) 'Blood as metaphor in proto-Indo-European', *Journal of Indo-European Studies*, 13(3/4): 333–376.

Loizos, P. (1975) *The Greek Gift*. Oxford: Blackwell.

Loizos, P. and Papataxiarchis, E. (1991) 'Gender, sexuality, and the person in Greek culture', in P. Loizos and E. Papataxiarchis (eds) *Contested Identities: Gender and Kinship in Modern Greece*. Princeton: Princeton University Press, 221–235.

Lorente, J.I. and Alonso, P.A. (2014) 'The global discourse – Narratives of scale and the informative management of climate change', *The Global Studies Journal*, 6(3): 1–12.

Lorimer, J. (2010) 'Elephants as companion species: The lively biogeographies of Asian elephant conservation in Sri Lanka', *Transactions of the Institute of British Geographers*, 35: 491–506.

Lourenço, R. (2009) 'Bandeira, porta-bandeira e mestre sala: Elementos de diversas culturas numa tríade soberanas das escolas de samba cariocas', *Textos Escolhidos de Cultura e Arte Populares*, 6(1): 7–18.

Lowenthal, D. (1985) *The Past is a Foreign Country*. Cambridge: Cambridge University Press.

Löwy, M. and Sayre, R. (2001) *Romanticism against the Tide of Modernity*. Durham: Duke University Press.

Luhmann, N. (1999) 'The Concept of Society', in A. Elliott (ed.) *Contemporary Social Theory*. Oxford: Blackwell: 143–155.

Luhrmann, T. (1991) *Persuasions of the Witch's Craft: Ritual Magic in Contemporary England*. Cambridge, MA: Harvard University Press.

Lury, C. (2004) *Brands: The Logos of Global Economy*. London: Sage.

Lyall, J. and Bell, C. (2002) *The Accelerated Sublime: Landscape, Tourism and Identity*. Westport, CT and London: Praeger.

Lynch, J. (1958) *Spanish Colonial Administration, 1782–1810: The Intendant System in the Viceroyalty of the Rio de la Plata*. London: Athlone.

Lynch, P., Germann Molz, J., McIntosch, A., Lugosi, P. and Lashley, C. (2011) 'Theorizing hospitality', *Hospitality & Society*, 1(1): 3–24.

MacCannell, D. (1973) 'Staged authenticity: Arrangements of social space in tourist settings', *American Journal of Sociology*, 79(3): 589–603.

MacCannell, D. (1989) *The Tourist*. London: Macmillan.

Machado-Borges, T. (2009) 'Producing beauty in Brazil', *Vibrant*, 6(1): 208–237.

Machado-Borges, T. (2014) '"Have you ever seen a thief wearing a uniform?!" Struggling for dignity in southeastern Brazil', *Ethnography* (published online 19 August 2014), www.eth.sagepub.com/content/early/2014/08/16/1466138114547623 (accessed 20 August 2014).

Maffesoli, M. (1993) 'The imaginary and the sacred in Durkheim's sociology', *Current Sociology*, 41(2): 59–68.

Maffesoli, M. (1996) *The Time of the Tribes*. London: Sage.

Maguire, J.A. (1999) *Global Sport: Identities, Societies, Civilization*. Cambridge: Polity.

Malbon, B. (1999) *Clubbing*. London: Routledge.

Maleuvre, D. (1999) *Museum Memories: History, Technology, Art*. Stanford, CA: Stanford University Press.

Mannheim, K. (1968 [1936]) *Ideology and Utopia*. New York: Harcourt, Brace & World.

Mannheim, K. (2003) 'The dynamics of spiritual realities', in J. Tanner (ed.) *The Sociology of Art: A Reader*. London: Routledge, 215–220.

Manning, S. and Sydow, J. (2011) 'Projects, paths, and practices: Sustaining and leveraging project-based relationships', *Industrial and Corporate Change*, 20(5): 1369–1402.

Maranhão, S. (2012) *Blood of the Sun: Poems*, translated by Alexis Levitin. Minneapolis: Milkweed Editions.

Marchetti, M.C. (2011) 'Space, mobility and new boundaries: The redefinition of social action', in G. Pellegrino (ed.) *The Politics of Proximity: Mobility and Immobility in Practice*. Aldershot: Ashgate, 17–30.

Marcuse, H. (1955) *Eros and Civilization: A Philosophical Inquiry into Freud*. New York: Beacon Press.

Marcuse, H. (1964) *One-Dimensional Man*. London: Sphere.

Marcuse, P. (1996) 'Space and race in the post-Fordist city', in E. Mingione (ed.) *Urban Poverty and the Underclass*. Oxford: Blackwell, 176–216.

Mason, T. (1995) *Passion of the people? Football in South America*. London: Verso.

Massey, D. (1993) 'Power-geometry and a progressive sense of place', in B. Curties, G. Robertson and L. Tickner (eds) *Mapping the Futures*. New York: Routledge, 59–69.

Massey, D. (1994) *Space, Place and Gender*. Cambridge: Polity.

Massey, D. (2005) *For Space*. London: Sage.

Massumi, B. (2002) *Parables of the Virtual: Movement, Affect, Sensation*. Durham, NC: Duke University Press.

Mauss, M. (1954) *The Gift: Forms and Functions of Exchange in Archaic Societies*. London: Free Press.

Mbembe, A. (2003) 'Necropolitics', translated by L. Meintjes. *Public Culture*, 15(1): 11–40.

McAleer, K. (1994) *Dueling: The Cult of Honour in Fin-de-Siècle Germany*. Princeton, NJ: Princeton University Press.

McCabe, S. and Stokoe, E.H. (2004) 'Place and identity in tourists' accounts', *Annals of Tourism Research*, 31(3): 601–622.

McClintock, A. (1995) *Imperial Leather: Race, Gender and Sexuality in the Colonial Context*. New York: Routledge.

McCreery, J. (1995) 'Negotiating with demons: The uses of magic language', *American Ethnologist*, 22(1): 144–164.

McKee, R. (1999) *Story*. London: Methuen.

McLuhan, M. (1962) *The Guttenberg Galaxy*. London: Routledge and Kegan Paul.

McLuhan, M. (1964) *Understanding the Media*. New York: McGraw.

McNeill, W.H. (1995) *Keeping Together in Time: Dance and the Drill in Human History*. Cambridge, MA: Harvard University Press.

McNulty, P. (2014) 'World Cup 2014: Brazil in shock after humiliation by Germany', BBC Sport, 9 July, www.bbc.co.uk/sport/0/football/28223066 (accessed 9 July 2014).

Meethan, K. (2001) *Tourism in Global Society: Place, Culture, Consumption*. Hampshire: Palgrave.

Melucci, A. (1989) *Nomads of the Present*. London: Hutchinson Radius.

Merleau-Ponty, M. (1962) *Phenomenology of Perception*. London: Routledge and Kegan Paul.

Merleau-Ponty, M. (1965) *The Structure of Behaviour*. London: Methuen.

Merleau-Ponty, M. (1968) *The Visible and the Invisible*. Evanston: Northwestern University Press.

Merton, R.K. (1948) 'The bearing of empirical research on the development of sociological theory', *American Sociological Review*, 13(5): 505–515.

Merton, R.K. and Barber, E. (2004) *The Travels and Adventures of Serendipity.* Princeton, NJ: Princeton University Press.

Metro Lyrics (n.d.a) 'Dar Um Jeito (We Will Find a Way) Lyrics', www.metrolyrics.com/dar-um-jeito-we-will-find-a-way-lyrics-santana.html (accessed 26 August 2014).

Metro Lyrics (n.d.b) 'We Are One (Ole Ola) Lyrics', www.metrolyrics.com/we-are-one-ole-ola-lyrics-pitbull.html (accessed 28 August 2014).

Meyer, M. and Molyneux-Hodgson, S. (2010) 'The dynamics of epistemic communities', *Sociological Research Online*, 15(2): 1.1–4.4. www.socresonline.org.uk/15/2/14.html (accessed 25 May 2010).

Middleton, R. (2000) 'Musical belongings: Western music and its low-other', in G. Born and D. Hesmondhalgh (eds) *Western Music and its Others.* Chicago: University of California Press, 59–85.

Miller, D. (1987) *Material Culture and Mass Consumption.* Oxford and Cambridge, MA: Basil Blackwell.

Miller, R.D. (1986) *A Study of Schiller's 'Letters on the Aesthetic Education of Man'.* Harrogate: The Duchy Press.

Mitchell, T. (1996) *Popular Music and Local Identity.* London: Leicester University Press.

Molotch, H. (2003) *Where Stuff Comes From: How Toasters, Toilets, Computers, and Many Other Things Come to be as They Are.* New York: Routledge.

Molotch, H. (2004) 'How art works: Form and function in the stuff of life', in R. Friedland and J. Mohr (eds) *Matters of Culture.* Cambridge: Cambridge University Press, 341–377.

Monteiro, M. (2009) 'Sedes da Copa de 1950 voltam a ter a honra no Mundial de 2014', Globoesporte.com, 31 May, www.globoesporte.globo.com/platb/memoriaec/2009/05/31/sedes-da-copa-de-1950-voltam-no-mundial-de-2014/ (accessed 25 July 2014).

Moraes, R. (2014) 'Less than half of Brazilians favor hosting World Cup, poll shows', Reuters, 8 April, www.reuters.com/article/2014/04/08/us-worldcup-brazil-idUSBREA3715H20140408 (accessed 27 July 2014).

Morales, E. (2003) *The Latin Beat: The Rhythms and Roots of Latin Music from Bossa Nova to Salsa and Beyond.* Cambridge, MA: Da Capo Press.

Moran, D. (2012) *Husserl's Crisis of the European Sciences and Transcendental Phenomenology: An Introduction.* Cambridge: Cambridge University Press.

Moreiras, A. (1999) 'The order of order: On the reluctant culturalism of anti-subalternist critiques', *Journal of Latin American Cultural Studies*, 8(1): 125–145.

Moreiras, A. (2001) *The Exhaustion of Difference.* Durham, NC: Duke University Press.

Morgan, N. and Pritchard, A. (2005) 'Security and social "sorting": Traversing the surveillance-tourism', *Tourist Studies*, 5(2): 115–132.

Morgan, N., Pritchard, A. and Piggott, R. (2003) 'Destination branding and the role of the stakeholders: The case of New Zealand', *Journal of Vacation Marketing*, 9 (3): 285–299.

Morinis, E.A. (1984) *Pilgrimage in the Hindu Tradition: A Case Study of West Bengal.* Delhi: Oxford University Press.

Morley, G. (2013) 'Brazil boosts World Cup security budget as crime rises', CNN, 5 December, www.edition.cnn.com/2012/12/05/sport/football/brazil-world-cup-security-football/ (accessed 27 July 2014).

Morphy, H. (1991) *Ancestral Connections: Art, and an Aboriginal System of Knowledge.* Chicago: University of Chicago Press.

Mowforth, M. and Munt, I. (1998) *Tourism and Sustainability.* London: Routledge.

Mowforth, M. and Munt, I. (2009) *Tourism and Sustainability,* third edn. London: Routledge.

Muñiz Jr, A.M. (2007) 'Brands and branding', in G. Ritzer (ed.) *The Blackwell Encyclopaedia of Sociology.* Oxford: Blackwell, 357–360.

Muñiz, A.M. and O'Guinn, T.C. (2001) 'Brand community', *Journal of Consumer Culture,* 27(4): 412–432.

Murray, B. (1996) *The World's Game: A History of Soccer.* Urbana, IL: University of Illinois Press.

Nagib, L. (2011) *World Cinema and the Ethics of Realism.* New York: Continuum.

Neder, A. (n.d.) 'Carlinhos Brown: Artist biography', All Music, www.allmusic.com/artist/carlinhos-brown-mn0000171711/biography (accessed 26 August 2014).

Nederveen Pieterse, J. (1998) 'Hybrid modernities: Mélange modernities in Asia', *Sociological Analysis,* 1(3): 75–86.

Nederveen Pieterse, J. (2004) *Globalization and Culture: Global Mélange.* Lanham: Rowman & Littlefield.

Nederveen Pieterse, J. (2006a) 'Globalization as hybridization', in M.G. Durham and D. Kellner (eds) *Media and Cultural Studies.* Malden: Blackwell, 658–680.

Nederveen Pieterse, J. (2006b) 'Emancipatory cosmopolitanism: Towards an agenda', *Development and Change,* 37(6): 1247–1257.

Nederveen Pieterse, J. (2008) 'Globalization the next round: Sociological perspectives', *Futures,* 40(8): 707–720.

Nederveen Pieterse, J. (2009) 'Multipolarity means thinking plural: Modernities', *Protosociology,* 26(1): 19–35.

Nederveen Pieterse, J. and Parekh, B. (1995) 'Shifting imaginaries: Decolonization, internal decolonization, postcoloniality', in J. Nederveen Pieterse and B. Parekh (eds) *The Decolonization of Imagination: Culture, Knowledge and Power.* London: Zed, 1–19.

Negus, K. (1999) *Music Genres and Corporate Cultures.* London: Routledge.

Nelson, M.R. and Deshpande, S. (2013) 'The prevalence of and consumer response to foreign and domestic brand placement in Bollywood movies', *Journal of Advertising,* 42(1): 1–15.

Nervo Codato, A. (2006) 'A political history of the Brazilian transition from military dictatorship to democracy', translated by M. Adelman, *Revista Sociologia e Politica,* 2 (25): 83–106.

Newitt, M. (2005) *A History of Portuguese Overseas Expansion, 1400–1668.* London: Routledge.

Nietzsche, F.W. (1996) *On the Genealogy of Morals.* Oxford: Oxford University Press.

Nora, P. (1989) 'Between memory and history: Les lieux de memoire', *Representations,* 26(2): 7–25.

Nussbaum, M. (2000) 'Aristotle, politics and human capabilities: A response to Anthony, Arneson, Charlesworth, and Mulgan', *Ethics,* 111(1): 102–140.

Nye, R. (1993) *Masculinity and Male Codes of Honor in Modern France.* New York and Oxford: Oxford University Press.

Obrador, P. (2003) 'Being-on-holiday: Tourist dwelling, bodies and place', *Tourist Studies,* 3(1): 47–66.

O'Callaghan, M. (1995) 'Continuities in imagination', in J. Nederveen Pieterse and B. Parekh (eds) *The Decolonization of Imagination: Culture, Knowledge and Power.* London: Zed, 22–42.

Olszewski, B. (2008) '*El cuerpo del baile*: The kinetic and social fundaments of tango', *Body Society*, 14(2): 63–81.

Ong, A. (1999) *Flexible Citizenship: The Cultural logics of Transnationality.* Durham, NC: Duke University Press.

Ong, A. (2006) *Neoliberalism as Exception: Mutations in Citizenship and Sovereignty.* Durham, NC: Duke University Press.

Ong, W. (1982) *Orality and Literacy.* London: Routledge.

O'Reilly, K. (2003) 'When is a tourist? The articulation of tourism and migration in Spain's Costa del Sol', *Tourist Studies*, 3(3): 301–317.

Ousby, I. (1990) *The Englishman's England.* Cambridge: Cambridge University Press.

Owen, J.G. (2005) 'Estimating the cost and benefit of hosting Olympic Games: What can Beijing expect from its 2008 games?', *Industrial Geographer*, 3(1): 1–18.

Panja, T. (2014) 'Corruption to blame for some Brazil World Cup cost', *Bloomberg News*, 23 May, www.businessweek.com/news/2014-05-22/corruption-to-blame-for-some-brazil-world-cup-cost-rises (accessed 27 July 2014).

Parker, R. (2009) *Bodies, Pleasures, and Passions: Sexual Culture in Contemporary Brazil.* Nashville, TN: Vanderbilt University Press.

Parmentier, R. (2006) 'Money walks, people talk: Systemic and transactional dimensions of Palauan exchange', *L'Homme*, 162: 49–80.

Parry, J. and Bloch, M. (1989) 'Introduction: Money and the morality of exchange', in J. Parry and M. Bloch (eds) *Money and the Morality of Exchange.* Cambridge: Cambridge University Press, 1–32.

Parry, R. (2003) 'Episteme and techne', in E.N. Zalta (ed.) *The Stanford Encyclopedia of Philosophy*, www.plato.stanford.edu/archives/sum2003/entries/episteme-techne/ (accessed 12 September 2014).

Passarinho, N. and Matoso, F. (2014) 'Em balanço da Copa, Dilma diz que Brasil derrotou prognósticos "terríveis"', *Globoesporte*, 14 July, www.g1.globo.com/politica/noticia/2014/07/em-balanco-da-copa-dilma-afirma-que-brasil-derrotou-pessimistas.html (accessed 25 July 2014).

Patke, R.S. (2000) 'Benjamin's arcades project and the postcolonial city', *Diacritics*, 30 (4): 2–14.

Pattullo, P. (1996) *Last Resorts: The Cost of Tourism in the Caribbean.* London: Cassell-Latin American Bureau.

Peck, J. (2003) 'Geography and public policy: Mapping the penal state', *Progress in Human Geography*, 27(2): 222–232.

Peirce, C. (1992) *The Essential Peirce: Selected Philosophical Writings, vol. I: 1867–93*, edited by N. Houser and C. Kloesel. Bloomington, IN: Indiana University Press.

Peirce, C. (1998) 'The Harvard lectures of pragmaticism', in Nathan Houser and Christian Kloesel (eds) *The Essential Peirce: Selected Philosophical Writings, vol. II: 1893–1913.* Bloomington, IN: Indiana University Press.

Pellauer, D. (2007) *Ricoeur: A Guide for the Perplexed.* New York: Continuum.

Pellegrino, G. (2007) 'Discourses on mobility and technological mediation: The texture of ubiquitous interaction', *PsychNology Journal*, 5(1): 59–81.

Pellegrino, G. (2011) 'Introduction: Studying (Im)mobility through a politics of proximity', in G. Pellegrino (ed.) *The Politics of Proximity: Mobility and Immobility in Practice.* Aldershot: Ashgate, 1–16.

Perkins, H.C. and Thorns, D.C. (2001) 'Gazing or performing? Reflections on Urry's tourist gaze in the context of contemporary experience in the Antipodes', *International Sociology*, 16(2): 185–204.

Petchesky, B. (2014) 'Meet "the Saddest Man in Brazil"', *Deadspin*, 9 July, www.deadspin.com/meet-the-saddest-man-in-brazil-1602350870 (accessed 23 September 2014).

Peterson, R.A. and Bennett, A. (2004) 'Introducing the scenes perspective', in A. Bennett and R.A. Peterson (eds) *Music Scenes*. Nashville: University of Vanderbilt Press.

Phillips, T. (2009) 'Brazil looks to transform sporting greatness into gold on world stage', *The Observer*, 4 October, www.theguardian.com/world/2009/oct/04/brazil-2016-olympics-economy (accessed 20 July 2014).

Picard, D. (1997) 'Cultural tourism, nation-building and regional culture', in M. Picard and R.E. Wood (eds) *Tourism, Ethnicity and the State in Asia and Pacific Societies*. Honolulu: University of Hawaii Press, 181–214.

Pillay, U. and Bass, O. (2008) 'Mega-events as a response to poverty reduction: The 2010 FIFA World Cup and it urban development implications', *Urban Forum*, 19: 329–346.

Plato (1974) *The Republic*. London: Hackett.

Polanyi, K. (1977) *The Livelihood of Man*, edited by H.W. Pearson. New York: Academic Press.

Popovitch, A. (2011) 'Debating Latin American aesthetic theory: Beatriz Sarlo on the autonomy of art', *Bulletin of Latin American Research*, 31(1): 36–50.

Pratt, M.L. (1992) *Imperial Eyes: Travel Writing and Transculturation*. London and New York: Routledge.

Presenza, A. (2013) 'Planning tourism through sporting events', *International Journal of Event and Festival Management*, 4(2): 125–139.

Production House (2014) 'FIFA World Cup Closing Ceremony 2014', YouTube, 14 July, www.youtube.com/watch?v=xxngFeLsd3U (accessed 24 July 2014).

Putnam, R. (1993) *Making Democracy Work: Civic Tradition in Modern Italy*. Princeton, NJ: Princeton University Press.

Radin, M.J. (1996) *Contested Commodities*. Cambridge, MA: Harvard University Press.

Ramchandani, G.M. and Coleman, R.J. (2012) 'The inspirational effects of three major sport events', *International Journal of Event and Festival Management*, 3(3): 257–271.

Rancière, J. (2004) *The Politics of Aesthetics*, translated by G. Rockill. London and New York: Bloomsbury.

Rancière, J. (2011) *The Emancipated Spectator*. London: Verso.

Reddy, W.M. (1984) *The Rise of Market Culture: The Textile Trade and French Society, 1750–1900*. Cambridge: Cambridge University Press.

RedShark News (2014) 'Sony's astonishing World Cup statistics', 22 May, www.redsharknews.com/business/item/1701-sony-s-astonishing-world-cup-statistics (accessed 28 July 2014).

Reichmann, R. (ed.) (1999) *Race in Contemporary Brazil: From Indifference to Inequality*. University Park, PA: University of Pennsylvania Press.

Reijnders, S. (2009) 'Watching the detectives: Inside the guilty landscapes of Inspector Morse, Baantjer and Wallander', *European Journal of Communication*, 24(2): 165–181.

Reuters (2013) 'Brazil beats Japan, protests spoil Confederations Cup opening day', 15 June, www.voanews.com/content/brazil-japan-confederations-cup/1682679.html (accessed 28 July 2014).

Reuters (2014) 'German soccer boss says players' "gaucho" dance not disrespectful', 16 July, www.sports.yahoo.com/news/german-soccer-boss-says-players-gaucho-da

nce-not-193001390–sow.html?soc_src=mediacontentsharebuttons (accessed 21 September 2014).

Ricoeur, P. (1988) *Time and Narrative*, vol. II. New York: Columbia University Press.

Ritchie, J.R. (2000) 'Turning 16 days into 16 years of through Olympic legacies', *Event Management*, 6(1): 155–165.

Ritzer, G. (2006) 'Globalization and McDonaldization: does it all amount to … nothing?', in G. Ritzer (ed.) *McDonaldization: The Reader*, second edn. Thousand Oaks, CA: Pine Forge Press, 335–348.

Ritzer, G. (ed.) (2012) 'Environment and Development, Rio Declaration 1992', in *The Wiley-Blackwell Encyclopedia of Globalization*. Oxford: Wiley Blackwell.

Ritzer, G. and Liska, A. (1997) '"McDisneyization" and "post-tourism": Contemporary perspectives on contemporary tourism', in C. Rojek and J. Urry (eds) *Touring Cultures: Transformations of Travel and Theory*. London and New York: Routledge, 96–112.

Robertson, R. (1992) *Globalization: Social Theory and Global Culture*. London: Sage.

Robertson, R. (1994) 'Globalisation or glocalisation?', *Journal of International Communication*, 1(1): 33–52.

Robertson, R. (1995) 'Glocalization: Time-space and homogeneity-heterogeneity', in M. Featherstone, S. Lash and R. Robertson (eds) *Global Modernities*. London: Sage, 25–44.

Robins, K. (2000) 'Encountering globalization', in D. Held and A. McGrew (eds) *The Global Transformations Reader: An Introduction to the Globalization Debate*. Cambridge: Polity, 239–246.

Roche, M. (1996) 'Mega-events and micro-modernization', in Y. Apostolopoulos, S. Leivadi and A. Yannakis (eds) *The Sociology of Tourism*. London: Routledge, 315–347.

Roche, M. (2000) *Mega-Events and Modernity*. London: Routledge.

Roche, M. (2002) 'The Olympics and "global citizenship"', *Citizenship Studies*, 6(1): 165–181.

Roche, M. (2006) 'Nations, mega-events and international culture', in G. Delanty and K. Kumar, *The Sage Handbook of Nations and Nationalism*. London: Sage, 260–272.

Rodowick, D. (1997) *Gilles Deleuze's Time Machine*. Durham, NC: Duke University Press.

Rodrigues, J.N. (2008) 'The two oldest matrixes of world discoveries', *Economia Global e Gestão*, 13(1): 9–23.

Rodrigues, J. and Devezas, T.C. (2007) *Pioneers of Globalization: Why the Portuguese Surprised the World*. Vila Nova de Famalicão: Centro Atlantico.

Román-Velázquez, P. (1999) *The Making of Latin London: Salsa Music, Place and Identity*. Aldershot: Ashgate.

Roper, M. (2014) 'World Cup witch doctor reveals magic formula to get England to the final in Brazil', *The Mirror*, 7 June, www.mirror.co.uk/news/uk-news/world-cup-witch-doctor-reveals-3659866 (accessed 2 October 2014).

Rosenau, J. (1990) *Turbulence in World Politics*. Brighton: Harvester.

Rowe, D. (2003) 'Sport and the repudiation of the global', *International Review for the Sociology of Sport*, 38(3): 281–294.

Rumford, C. (2006) 'Theorizing borders', *European Journal of Social Theory*, 9(2): 155–170.

Rumford, C. (2008) 'Citizens and borderwork in Europe', *Space and Polity*, 12(1): 1–12.

Russell-Wood, A.J.R. (2002a) 'Centers and peripheries in the Luso-Brazilian world, 1500–1808', in C. Daniels and M.V. Kennedy (eds) *Negotiated Empires: Centers and Peripheries in the Americas, 1500–1820*. New York: Routledge, 105–142.

Russell-Wood, A.J.R. (2002b) *Slavery in Freedom in Colonial Brazil*, new edn. Oxford: Oneworld.

Sacks, O. (2011) *Musicophilia*. London: Picador.

Sahlins, M. (1965) 'On the sociology of primitive exchange', in M. Banton (ed.) *The Relevance of Models for Social Anthropology*. London: Tavistock, 139–236.

Sahlins, M. (1972) *Stone Age Economics*. Chicago: Aldine.

Sahlins, M. (1976) *Culture and Practical Reason*. Chicago: University of Chicago Press.

Sahlins, M. (2013a) 'On the Culture of Material Value and the cosmography of riches', *HAU: Journal of Ethnographic Theory*, 3(2): 161–195.

Sahlins, M. (2013b) *What Kinship is – and is Not*. Chicago: University of Chicago Press.

Said, E. (1978) *Orientalism*. London: Penguin Books.

Said, E. (1994) *Culture and Imperialism*. London: Vintage.

Salazar, N. (2012) 'The (im)mobility of tourism imaginaries', in M. Smith and G. Richards (eds) *The Routledge Handbook of Heritage Tourism*. London: Routledge, 34–39.

Sallnow, M.J. (1981) 'Communitas reconsidered: The sociology of Andean pilgrimage', *Man*, 16(2): 163–182.

Sallnow, M.J. (1987) *Pilgrims of the Andes: Regional Cults in Cusco*. Washington, DC: Smithsonian Institution Press.

Salvatore, R. (1998) 'The enterprise of knowledge: Representational machines of informal empire', in G. Joseph, C. Legrand and R. Salvatore (eds) *Close Encounters of Empire: Writing the Cultural History of U.S.-Latin American Relations*. Durham, NC: Duke University Press, 69–104.

Samuels, D.W., Maintjes, L., Ochoa, A.M. and Porcello, T. (2010) 'Soundscapes: Toward a sounded anthropology', *Annual Review of Anthropology*, 39: 329–345.

Sánchez Taylor, J. (2000) 'Tourism and "embodied" commodities: Sex tourism in the Caribbean', in S. Clift and S. Carter (eds) *Tourism and Sex*. London and New York: Pinter, 168–178.

Sandywell, B. (2011) *Dictionary of Visual Discourse*. Surrey: Ashgate.

Santana (The Official Carlos Santana Website) (n.d.) 'Carlos Santana Biography', www.santana.com/Carlos-Santana-Biography/ (accessed 26 August 2014).

Santana, G. (2000) 'An overview of contemporary tourism development in Brazil', *International Journal of Contemporary Hospitality Management*, 12(7): 424–430.

Santos, A.C. (2004) 'Framing Portugal: Representational dynamics', *Annals of Tourism Research*, 31(1): 122–138.

Sassen, S. (2001) *The Global City*. Princeton, NJ: Princeton University Press.

Sassen, S. (ed.) (2002) *Global Networks, Linked Cities*. London: Routledge.

Savelli, A. (2009) 'Tourism in Italian sociological thought and study', in G.M.S. Dann and G. Parrinello (eds) *The Sociology of Tourism: European Origins and Developments*. Bingley: Emerald, 131–168.

Sayer, A. (1999) 'Valuing culture and economy', in L. Ray and A. Sayer (eds) *Culture and Economy After the Cultural Turn*. London: Sage, 53–75.

Sayer, A. (2000) 'Moral economy and political economy', *Studies in Political Economy*, 61(2): 9–103.

Sayer, A. (2003) '(De-)commodification, consumer culture and moral economy', *Environment and Planning D*, 21(3): 341–357.

Schafer, R.M. (1994) *The Soundscape*. Rochester: Destiny.

Scheler, M. (2003) *Ressentiment*. Madison, WI: Marquette University Press.

Schmitt, C. (1996) *Land and Sea*. Corvallis, OR: Plutarch Press.

Schmitt, C. (2006) *The Nomos of the Earth in the International Law of Jus Publicum Europaeum*. New York: Telos.

Schütz, A. (1945) 'On multiple realities', *Phenomenology and Social Research*, 5(4): 533–576.

Schütz, A. and Luckmann, T. (1973) *Structures of the Life-World*. Evanston: Northwest University Press.

Selwyn, T. (1996) *The Tourist Image: Myths and Myth-Making in Tourism*. Chichester: Wiley.

Sen, A. (1999) *Development as Freedom*. Oxford: Oxford University Press.

Shapiro, M. (2002) *Carlos Santana: Back on Top*. New York: St Martin's Press.

Shaw, L. (1999) *The Social History of the Brazilian Samba*. Aldershot: Ashgate.

Sheller, M. (2000) *Democracy after Slavery: Black Publics and Peasant Radicalism in Haiti and Jamaica*. Oxford and London: Macmillan.

Sheller, M. (2003) *Consuming the Caribbean: From Arawaks to Zombies*. New York: Routledge.

Sheller, M. (2004) 'Demobilizing and remobilizing Caribbean paradise', in M. Sheller and J. Urry (eds) *Tourism Mobilities: Places to Play, Places in Play*. London: Routledge, 13–21.

Sheller, M. (2012a) *Citizenship from Below: Erotic Agency and Caribbean Freedom*. Durham, NC: Duke University Press.

Sheller, M. (2012b) 'Mobilities', in G. Ritzer (ed.) *The Wiley-Blackwell Encyclopaedia of Globalization*. New York: Wiley Blackwell.

Sheller, M. (2014a) 'Sociology after the mobilities turn', in P. Adey, D. Bissell, K. Hannam, P. Merriman and M. Sheller (eds) *The Routledge Handbook of Mobilities*. London and New York: Routledge, 45–54.

Sheller, M. (2014b) 'The new mobilities paradigm for a live sociology', *Current Sociology*, 1(23) (published online, 23 May 2014), www.csi.sagepub.com/content/early/2014/05/23/0011392114533211.abstract (accessed 25 September 2014).

Sheller, M. and Urry, J. (2004) 'Places to play, places in play', in M. Sheller and J. Urry (eds) *Tourism Mobilities: Places to Play, Places in Play*. London: Routledge, 1–10.

Sheller, M. and Urry, J. (2006) 'The new mobilities paradigm', *Environment and Planning A*, 38(2): 207–226.

Shields, R. (1991) *Places on the Margin: Alternative Geographies of Modernity*. London: Routledge.

Shilling, C. (1999) 'Towards an embodied understanding of the structure/agency relationship', *British Journal of Sociology*, 50(4): 543–562.

Shils, E. (1975) *Center and Periphery: Essays in Macrosociology*. Chicago: University of Chicago Press.

Shohat, E. (1992) 'Notes on the "post-colonial"', *Social Text*, 31/32: 99–113.

Shurmer-Smith, P. and Hannam, K. (1994) *Worlds of Desire, Realms of Power: A Cultural Geography*. London: Edward Arnold.

Silk, M. (2001) 'Together we're one? The "place" of the nation in media representations of the 1998 Kuala Lumpur Commonwealth Games', *Sociology of Sport Journal*, 18(3): 277–301.

Silva, M.L. (2014) 'Queer sex vignettes from a Brazilian favela: An ethnographic striptease', *Ethnography* (published online, 20 May 2014), www.eth.sagepub.com/content/early/2014/06/10/1466138114534335 (accessed 3 October 2014).

Simmel, G. (1906) 'The sociology of secrecy and secret societies', *American Journal of Sociology*, 11(4): 441–498.

Simmel, G. and Wolff, K.H. (1950) *The Sociology of Georg Simmel*. New York: Free Press.

Simoni, V. (2008) 'Shifting power: The destabilisation of asymmetries in the realm of tourism in Cuba', *Tsantsa*, 13: 89–97.

Simoni, V. (2013) 'Intimate stereotypes: The vicissitudes of being Caliente in touristic Cuba', *Civilizations*, 61(2): 181–198.

Singh, S. (2012) 'Slow travel and Indian culture: Philosophical and practical aspects', in S. Fullagar, K. Markwell and E. Wilson (eds) *Slow Tourism: Experiences and Mobilities*. Bristol: Channel View, 214–226.

Skalník, P. (2003) 'Gellner on modernity', *Social Evolution & History*, 2(2): 203–224.

Skeggs, B. (1997) *Formations of Class and Gender*. London: Sage.

Skeggs, B. (2004) *Class, Self, Culture*. London: Routledge.

Skidmore, T.E. (2003) 'Racial mixture and affirmative action: The cases of Brazil and the United States', *American Historical Review*, 108(5): 1391–1396.

Skoll, G.R. and Korstanje, M. (2014) 'Urban heritage, gentrification and tourism in Riverwest and Albasto', *Journal of Heritage Tourism* (published online, 15 April 2014), www.tandfonline.com/doi/abs/10.1080/1743873X.2014.890624#.U8kgTPldWSo (accessed 18 July 2014).

Skouteri-Didaskalou, N. (1980) 'I thlipsi ton *Thliveron Tropikon* kai o vathos miden tis anthropological grafis' [The sadness of *Pitiable Tropics* and the mark of zero for anthropological writing], *Ethologia*, 31: 57–65.

Slater, J. (2004) 'Brand Louisiana: Capitalising on music and cuisine', in N. Morgan, A. Pritchard and R. Pride (eds) *Destination Branding: Creating the Unique Destination Proposition*. Oxford: Elsevier Butterworth-Heinemann, 226–241.

Slatta, R.W. (1992) *Gauchos and the Vanishing Frontier*. Lincoln: University of Nebraska Press.

Sloterdijk, P. (2009) 'Geometry in the Colossal: The project of metaphysical globalization', *Environment and Planning D: Society and Space*, 27(1): 29–40.

Smith, A.D. (1995) *Nations and Nationalism in a Global Era*. Cambridge: Polity.

Smith, A.D. (1999) *Myths and Memories of the Nation*. Oxford and New York: Oxford University Press.

Smith, A.D. (2000) *The Nation in History*. Hanover, NH: University Press of New England.

Smith, A.D. (2006) 'Ethnicity and nationalism', in G. Delanty and K. Kumar (eds) *The SAGE Handbook of Nations and Nationalism*. London: Sage, 169–181.

Smith, P. (2008) 'The Balinese cockfight decoded: Reflections on Geertz, the strong programme and structuralism', *Cultural Sociology*, 2(2): 169–186.

Smith, R. (2007) *Being Human: Historical Knowledge and the Creation of Human Nature*. New York: Columbia University Press.

Spivak, G. (1988) 'Can the subaltern speak?', in C. Nelson and L. Grossberg (eds) *Marxism and the Interpretation of Culture*. Urbana: University of Illinois Press, 271–313.

Spivak, G. (1993) *Outside the Teaching Machine*. London: Routledge.

Spivak, G. (1999) *A Critique of Postcolonial Reason: Towards a Critique of the Vanishing Present*. Cambridge, MA: Harvard University Press.

Squires, N. (2014) 'World Cup 2014: Amazonian shaman predicts defeat for England against Italy', *The Telegraph*, 11 June, www.telegraph.co.uk/sport/football/world-cup/10891482/World-Cup-2014-Amazonian-shaman-predicts-defeat-for-England-against-Italy.html (accessed 2 October 2014).

Stasch, R. (2009) *Society of Others: Kinship and Mourning in a West Papuan Place.* Berkeley: University of California Press.

Steger, M.B. (2008) *The Rise of the Global Imaginary: Political Ideologies from the French Revolution to the Global War on Terror.* Oxford: Oxford University Press.

Steinberg, P. (2000) 'Lines of division, lines of connection: Stewardship in the world ocean', *The Geographical Review*, 89(2): 254–264.

Stephens, T. (1989) *Dictionary of Latin American Racial and Ethnic Terminology.* Gainesville: University of Florida Press.

Stevenson, N. (2002) *Cultural Citizenship.* Buckingham and Philadelphia, PA: Open University Press.

Stewart, F.H. (1994) *Honour.* Chicago: University of Chicago Press.

Stiegler, B. (1998) *Technics and Time, vol. I: The Fault of Epimetheus.* Stanford, CA: Stanford University Press.

Stiegler, B. (2003) 'Technics of decision', *Anglaki*, 8(2): 151–168.

Stocking, G. (1982) 'Afterword: A view from the center', *Ethnos*, 47(1/2): 172–186.

Strain, E. (2003) *Public Places, Private Journeys: Ethnography, Entertainment and the Tourist Gaze.* New Jersey: Rutgers University Press.

Straw, W. (1991) 'Systems of articulation, logics of change: Communities and scenes in popular music', *Cultural Studies*, 5(3): 368–388.

Szerszynski, B. and Urry, J. (2006) 'Visuality, mobility and the cosmopolitan: Inhabiting the world from afar', *The British Journal of Sociology*, 57(1): 113–131.

Tanner, J. (ed.) (2003) *The Sociology of Art.* London: Routledge.

Tarde, G. (1903) *The Laws of Imitation.* New York: Henry Holt & Co.

Tate, S. (2011) 'Heading South: Love/sex, necropolitics and decolonial romance', *Small Axe*, 35: 43–58.

Taylor, C. (2004) *Modern Social Imaginaries.* Durham, NC: Duke University Press.

Taylor, T. (2010) *The Artificial Ape.* New York: Palgrave Macmillan.

Telles, E.E. (2006) *Race in Another America: Race Mixture, Exclusion and State in Brazil.* Princeton, NJ: Princeton University Press.

Therborn, G. (1995) 'Routes to/through modernity', in M. Featherstone, S. Lash and R. Robertson (eds) *Global Modernities.* London: Sage, 124–139.

Thomas, N. (1994) *Colonialism's Culture: Anthropology, Travel and Government.* Cambridge: Polity.

Thompson, J. (1995) *The Media and Modernity.* Cambridge: Polity.

Thompson, P. (2012) 'What is concrete about Ernst Bloch's "concrete utopia"?', in M. Hviid Jacobsen and K. Tester (eds) *Utopia: Social Theory and Future.* Farnham: Ashgate.

Thompson, R.F. (1984) *Flash of the Spirit: African and Afro-American Art and Philosophy.* New York: Vintage.

Thompson Drewal, M. (1992) *Yoruba Ritual: Performers, Play, Agency.* Bloomington, IN: Indiana University Press.

Thornton, T.M. (1988) 'On the trail of voodoo: African Christianity in Africa and the Americas', *The Americas*, 55: 261–278.

Thrift, N. (1996) 'Inhuman geographies: Landscapes of speed, light and power', in N. Thrift (ed.) *Spatial Formations.* London: Sage, 256–310.

Thrift, N. (2006) 'Re-inventing invention: New tendencies in capitalist commodification', *Economy and Society*, 36(2), 279–306.

Thrift, N. (2007) *Non-representational Theory: Space, Politics, Affect*. London: Routledge.

Thrift, N. (2011) 'Lifeworld Inc – and what to do about it', *Environment and Planning D: Society and Space*, 29(1): 5–26.

Till, K.E. (2005) *The New Berlin: Memory, Politics, Place*. Minneapolis: University of Minnesota Press.

Todd, S.C. (2008) 'Nature, Beauty and Tourism', in J. Tribe (ed.) *Philosophical Issues in Tourism*. Bristol and Toronto: Channel View Publications, 154–170.

Tolia-Kelly, D.P. (2010) *Landscape, Race and Memory: Material Ecologies of Home*. Farnham: Ashgate.

Tomaselli, K.G. (2007) '"Op die grond": Writing in the san/d, surviving crime', in K.G. Tomaselli (ed.) *Writing in the San/d*. New York: Altamira Press, 39–58.

Tomlinson, A. (1996) 'Olympic spectacle: Opening ceremonies and some paradoxes of globalization', *Media, Culture & Society*, 18(4): 583–602.

Tomlinson, A. (2005) *Sport and Leisure Cultures*. Minneapolis, MN: University of Minnesota Press.

Tomlinson, A. and Young, C. (2006) 'Introduction', in A. Tomlinson and C. Yound (eds) *National Identity and Global Sports Events*. New York: SUNY, 1–14.

Tomlinson, J. (2000) 'Proximity politics', *Information, Communication and Society*, 3(3): 402–414.

Tonkonoff, S. (2013) 'A new social physic: The sociology of Gabriel Tarde and its legacy', *Current Sociology*, 61(3): 267–282.

Tönnies, F. (1957) *Community and Society: Gemeinschaft und Gesellschaft*. East Lansing: Michigan State University Press.

Tribe, J. (2004) 'Knowing about tourism: Epistemological issues', in J. Phillimore and L. Goodson (eds) *Qualitative Research in Tourism: Ontologies, Epistemologies and Methodologies*. London: Routledge, 46–62.

Tribe, J. (2008) 'Philosophical issues in tourism', in J. Tribe (ed.) *Philosophical Issues in Tourism*. Bristol and Toronto: Channel View Publications, 3–22.

Trondman, M. (2011) '"To locate in the tenor of their setting the sources of their spell": Clifford Geertz and the "strong" programme in cultural sociology', in J.C. Alexander, P. Smith and M. Norton (eds) *Interpreting Clifford Geertz: Cultural Investigation in the Social Sciences*. New York: Palgrave Macmillan, 145–166.

Tuan, Y.F. (1974) *Topophilia*. New York: Columbia University Press.

Tudor, A. (1992) 'Them and us: Story and stereotype in TV World coverage' *European Journal of Communication*, 7(3): 391–413.

Turner, B.S. (1984) *The Body and Society: Explorations in Social Theory*. London: Sage.

Turner, V. (1969) *The Ritual Process: Structure and Anti-Structure*. New York: Aldine de Gruyter.

Turner, V. (1974a) *Dramas, Fields and Metaphors: Symbolic Action in Human Society*. Ithaca, NY: Cornell University Press.

Turner, V. (1974b) 'Liminal to liminoid, play flow and ritual: An essay in comparative symbolology', *Rice University Studies*, 50: 53–92.

Turner, V. and Turner, E. (1978) *Image and Pilgrimage in Christian Culture: Anthropological Perspectives*. Oxford: Basil Blackwell.

Turner Bushnell, A. and Greene, J.P. (2002) 'Peripheries, centers and the construction of early modern American empires', in C. Daniels and M.V. Kennedy (eds)

Negotiated Empires: Centers and Peripheries in the Americas, 1500–1820. New York: Routledge, 1–14.

Turton, A. (2000) 'Introduction to civility and savagery', in A. Turton (ed.) *Civility and Savagery: Social Identity in Tai States*. Surrey: Curzon Press, 3–32.

Tyers, A. (2014) 'World Cup 2014 opening ceremony: Live', *The Telegraph*, 12 June, www.telegraph.co.uk/sport/football/world-cup/10894619/World-Cup-2014-opening-ceremony-live.html (accessed 19 July 2014).

Tzanelli, R. (2002a) 'Haunted by the "enemy" within: Brigandage, Vlachian/Albanian Greekness, Turkish "contamination" and narratives of Greek nationhood in the Dilessi/Marathon affair (1870)', *Journal of Modern Greek Studies*, 20(1): 47–74.

Tzanelli, R. (2002b) 'Unclaimed colonies: Anglo-Greek identities through the prism of the Dilessi (Marathon) Murders (1870)', *Journal of Historical Sociology*, 15(2): 169–191.

Tzanelli, R. (2004) 'Giving Gifts (and then Taking Them Back): Identity, Reciprocity and Symbolic Power in the Context of Athens 2004', *The Journal of Cultural Research*, 8(4): 425–446.

Tzanelli, R. (2006) '"Impossible is a fact": Greek nationalism and international recognition in Euro 2004', *Media, Culture & Society*, 28(4): 483–503.

Tzanelli, R. (2007) *The Cinematic Tourist: Explorations in Globalization, Culture and Resistance*. London: Routledge.

Tzanelli, R. (2008) *Nation-Building and Identity in Europe: The Dialogics of Reciprocity*. Basingstoke: Palgrave Macmillan.

Tzanelli, R. (2010) 'Mediating Cosmopolitanism: Crafting an Allegorical Imperative through Beijing 2008', *International Review of Sociology*, 20(2): 215–241.

Tzanelli, R. (2011) *Cosmopolitan Memory in Europe's 'Backwaters': Rethinking Civility*. Abingdon and New York: Routledge.

Tzanelli, R. (2012a) 'Domesticating Sweet Sadness: Thessaloniki's Glyká as a Travel Narrative', *Cultural Studies – Critical Methodologies*, 12(2): 159–172.

Tzanelli, R. (2012b) 'Domesticating the tourist gaze in Thessaloniki's Prigipos', *Ethnography*, 13(3): 278–305.

Tzanelli, R. (2012c) 'The Greek Fall: Simulacral thanatotourism in Europe', *The Global Studies Journal*, 5(1): 105–120.

Tzanelli, R. (2013a) 'From (dis)embodied journeys to "artscapes": Belly dancing as a digital "travelling culture"', in S. Cohen, T. Duncan and M. Thulemark (eds) *Lifestyle Mobilities: Intersections of Travel, Leisure and Migration*. Aldershot: Ashgate, 65–82.

Tzanelli, R. (2013b) *Heritage in the Digital Era: Cinematic Tourism and the Activist Cause*. London: Routledge.

Tzanelli, R. (2013c) *Olympic Ceremonialism and the Performance of National Character: From London 2012 to Rio 2016*. Basingstoke: Palgrave Pivot.

Tzanelli, R. (2014) 'Embodied art and aesthetic performativity in the London 2012 handover to Rio (2016)', *The Global Studies Journal*, 6(2): 13–24.

Tzanelli, R. and Yar, M. (2014) '*Breaking Bad*, making good: Notes on a televisual tourist industry', *Mobilities* (published online, 10 July 2014), www.tandfonline.com/doi/abs/10.1080/17450101.2014.929256#.VCQ5dfldWSo (accessed 25 September 2014).

UNESCO (2003) 'Convention on the safeguarding of immaterial cultural heritage', www.unesco.org/culture/ich/index.php?pg=00006 (accessed 14 July 2014).

UNESCO Culture Sector – Intangible Heritage (2003) 'The States Parties to the Convention for the Safeguarding of the Intangible Cultural Heritage', www.unesco.org/culture/ich/?pg=00024 (accessed 14 July 2014).

Urquìa, N. (2005) 'The rebranding of salsa in London's dance clubs: How an ethnicised form of cultural capital was institutionalised', *Leisure Studies*, 24(4): 385–397.

Urry, J. (1995) *Consuming Places.* London: Routledge.

Urry, J. (2002) *The Tourist Gaze*, second edn. London: Routledge.

Urry, J. (2003) *Global Complexity.* Cambridge: Polity.

Urry, J. (2004) 'Death in Venice', in M. Sheller and J. Urry (eds) *Tourism Mobilities: Places to Play, Places in Play.* London and New York: Routledge, 205–215.

Urry, J. (2007) *Mobilities.* Cambridge: Polity.

Urry, J. (2011) *Climate Change and Society.* Cambridge: Polity.

Urry, J. (2014) *Offshoring*. Cambridge: Polity.

Urry, J. and Larsen, J. (2011) *The Tourist Gaze 3.0*, third edn. London: Sage.

Uteng, T.P. and Cresswell, T. (2008) *Gendered Mobilities.* Aldershot: Ashgate.

Valente, F.L. (2012) 'Afterword', in S. Maranhão, *Blood of the Sun – Poems*, translated by A. Levitin. Minneapolis, MN: Milkweed, 147–151.

van der Westhuizen, J. (2004) 'Marketing Malaysia as a model modern Muslim state: The significance of the 16th Commonwealth Games', *Third World Quarterly*, 25(7): 1277–1297.

Van Gennep, A. (1960 [1909]) *The Rites of Passage.* Chicago: University of Chicago Press.

Varela, F.J. (1999) 'The specious present: A neurophenomenology of time consciousness', in J. Petitot, F.J. Varela, G. Pachoud and J.M. Roy (eds) *Naturalizing Phenomenology: Issues in Contemporary Phenomenology and Cognitive Science.* Stanford, CA: Stanford University Press, 265–314.

Veblen, T. (1899) *The Theory of the Leisure Class.* New York: Macmillan.

Veblen, T. (1904) *The Theory of Business Enterprise.* New York: Schreibner's Sons.

Veblen, T. (1914) *The Instinct of Workmanship and the State of the Industrial Arts.* New York: Macmillan.

Veijola, S. (2009) 'Tourism as work', *Tourist Studies*, 9(2): 83–87.

Veijola, S. and Jokinen, E. (1994) 'The body in tourism', *Theory and Society*, 11(3): 125–151.

Veijola, S. and Valtonen, A. (2007) 'The body in tourism industry', in A. Pritchard, N. Morgan, I. Ateljevic and C. Harris (eds) *Tourism and Gender: Embodiment, Sensuality and Experience.* Wallingford: CABI, 13–31.

Veloso, C. (2003) *Tropical Truth: A Story of Music and Revolution in Brazil.* London: Bloomsbury.

Vinod, T. (2006) *From Inside Brazil: Development in the Land of Contrasts.* Stanford, CA: Stanford University Press.

Viveiros de Castro, E. (1992) *From the Enemy's Point of View: Humanity and Diversity in an Amazonian Society*, translated by C.V. Howard. Chicago: University of Chicago Press.

Wacquant, L. (2004) *Body and Soul.* New York: Oxford University Press.

Waddington, D.P. (2010) 'Applying the flashpoints model of public disorder to the 2001 Bradford riot', *British Journal of Criminology*, 50(2): 342–359.

Wade, P. (2001) 'National identity and nationalism: A theoretical view from Latin America', *Racial and Ethnic Studies*, 24(5): 845–865.

Wagner-Pacifici, R. (2011) '"Malarial and diffident": The vision of Clifford Geertz', in J.C. Alexander, P. Smith and M. Norton (eds) *Interpreting Clifford Geertz: Cultural Investigation in the Social Sciences.* New York: Palgrave Macmillan, 93–102.

Walby, S. (1990) *Theorising Patriarchy.* Oxford: Blackwell.

Walby, S. (1994) "Is Citizenship Gendered?", *Sociology*, 28(2): 379–395.

Wallace, S. (2014) 'Brazil vs Germany match report World Cup 2014: Utter humiliation for hosts as Thomas Muller and Toni Kroos help Germany hit seven past Selecao', *The Independent*, 9 July, www.independent.co.uk/sport/football/worldcup/brazil-vs-germany-match-report-world-cup-2014-utter-humiliation-for-brazil-as-germany-hit-seven-9593317.html (accessed 9 July 2014).

Wallerstein, I. (1974) *The Modern World System*, vol. I. New York: Academic Press.

Wallerstein, I. (1980) *The Modern World System*, vol. II. New York: Academic Press.

Walter, T. (2009) 'Dark tourism: Mediating between the dead and the living', in *The Darker Side of Travel: The Theory and Practice of Dark Tourism*. Bristol: Channel View Publications, 39–55.

Warnke, G. (2011) 'Geertzian irony', in J.C. Alexander, P. Smith and M. Norton (eds) *Interpreting Clifford Geertz: Cultural Investigation in the Social Sciences*. New York: Palgrave Macmillan, 45–54.

Watts, J. (2014) 'Disbelief as Germany break hosts Brazil's hearts in 7–1 defeat', *The Guardian*, 9 July, www.theguardian.com/football/2014/jul/09/germany-brazil-7-1-defeat-dejection-disbelief-world-cup (accessed 9 July 2014).

Weber, M. (1978a) *Economy and Society*. Berkeley, CA: University of California Press.

Weber, M. (1978b) *Selections in Translation*. Cambridge: Cambridge University Press.

Weber, M. (1985) *The Protestant Ethic and the Spirit of Capitalism*, translated by T. Parsons. London: Unwin Hyman.

Wenning, M. (2009) 'The return of rage', *Parrhesia*, 8: 89–99.

Wheeller, B. (1996) 'No particular place to go: Travel, tourism and music', in M. Pobinson, N. Evans and P. Callaghan (eds) *Tourism and Cultural Change*. Sunderland: Business Education, 323–340.

Whitson, D. (2004) 'Bringing the world to Canada: "The periphery of the centre"', *Third World Quarterly*, 25(7): 1215–1232.

Wikipedia (2014) '2014 FIFA World Cup', www.en.wikipedia.org/wiki/2014_FIFA_World_Cup (accessed 16 July 2014).

Williams, R. (1977) *Marxism and Literature*. Oxford: Oxford Paperbacks.

Willis, P. (1990) *Common Culture*. Buckingham: Open University Press.

Wiltz, T. (2004) 'Hustling to the beat: Pitbull Perez has worked his way into the hip-hop mix', *The Washington Post*, 25 July, www.washingtonpost.com/wp-dyn/articles/A9488-2004Jul23.html (accessed 27 August 2014).

Witkin, R. (2005) 'A "new" paradigm for the sociology of aesthetics', in D. Inglis and J. Hughson (eds) *The Sociology of Art: Ways of Seeing*. London: Palgrave, 73–86.

Wolff, J. (1984) *The Social Production of Art*. New York: New York University Press.

Wolff, J. (1987) 'The ideology of autonomous art', in R. Leppert and S. McClary (eds) *Music and Society: The Politics of Composition, Performance and Perception*. Minneapolis: University of Minnesota Press, 1–12.

Worden, M. (2008) *China's Great Leap: The Beijing Games and Olympian Human Rights Challenges*. New York: Seven Stories Press.

World Cup Portal (2014a) 'The World Cup of World Cups – Article by President Dilma Rousseff', 8 June, www.copa2014.gov.br/en/noticia/world-cup-world-cups-article-president-dilmarousseff (accessed 11 July 2014).

World Cup Portal (2014b) 'Nature, dance, football and science: find out more details about the World Cup opening ceremony', 9 June, www.copa2014.gov.br/en/noticia/nature-dance-football-and-science-find-out-more-details-about-world-cup-opening-ceremony (accessed 11 July 2014).

World Cup Portal (2014c) 'Brazil has overcome major obstacles towards organising World Cup, says President Dilma Rousseff during official address', 10 June, www.copa2014.gov.br/en/noticia/brazil-has-overcome-major-obstacles-towards-organising-world-cup-says-president-dilma (accessed 11 July 2014).

World Cup Portal (2014d) '"We have worked for the World Cup as hard as we want to win it", says Dilma Rousseff in message read by Minister Aldo Rebelo', 11 June, www.copa2014.gov.br/en/noticia/we-have-worked-world-cup-hard-we-want-win-it-says-dilma-rousseff-message-read-minister-aldo (accessed 11 July 2014).

Wren-Lewis, J. and Clarke, A. (1983) 'The World Cup – A political football', *Theory, Culture and Society*, 1(3): 123–132.

Yahoo News (n.d.) 'World Cup 2014: Goal Control goal-line technology to be used in Brazil', www.news.yahoo.com/video/world-cup-2014-goal-control-051750367.html (accessed 27 July 2014).

Yar, M. (2014a) *Crime, Deviance and Doping: Fallen Sports Stars, Autobiography and the Management of Stigma*. Basingstoke: Palgrave Macmillan.

Yar, M. (2014b) *The Cultural Imaginary of the Internet: Virtual Utopias and Dystopias*. Basingstoke: Palgrave Macmillan.

Young, R. (2001) *Postcolonialism: A Historical Introduction*. Oxford: Blackwell.

Yuval-Davis, N. and Webner, P. (1999) *Women, Citizenship and Difference*. London: Zed.

ZH (2009) 'Governo estadual considera positiva viagem do Gaúcho da Copa com verbas públicas', 19 August, www,zh.clicrbs.com.br/rs/noticia/2009/08/governo-estadual-considera-positiva-viagem-do-gaucho-da-copa-com-verbas-publicas-2624213.html (accessed 23 September 2014).

Ziakas, V. and Costa, C.A. (2011) 'The use of an event portfolio in regional community and tourism development: Creating synergy between sport and cultural events', *Journal of Sport and Tourism*, 16(2): 149–175.

Zukin, S. (2003) 'Home-shopping in the global marketplace', paper presented to 'Les sens du mouvement' colloquium, Cerisyla-Salle, Normandy.

Index

aboriginal internal others, primitivist construction of 72
absent presence 26–7
actor-network theoretical schema 57–8
Adey, P. 2, 27, 45, 46, 56, 58, 66
Adler, J. 40
Adorno, T. and Horkheimer, M. 39
aesthetic cosmopolitan practice and epistemology 126–7
aesthetic styles, principles of social formation of 65
aesthetics of 'sedentary' *indigenismo* 21
affiliative communities 53
African religions, native lifestyles and 24
African spirituality, absence of 72–3
Afro-Brazilian ancestry 122
Ahmad, A. 126
Ahmed, S. 46
Aïnouz, Karim 89
Alabarces, P. 117
Alabarces, P., Tomlinson, A. and Young, C. 63
Albertsen, N. and Diken, B. 33, 53
Albiceleste 92
Albrow, M. 73
Albrow, M., Eade, J., Dürrschmidt, J. and Washbourne, N. 54, 55, 67
alegria (joy), good life and 45–6
Alexander, J.C. 26, 33, 45, 46, 53, 101, 112
Alexander, J.C. and Smith, P. 53, 62
Alexander, J.C., Eyerman, R., Giesen, B., Smelser, N.J. and Sztompka, P. 41
Amazonian *indigenismo* 72–3
Amazonian nature 69, 70
Americas Program of the Center for International Policy 102
Anastasiou, D. and Schäler, R. 61
ancestral honouring 9–10
Anderson, B. 39, 51
André, S. 31
Andrews, D.L. and Clift, B.C. 6
Andrews, D.L. and Mower, R.L. 2, 5
Andrews, D.L. and Ritzer, G. 18
anthropological understandings 14–15, 22, 51–2, 61, 64; global aesthetic, Brazilian anthropology and 111–18
anti anti-relativism 11
Aparicio, F.R. and Chávez-Silverman, S. 72
Appadurai, A. 19, 43, 63, 91, 111
Aravamudan, S. 21, 55, 57, 64, 69, 71, 77
Archer, M. 53, 55, 62, 67
Archetti, E. 80, 81, 117
architectural innovation 7
Ardener, E. 123
Argyrou, V. 19, 25
Aries, P. 81
Aristotle 27, 29
Armstrong, D. 113
Armstrong, G. and Giulianotti, R. 45, 108
Arnason, J.P. 115
Arreguin, Raelene 94
art and politics, historic entanglement of 73–4
artistic contexts, political backgrounds and 66
artistic cosmopolitan ethos 21
artistic technopoetic groups 54
artistic temperament 84–5
Ashcroft, B. 49
Ashworth, G.J. and Voogd, H. 9
Ateljevic, I. 47, 48, 49
Ateljevic, I. and Hall, D. 48
Ateljevic, I., Pritchard, A. and Morgan, N. 42

Atkins, C. 102
Attwood, F. 94
audiovisual templates 7
Augé, M. 14, 62
authoritarianism in 23, 25, 36–7
Avatar (James Cameron film) 104
Avelar, I. 75
Averill, G. 53
axé dancing style 83–4, 96–7
Ayikoru, M. 62

Baerenholdt, J.E. 13
Baerenholdt, J.E. and Graså̊s, B. 12
Bajc, V., Coleman, S. and Eade, J. 46
Bakhtin, M.M. 76, 90
Bales, K. 27
Balkovicius, Jimmy 71, 86, 88, 89, 93
Balotelli 'magic' 119, 120
banditry 74
Banfield, E. 104
Barbosa, L.N. 20
Bærenholdt, O. 121
Bærenholdt, O., Haldrup, M., Larsen, J. and Urry, J. 21
Barrabi, T. 120
Barreira, I.A.F. 24, 26, 103
Barros, Paulo 68
Barth, F. 18
Barthes, R. 97
Bauman, Z. 15, 24, 31, 44, 47, 57, 100, 115, 120
BBC Sport 106
beauty, curse of 27–37
Beck, U. 44, 47, 55, 86, 94, 104
Beck, U., Giddens, A. and Lash, S. 55
Becker, H.S. 110
Beckham, David 87
Beijing 2008 Olympic Games 4
Belo Monte Dam in Amazonia (and controversy) 102–4
Bendix, R. 9
Benjamin, 22, 72, 110
Bennett, A. 64
Berleant, A. 70
Best, D. 32
Bhabha, H.K. 75
Bhatt, C. 51
Bianchi, R. and Stephenson, M. 100
Billig, M. 110
bio-geographies, embodied performance of 70
biographical storytelling 9–10
biomechanics 48–9, 52, 55, 66
'black' and 'white,' flexibility of spectrum between 63–4
Blanton, R. 70
Blatter, Sepp 100, 109
Bloch, M. and Adler, S.A. 81
Bonsam, Nana Kwaku 120
Born, G. and Hesmondhalgh, D. 27
Bottenburg, M.V. 2, 79
Bourdieu, Pierre 13, 32, 34, 67
Bowman, G. 12
Brasilidade (Brazilian-ness) 2, 54, 58, 66, 67, 70, 71, 75, 99, 113, 124, 125; practical action, aesthetics and 24, 30, 32–3, 34
Brazilian artistry, myth of Afro-European play as 33–4
Brazilian character and 'person,' recreation of 57–61
'Brazilian Dilemma,' DaMatta's conception of 12, 14, 28, 31–2, 37, 63, 125
Brazilian mannerisms as performative events 59–60
'Brazilian Truth' 27
Brazuca 90–91
Brecht, Berthold 31
Brennan, T. 46
Britain, colonial sensitivities of 4
broadcasting rights 6
Broderick, Ryan 112
Brooks, P. 46, 78
Brown, Carlinhos 83, 92, 93, 94, 95
Bruner, E. 45, 111
Bruno, G. 46
Budd, M. 69
bureaucratic tropes, rejection of 25–6
Buscema, C. 52, 66
Büscher, M. and Urry, J. 42, 61, 112
Büscher, M., Urry, J. and Witchger, K. 42, 61
Butler, B. 39, 40, 42

Caldas, Luiz 83
Cameron, James 104
Campbell, J. 14, 23, 59, 116
Candomblé 33, 72, 75, 83
Cannadine, D. 4, 31, 32, 118
Cannella, G. and Viruru, R. 81
capital: football and 33; plutocratic pursuit of 15
capoeira and *capoeiragem* 74–8
Carmo, M. 117
Carmon, I. 89, 90

Carnival *(Carnaval)* 8, 19, 25, 69, 75, 77, 82, 83, 85, 86, 87, 91, 92, 97
Carr, N. 61
Cartesian epistemology 74
cartographic representation: colonial jurisdiction and 16–17; 'grobalisation' and 18–19
Castells, M. 6, 56, 104
Castree, N. 70
catachresis 55–6
catastrophe 106
Catholic cosmologies in Brazil 40
Cavanaugh, W. 46
cavaquinhos (street musicians) 89
'I am Going to Celebrate' (samba song) 107–8
ceremonial control 59
ceremonial representations of liquid routes 69
ceremonial spectacles 1–2, 3, 13, 17–18, 67–85, 86–7, 121; complementary articulations 54, 57, 58, 62, 66; defeat, loss of riches and 99, 100, 102, 113–14, 115; practical action, aesthetics and 24–5, 30, 43, 46
ceremony and protest, embodied mobilities of 42
Chagas, P. 107
Chakrabarty, D. 75
Chateau, D. and Lefebvre, M. 79
Chatterjee, P. 22
Chia-Ling, L. 51
Cholbi, Rosemeri 118
Chowdry, G. 50
Christ (the Redeemer) 101
Christianity 24
chrono-spatiality, moving systems of 2
Chvaicer, M.T. 74, 76
Cirkut 94
cities, privileged position of 4
citizenship 38, 119, 122; deficit in 23–4; flexible citizenship 55; global citizenship 99, 100
civil society 3; creation of 27
civilisational hierarchy, harmonisation of 29
Claeys, G. and Sargent, L. 106
Clark, T. 82
'Claudinha' (Claudia Leite) 83
Clifford, J. 3, 74, 97
climate zones 7, 8
co-parenthood *(compadrazgo, compadrío)* 23
Coghlan, A. 32
Cohen, E. 63, 68, 106
Cole, M. 48
Coleman, J. 54, 104
Coleman, S. and Eade, J. 69
collective identity 10–11
collective memory 9; collective memory work 38
Collins, J. 118
colonial epistemologies 20
colonial society, 'social body' of 76
Comaroff, J. and Comaroff, J. 121, 122
commercialization 100
communal narratives of cultural and intellectual property 38
communal solidarity, maintenance of 101
communication, styles of 44–5
communitas 106–7
competing nations, national embodiments of 91
Confederação Brasileira de Futebol (CBF) 36
connections, 'being in the world,' global mobility and 21–2, 24
Connell, J. and Gibson, C. 89, 90
Connell, R.W. 25, 85
Connerton, P. 75, 110
Conselho Nacional de Desportos (CND) 36
Constitution of Brazil (1934) 35
consumption, tourism and protest, interconnections of 10–11
Conte Jr. John J. 94
contemporary consumption, ethics of 56–7
Convention on Heritage Monuments and Sites (1973) 38
Convention on the Safeguarding of the Intangible Cultural Heritage of Humanity (2003) 37–8
Cordey, H. 94
corporate social responsibility (CSR) 3
corruption 14, 20, 36, 81, 102, 114, 125
Coscarelli, J. 108
Cosgrove, D. 18
cosmetic-individualist principles 76
cosmetic phenomenology 125–6
cosmographies 14, 16, 17, 18, 19; riches, Brazilian cosmography of 20, 52, 54, 69, 91, 98–9, 104, 114, 116, 119, 120
cosmologies 14, 33–4, 38, 42–3, 46, 58, 60–61, 69, 75–6, 80–81, 92, 122–3, 124, 127; African cosmologies 30; bureaucracy and 23; Catholic

cosmologies 40; cosmological aesthetics 99; cosmological autonomy 18; cosmological self-narration 119; cosmological statement 100–101; cosmologies before colonisation 58; cultural-cosmological constructions 48, 57; global cosmological core 19; homeland, cosmologies of 32; life rituals and 25; national cosmological centres 114–15; recognition, cosmologies of 16; regional cosmological scenarios 116; secular cosmology 55; tribalist conceptual frameworks and 15; Western cosmological frameworks 64
cosmopolitan desires 17–18
cosmopolitan horizons 9
Couldry, N. 54, 114
counter-colonial games 28
Crang, M. and Franklin, A. 42
Cresswell, T. 37, 52, 62, 65, 66, 71, 72
Crompton, J. 5
Cronin, M. 52, 53
Crouch, C. 38
Crouch, D. 107
Crouch, G.I. and Ritchie, B.J.R. 9
cultural capital, mobility of 12–13
cultural codes, vertical ethics in 100
cultural hierarchies 27
cultural intimacy 14–15, 23–4, 122–7
cultural nationalism 42
culture: ceremonial marketing of 15; cultural project, clash within 27; moving systems of 2; narratives of 9–10; nature of 38
Czeglédy, A.P. 15

daimonáõ (being possessed by demons) 43
DaMatta, R. 10, 12, 17, 19, 20, 23, 28, 37, 40, 41, 51, 54, 58, 61, 65, 70, 76, 77, 81, 82, 85, 87, 95, 100, 101, 106, 108, 109, 112, 115, 123, 124
dances: ceremony and national meaning in 46; dance routines 46, 113–14, 115; music and dance sub-cultures 64; *see also* samba
D'Andrea, A. 62
Dann, G.M.S. 21, 81
Dann, G.M.S. and Liebman Parrinello, G. 75
Dann, G.M.S. and Seaton, A.V. 10, 26, 28
Davis, D.J. 76
Davis, M. 72
Davis, W. 123
Dayan, J. 73
De Certeau, M. 42, 77, 99, 105, 107
De Coubertin, Pierre 100
De Gama, Vasco 35
De Kadt, E.J. 3
De la Fuente, E. 30, 61, 66
De Navarro, Autlán 92
De Pina-Cabral, J. 27
De Sousa Santos, B. 26, 103
De Souza e Silva, A. and Frith, J. 6
De Souza e Silva, A. and Sheller, M. 6, 11
De Souza e Silva, A. and Sutko, D. 6
Dean, J. 51
Debord, G. 57, 87, 123
defeat as 'paradigmatic human event' 98–9
Deichmann, J. 3, 118
Delanty, G. 47, 119
Delanty, G. and O'Mahony, P. 85
Deleuze, G. and Guattari, F. 24
demographics, diversity in 26
Denning, M. 89
DeNora, T. 66, 93, 107, 110
Dentsu 6
Denzin, N. 28
Derrida, J. and Dufourmantelle, A. 101
Derrida, Jacques 10, 24, 29, 41, 53, 72, 101
Descola, P. 69
development, underdevelopment of 4, 9–13
developmental policies, appropriation of 12
Devezas, T. and Modelski, G. 19
Didi 78
Dikötter, F. 28
Dimitrova Savova, N. 75, 79
Disney, Walt 92
domestic elite practices 9
Domingues, J.M. 101, 114
Donald, S.H. and Gammack, J.G. 80
dos Santos, João Francisco 90
Dredge, D. 44
Dredge, D. and Jamal, T. 44, 52
Drewal, Thompson 76
Dudko, J. 97
Duffy, M. 82
Dumont, L. 17
Duncan, J. 21
Durkheim, Emile 23, 24, 49, 50, 73, 108
Dürrschmidt, J. 62, 111

Dussel, E. 48
Duval, D.T. 106

Eade, J. 107, 124
Eade, J. and Sallnow, M.J. 106
Eco, U. 79
economics 2, 4; commodity economy 81; contingent economic and political complications 127; day-to-day economic life, asymmetries of 10; economic activity, nodes of 71; economic benefits 8–9, 121; economic connectivity 56; economic expansion 3; economic process 57; economic prowess, demonstration of 17; economic subjection 34; economic well-being 79; economies of signs and thought 25, 59; economies of touch 76; globalised economy 5, 11; international economic system 44; knowledge economies 30; leisure economics 101; market economics 13, 100–101; 'money economies' 20, 104; neoliberalisation of Brazilian economy 126; night-time economies 121; political and economic intent 62; political-economic disputes 16; political economy of movement 110; political-moral economy 123; regional economic development 12–13; social and economic ascent 108; spatialised economy of flows 77; tourism sector, economics of 7, 11; unequal socio-economic distribution 125
Edensor, T. 62, 76, 109
Eisenstadt, S.N. 18
Eliade, M. 10, 11, 68
Elias, N. 14, 75
Elias, N. and Dunning, E. 79
Elizabeth II 118
Elliot, A. and Urry, J. 104
Ellul, J. 13
emotion: affect and 45; emotional reactions of football folk 2; human emotional, ideational and material mobilities 57–8, 63, 74, 98, 107; moral reason and de-territorialised emotion 85
Engelbrekt, K. 107, 116
Enlightenment cosmopolitanism 55–6
Enloe, C. 30, 56
environmental management and development 44
environmental sustainability 44–5
epistemic communities 54
epistemologcal articulations 14
epistemologcal convictions 4
epistemological boundaries 49
epistemological particularities 18
epistemology, methodology and 61–6, 75–6
Erlmann, V. 53
Errington, J. 62
Estefan, Gloria 96
ethics of contemporary consumption 56–7
ethnic communities as embodied subjects 58
ethnic territories 103
ethno-cultural peripheries, 'anthropologisation' of 17
ethno-racial and class inequalities, amelioration of 5
eudomonia 42–3, 66, 76, 82, 91, 95, 99, 115
European Broadcasting Union 6
European epistemologies 80–81
Evans-Pritchard, E.E. 14, 116, 119
exoticism 12–13, 17, 19, 22, 25, 28–9, 56, 61, 69, 70–71, 74, 75, 87

Fabian, J. 37
Falk, I. and Kilpatrick, S. 79
Fanon, F. 77
Farnell, B. 57, 73
Faubion, J. 102
favela cultures 73
favela evictions 102
favela poverty 73, 121
favela rebelliousness 109
favela scapes 80
Featherstone, M. 76, 126
Feixa, C. and Juris, J.S. 45
felicidade (happiness, prosperity), romanticism in 12, 34, 43–4, 45–6
Fennell, D. 43
Ferguson, N. 114
Fernandes, Clovis Acosta 112, 114
fibre-optic networks 101
FIFA (Féderation Internationale de Football Association) 1, 6–8, 9, 41, 61, 88, 96, 98–9, 100, 106, 109, 112, 114; Fan Fest 7–8; São Paulo, 64th FIFA Congress in 100; World Cup closing ceremony 54, 83, 86–97, 113–14; belonging, conceptions of 86, 92; identity and belonging, negotiation of 86–7; World Cup

opening ceremony 1–2, 3, 17–18, 24–5, 58, 86–7, 99, 100, 102; dance routines in 46, 113–14, 115; indigenous tropicopolitans and 67–85
Filho, Màrio Rodrigues 35, 36
filiative communities 53
filiative-to-affiliative code switching 68
Firth, R. 17
flexible citizenship 55
football: football fandom 3; footballing nationalism 108–9; social realm, football as supplanting 98; sociological perspective on 98; as *téchne* 78
football in Brazil 2; 'black masculine ethos' of 31; as celebration of life 79; democracy in, feelings of 98; football style, immanence of 78, 80; importation and adaptation on 35; mesmeric tendencies of 78; *see alsofutebolarte*
Foster, K. 34, 36
Foucault, Michel 6, 7, 29, 49, 63, 72
Frabetti, F. 29, 58
Frank, André Gunder 4, 13
Franko Aas, K. 56
Freire-Madeiros, B. 72
Freud, Sigmund 25, 26, 39
Freyre, Gilberto 34, 35, 76
Frisby, D. 56
Frith, S. 89
Frye, N. 106
Fryer, P. 109
Fuleco (FIFA mascot) 96–7
FUNAI (National Indian Foundation) 120
Furler, Sia 84
futebolarte: artisticity of 110–11; deep play in 32–7; European Apollonian and Brazilian Dionysian spirits, binary stylistic oppositions between 34–5, 36, 37; professionalism of, Filho's unequivocal defence of 35–6; public self-presentations of 80; samba and, connection between 95

Gallant, T.W. 113
Gallope, M. 40
Gardiner, M. 53
Garland, J. and Rowe, M. 75
Garrincha 78
Garrison, J.W. 24
Gaúcho da Copa 111–12, 115
Gauntlett, D. 53
Geertz, Clifford 1, 4, 11, 12, 18, 25, 26, 33, 38, 43, 45, 61, 81, 87, 98, 101, 118, 122
Gellner, Ernest 15, 38, 51, 61, 64, 78, 108
gender: cultural allegory, 'gender order' as 122–7; 'gender order' 25, 30–31, 126; interactions with 25; unity of class and race/ethnicity in Brazil 31–2
gentrification, ambivalence towards 90
geomorphological idiosyncrasy 69
Germann Molz, J. 54
Gerth, H.H. and Mills, W. 29, 99
Gibson, O. 109
Giddens, Anthony 10, 44, 54, 62, 69, 94, 122
Giesen, B. 4, 11, 33
Gikandi, S. 49
Gill, K. 87, 116
Giulianotti, R. 3, 110
Giulianotti, R. and Robertson, R. 2, 79, 85, 98, 100, 104
global civilisational hierarchy, offshoring and 4–9
global public spheres 61
global sports tourism, mega-events and 62, 67, 73
global structural movements 125
globalisation: converging pressures of 100–101; 'deep plot' of 4, 5, 6, 7, 9, 13, 22, 97; global civilisational hierarchy, offshoring and 4–9; mobility, football and, interrelationships between *2*
globes and maps, European production of 16
GloboEsporte 105
Gluckman, M. 14
Goal Control system 7
Gobineau, Arthur de 31
godparenthood *(padrinazgo)* 23
Goffman, Erving 11, 90
Goldmann, L. 51
Goldschmidt, E.M.R. 19
Goodman, N. 51
Gordon, C. and Helal, R. 35, 36, 37
Gottwald, Lukasz 84
Gourgouris, S. 87, 107
governance 22–3
governmentalization 100
Graburn, N.N.H. 10, 34
Graham, S. and Marvin, S. 77
Graml, R. 126
Greenblatt, S. 57, 127

Greene, R. 21
Greenfeld, L. 114, 115
Gregg, M. 84
Gregory, R. 122
Grodona, Julio 113
Grugulis, I. and Stoyanova, D. 53
Gudeman, S. 13
guilty landscapes 9–10
Gunn, G.C. 16, 30
Gutman, H.G. 23
Gwerner, S. 77

Haas, P. 54
Habermas, J. 38, 68, 111
habitus, Bourdieu's concept of 19–20, 32–3, 48, 64, 77, 116, 117, 126; Brazil, Western cultural perceptions of *habitus* of 19–20; feminine *habitus* 25; national *habitus* 79
Hajer, M.A. 63
Hall, C.M., Timothy, D.J. and Duval, D.T. 106
Hall, S. 125
Hand, M. and Sandywell, B. 53
Handleman, D. 48
Hannam, K. 52, 65
Hannam, K., Sheller, M. and Urry, J. 2, 52
Hannerz, U. 3, 54
Haraway, D. 82
Hardt, M. and Negri, A. 53
harmony, scriptures of 3
Harrison, D. 18, 39
Hart, K. 15
Harvey, D. 57
Havelange, João 98
Haybron, D.M. 43, 46
HBS (Host Broadcast Services) 6
Heidegger, Martin 21, 37; epistemology of 50
Henning, C. 21, 51
Hennion, A. and Latour, B. 95
Herder, Johann Gottfried 51
heritage 6, 7, 33, 40–41, 53, 54, 67, 75, 80, 86, 105, 125; art and 31; authoritarian heritage 6; colonial heritage 114; cultural heritage 37–8; 'dissonant heritage' 10; football as, projection of 78; football heritage 109–10; *gaúcho* heritage 114; gender-bending heritage 89–90; global notions of time-space and 39; Hellenic heritage 29; heritage conservation 105; heritage kinaesthetics 41–2, 45, 46, 52, 87; heritage politics 126; heritage sites 79; legacy and, interplay between 85, 104; memory and 42; migration heritage 122; mobility of 127; national heritage 44; Nyorican heritage 82; Puerto Rican heritage 82–3; racial heritage 34; synaesthetic heritage 122; trans-modernity and 48
Herzfeld, M. 11, 12, 14, 15, 17, 23, 25, 27, 29, 41, 48, 56, 61, 64, 65, 78, 80, 87, 91, 102, 103, 105, 109, 110, 116, 118, 122, 123, 126
Hesmondhalgh, D. 89
Hesmondhalgh, D. and Baker, S. 84
Hetherington, K. 77
Hewison, R. 39
hierarchical integration 55
Highmore, B. 77
Hinchberger, B. 83, 84
Hochschild, A. 126
Hollinshead, K. 62
Holt, R.J. 79
Holton, R. 18, 71, 100
Honneth, A. 84
hooks, b. 76
Hooton, C. 106
Horne, J. 41
Horne, J. and Manzenreiter, W. 3
hospitality 5, 15, 21, 22, 67, 101, 105, 112
hospitality norms 15
host-guest reciprocities, tourist flows and 40–41
Houlihan, B. and Green, M. 100
Howells, R. 91
Hugh-Jones, S. 18
Hughson, J. 32
human diversity, gendering and racialising of 127
human experience, linguistic apparatus of 39
humiliation 106
Humphrey, J. 80
Humphreys, B.R. and Prokopowizc, S. 3
Hunt, P. and Frankenberg, R. 81
Husserl, Edmund 39, 49–50
hybridisation as 'travelling culture' 74

iconicity: imagological semblance and 122; national modernisation and 64–5
identity: bifurcated narrative of 27–8; ceremonial expressions of 45–6; identity narratives 85; national

identity 27–8; synaesthetic narratives of 68
image, symmetry and architectonics of 27
industrial modernity 12, 21, 101
industrialization 17
industriousness, discourse of 101
infrastructural investment 101–2
infrastructural variables 8
Inglesias, Julio 96
Inglis, D. 16, 19, 30, 63, 69
Inglis, D. and Hughson, J. 32, 33, 58, 61, 81, 110
Inglis, D. and Robertson, R. 17
Ingold, T. 16, 28, 33, 54, 71, 107
Instituto Raoni 104
integrated mobility systems 55
interactional levels 6
intergenerational reciprocity 38–9
internal colonisation 56
International Broadcast Centre 6
International Media Content 6
International Union for Conservation of Nature (IUCN) Red List 97
interpersonal communication 25–6
Irizarry, D. 93
Ivy, M. 17

Jackson, W. 114
Jaguaribe, B. and Hetherington, K. 57, 72, 73
Jamal, T. and Hill, S. 72
Jamal, T., Everett, J. and Dann, G.M.S. 70
James, P. 102
Jameson, Frederic 126
Jaraquii, Doctor 119, 120
Jardine, L. 16
Jardine, L. and Brotton, J. 16
Jay, M. 122
Jean, W. and Pires, A. 95, 96
Jean, Wyclef 92, 93
Jennings, W. 6
Jensen, B.B. 6, 46, 77, 109
Jensen, O.B. and Richardson, T.D. 56
John, Elton 83
Johnson, M. 126
Jomphe-Lepine, Mathieu 94

Kaka 87
Kaplan, A. 52
Kaufmann, V. 5, 94
Kaufmann, V. and Mantulet, B. 55
Kaufmann, V., Bergman, M. and Joye, D. 5, 94
Keft-Kennedy, V. 94
Khayat, Nadir 84
Kiddy, E.W. 19
Kinney, J. 114
kinship, family and 14, 20, 54, 59, 78, 126; horizontal kinship, principles of 76; kinship rules 23, 37–8, 44; kinship values, maintenance of 36; networks of kinship 42–3, 59, 124; structures of kinship 60
Kirshenblatt-Gimblett, B. 45, 68
knowledge pathways 24
Kohn, H. 114
Korstanje, M. 3, 10, 16, 59, 117, 118
Korstanje, M. and George, B. 9, 10, 105
Korstanje, M.E., Tzanelli, R., and Clayton, A. 106
Kulick, D. 126

'La, La, La' (Shakira's performance of) 93–5, 96
Lalalila, Lisa 94
Lance! 105
Landry, D. and MacLean, G. 76
landscapes of guilt 10
Langlois, G. 53, 95
language, subtle intimacy between technology and 53
Lash, S. and Urry, J. 3, 25, 37, 55, 59, 97, 110
Lasseter, John 83
Law, J. 16, 28, 38
Lee, C. and Taylor, T. 9
legacy impacts 3
Leite, Claudia 68, 82, 83, 84
Leite Inácio Pedreira, Claudia Cristina 83
Leite Lopes, J.S. 35, 100
Lemke, T. 66
Lennon, J. and Foley, M. 10
Leoussi, A. 51
Lessnoff, M. 15
Lever, J. 37
Lévi-Strauss, C. 43, 60, 73, 80
Levine, R. 34, 36, 118
Lewis, L.J. 75
Lichrou, M., O'Malley, L. and Patterson, M. 9
Lichterman, P. 11
linda Lapiana's téchne of bodily movement 90–91

linda maravilhosa (marvellously beautiful) 28–9, 75, 124, 127
linguistic variations 3–4
'living museum,' discourses on 19–20
local epistemologies 17
logocentrism 53
Loizos, P. 12
Loizos, P. and Papataxiarchis, E. 34
London 2012 handover ceremony to Rio 24–5
Lopez, Jennifer 68, 82, 83, 84
Lorente, J.I. and Alonso, P.A. 44
Lorimer, J. 70
Lourenço, R. 91
Low, Joachim 92
Lowenthal, D. 28
Löwy, M. and Sayre, R. 50
Luhmann, N. 111
Luhrmann, T. 119
Luiz, David 115
Luke, Dr. 94
Lula da Silva, Luiz Inácio 5, 100, 104
Lury, C. 81, 94
Luske, H. 114
Lusotropical perception 31, 34
Lyall, J. and Bell, C. 54
Lynch, J. 15, 114
Lynch, P., Germann Molz, J., McIntosch, A., Lugosi, P. and Lashley, C. 21

McCabe, S. and Stokoe, E.H. 9
MacCannell, D. 21, 64
McClintock, A. 30, 50
McCreery, J. 33
Machado-Borges, T. 31
McKee, R. 59, 65
McLuhan, M. 51
McNeill, W.H. 46
McNulty, P. 106
Maffesoli, M. 51, 64
Maguire, J.A. 2, 79
Malandro (male rogue) 40, 41, 77, 80, 84, 91, 96, 108, 123, 127
Malbon, B. 64, 82, 95
Maleuvre, D. 41
Mannheim, K. 10, 25
Manning, S. and Sydow, J. 53
mappamundi (world map) 16, 18
maps and globes, European production of 16
Maradona, Diego 117
Marchetti, M.C. 4, 49
Marcuse, Herbert 10, 26, 73, 81, 89
Márquez, García 94
Martí, José 84
Martin, Max 94
Martin, Ricky 83
Marx, Karl 29
Mason, T. 34
Massey, D. 73, 125
Massumi, B. 46
material production 9
material value, transformation into social value 17–18
Mauss, M. 38, 59
Mbembe, A. 28
Meethan, K. 9, 62
mega-events 2–3, 5, 7, 9, 18–19, 21, 22, 73, 75–6, 78, 99, 115; aesthetics of 32; consumption of 43; creative capital and 59; global advertising in context of 55; global communities of viewers for 69; global cosmography of riches and 104; global sports tourism and 62, 67, 73; ideoscapal classification of 63; inter-cultural communication and 51–2; intercultural dialogue and athletic events 56; management of 3; 'Mega-Events and Human Rights Violations in Brazil' (*A Publica,* 2012) 102; transnational artistic communities in 52–3; *see also* World Cup (2014)
Melucci, A. 49
memory: historical discourse and 3; *lieux de mémoire* (sites of memory) 41; loss of 29–30; *mnemonists* and preservation of 39; present and 22–3
Merleau-Ponty, M. 33, 38, 58
Merry, Eagle 104
Merton, R.K. 33
Merton, R.K. and Barber, E. 115, 119
Messi, Lionel 91, 120
mestre de sala, exhibitionist function of 91–2
metaphysical background 28
Meyer, M. and Molineaux-Hodgson, S. 9
micro-cultures and macro-sociology of 15
micro-globalisation of global cities 62
Middleton, R. 90
military dictatorship in 22, 36
Miller, R.D. 33, 110
Mitchell, T. 82
mnemotechnical technologies 53

mobilities: actualisation of 37; aeromobilities 5; Brazilian history, multiple mobilities of 47–8; of capitalist environments 39; Caribbean mobilities 49; ceremony and protest, embodied mobilities of 42; cinematic mobilities 90; collective mobilities 66; cosmographic mobilities 18; cultural capital, mobility of 12–13; cultural mobilities 20, 101; current Brazilian mobilities, cosmetics of 4; embodied mobilities 26, 42; enablement of 19; Euro-African experiential mobilities 76; European linkages of spatiality and 56; financial mobilities 56, 111; First World mobilities 71; football mobility, magic of 119–21; global mobilities 67; globalisation theory and theory of mobilities 49; 'governmobilities' 13, 121, 123; human emotional, ideational and material mobilities 57–8, 63, 74, 98, 107; informational mobilities 57; interconnected mobilities 56; Latin American mobilities 90; migrant mobilities 24; mobilities paradigm 2, 45, 61, 125; multiple mobilities of local custom and sustainable tourism, tensions between 44; mythological mobilities 114; new mobilities agenda, development of 42; new mobilities paradigm 3, 45; place, confliction mobilities of 104; post-modern mobilities 77; real and symbolic mobilities, football and 117; social (im)mobilities 52; sociology of mobility 110–11; status symbol of mobility 8; streets and public sites, multiple mobilities of 106; tourism mobilities 9, 28, 62, 75; trans-modernity, multiple mobilities of 125; transnational mobilities 52
modernity, imported ideas of 3, 12
Molotch, H. 30
monadic nomads 106
Monte, Marisa 94
Monteiro, M. 8
Moraes, R. 102
moral spoliation of Brazilian personhood 40
Morales, E. 82, 84
Moran, D. 29
Moreiras, A. 22
Morgan, N. and Pritchard, A. 77
Morinis, E.A. 107
Morley, G. 6
Morphy, H. 71
motivational specificity 45
Moura, Alfredo 83
mourning at failure in World Cup 1–2, 3
Mowforth, M. and Munt, I. 72
multiculturalism and hybridity, language of 70–71
Muñiz, A.M. and O'Guinn, T.C. 80
Murcia, Daniel 84
Murray, B. 36, 118
'museumification,' processes of 16
music: dance sub-cultures and 64; mobilisation in action of 107–8; musicology 66
Mussolini, Benito 35
myths and fantasies 9

Nachträglichkeit 64, 120
Nagib, L. 26, 80
national 'archaeology' of Brazilian football 35–6
national desires, cosmologies of 18
national identity 27–8
national unity and racial democracy in 35
nationalisation, trans-modernisation and 30
Nationalmannschaft 92
necropolitics 28
Nederveen Pieterse, J. 27, 31, 47, 55, 56, 57, 61, 66, 71, 74, 102
Nederveen Pieterse, J. and Parekh, B. 56, 71, 74
Negus, K. 89
Nelson, M.R. and Deshpande, S. 80
'neo-tribal' theory 64
Nervo Codato, A. 22
network sociatities, kinship bonds and 23
Neymar 105, 112
Niersbach, Wolfgang 113
Nietzsche, F.W. 26
Nora, P. 41, 110
North-South gap 56
nostalgia, football spaces and 79
Nussbaum, M. 45

Obrador, P. 58
O'Callaghan, M. 51
offshoring: global civilisational hierarchy and 4–9; riches, offshoring and cosmology of 13–20

Olodum band 68, 82, 83
Ong, A. 55
Ong, W. 27, 71
ontological considerations 14, 24, 32–3, 37, 40, 62, 122–3
O'Reilly, K. 50
Organización de Televisión Iberoamericana 6
orientalisation-as-racialisation, British perceptions of 32
ornapentation, art and 30–31
Ousby, I. 115
Owen, J.G. 3

Panja, T. 102
Parker, R. 126
Parmentier, R. 17
Parry, J. and Bloch, M. 20
Parry, R. 29
Passarinho, N. and Matoso, F. 7
Patke, R.S. 10
patrimony 104–5
Pattullo, P. 56
Peck, J. 56
Peirce, C. 45
Pelé 78, 80, 87, 92, 117, 118
Pellauer, D. 60
Pellegrino, G. 2, 52, 116
perceptions, varied ideas of 'visibility' and 33
Pérez, Armando Christian 10, 84
performance epistemology 45
performative museology 68
Perkins, H.C. and Thorns, D.C. 65
Perry, Katy 83
Petchesky, B. 112, 113
Peterson, R.A. and Bennett, A. 64
Phillips, T. 5
Picard, D. 12
Pillay, U. and Bass, O. 3
Pique, Gerard 93
Pires, Alexandre 92, 96
Pitbull (rapper) 68, 82, 84
place: demobilisation of places and human groups 71; marketing and promotion of 5; narratives of 9–10; notion of 62
Plano de Modernização do Futebol Brasileiro 36–7
Plato 29, 43, 53, 64
play principle, Marcuse's discussion of 81
Poe, Edgar Allan 58
Polanyi, K. 13
political secrecy 11–12, 125
politics: art and, disconnections between 2525; ceremonial spectacle and 1–2, 3; football and politics of leisure, separation of 3; participation in 99; political-cultural flexibility 55–6; political transition 22, 26; theatre of 1–2
polyphony 11, 103
Popovitch, A. 22, 26
popular performance, audiovisual 'snapshots' of 11
Portugal, colonial sensitivities of 4
post-colonial federation 5
post-colonial polities 56–7
postpositivist epistemologies, borrowings from 62
power: collusion of power alliances 32–3; geometries of 27; hierarchical power systems 17–18; moving systems of 2; power resources 126
Pratt, M.L. 72
Presenza, A. 2
protest, tourism and consumption, interconnections of 10–11
Protestant ethic 40
proto-national craft, hermeneutics of *téchne* as 29
public funds, complaints about displacement of 3
public sites, social practices and 106–7
Putnam, R. 53, 104

racial and class hierarchies in 27, 31–2, 42–3
racial criss-crossings 74
Ramchandani, G.M. and Coleman, R.J. 5
Rancière, J. 26, 32, 42, 45, 48, 103, 111, 120
Rebelo, Aldo 7
recognition: cosmologies of 16; politics of 100; pragmatic obstacles of 22
Reddy, W.M. 13
redemption, ideas of 12, 101
regional economic development 12–13
Reijnders, S. 10
relatiional machines 52–3
remembrance rituals 43
representation, western machineries of 126
representational machine 57
resentment: articulations of 105–11; nationalism and 109–10

rhythmic terms, idea of thinking and interpreting in 65–6
riches, cosmography of 20, 52, 54, 69, 91, 114, 116, 119, 120; global cosmography of riches and 104; officialisation of 98–9
riches, offshoring and cosmology of 13–20
Ricoeur, P. 59
Rihanna 83
Rio Declaration on Environment and Development (2012) 44
Rio Olympics (2016) 99, 114–15
Ritchie, J.R. 3
rites of passage 11
ritual looting, performativity of 39–40
rituals of life, ceremonial borrowing from 25
Ritzer, G. 18
Ritzer, G. and Liska, A. 81
Roberts, W. 114
Robertson, R. 47, 49, 54, 74, 125
Robins, K. 58
Roche, M. 63
Rodowick, D. 63
Rodrigues, J. and Devezas, T.C. 19
Rodrigues, J.N. 19
Román-Velázquez, P. 83
Ronaldo 120
Roper, M. 120
Rosenau, J. 57
Rousseff, Dilma 1, 78, 79, 99, 100, 101, 102, 104, 105, 108, 109, 112, 113, 124
Rowe, D. 107
RS International Broadcasting & Sports Management 6
Rumford, C. 56
Russell-Wood, A.J.R. 4, 17, 19, 23, 24, 31, 34, 63, 124
ruthlessness of bureaucracy in (and survival of people within) 20

Sabella, Alejandro 92
Sacks, O. 42
sacralised rites of passage 11
Sahlins, M. 13, 14, 16, 19, 67, 69, 117
Said, E. 11, 32, 50
Sallnow, M.J. 106, 107
Salvatore, R. 57, 127
samba 19, 25, 29, 64, 68, 72–3, 75, 83–4, 87, 88, 89–90, 94–5, 96–7, 107–8, 118; hybrid samba-reggae 83, 97; Lapa samba dancers 91; Portela samba dancers 92; samba *favelarte* 109; sambadrome 91
Samuels, D.W., Maintjes, L., Ochoa, A. M. and Porcello, T. 116
Sánchez Taylor, J. 87
Sandywell, B. 50, 122
Sangalo, Ivete 92, 96, 97
Santana, Carlos 92, 93, 96
Santana, G. 7, 96
Santos, Antonio Carlos 9, 94
São Paulo, 64th FIFA Congress in 100
Sarajane 83
Sarlo, Beatriz 26
Sassen, S. 6, 9, 51
saudade (nostalgia), romanticism in 12, 34
Savelli, A. 10
Savova, Dimitrova 41, 109
Sayer, A. 13
scene theory 64
Schafer, R.M. 116
Scheler, M. 26, 55
Scherper-Hughes, Nancy 65
Schiller, F. 33
Schmitt, C. 22
Schütz, A. 24, 51, 55, 107
Schütz, A. and Luckman, T. 28
Schweinsteiger, Bastian 91
Scolari, Luiz Felipe 106, 109
secrecy, cultures of 20
self-characterisations 127
Selwyn, T. 9
Sen, A. 45
Sengalo, Ivete 83
sensory holism, promotion of 65
sentimental education 45
Shakira 54, 90, 92, 93, 94, 95, 97, 113
Shapiro, M. 96
Shaw, L. 76
Sheller, M. 2, 11, 13, 21, 27, 34, 49, 56, 61, 71, 73, 76, 90, 100, 119, 122, 125
Sheller, M. and Urry, J. 2, 63, 65, 74
Shields, R. 80
Shilling, C. 55
Shils, E. 18, 103
Shohat, E. 38
Shurmer-Smith, P. and Hannam, K. 62
Silk, M. 4
Silva, M.L. 126
Simmel, G. 14, 15
Simmel, G. and Wolff, K.H. 56, 68
Simoni, V. 40
Singh, Jay 94
Singh, S. 76

Singleton, John 84
'situational value' of Brazilian culture in global cosmographies of riches 19
Skalník, P. 15
Skeggs, B. 31
Skidmore, T.E. 119
Skouteri-Didaskalou, N. 60, 112
Slater, J. 9
Slatta, R.W. 113
slavery: legacies of 10; pernicious effects of 24
Sloterdijk, P. 39, 69
Smith, A.D. 24, 25, 38, 39, 62, 65, 113
social actors, 'natural character' and 78
social *chromophobia* 79
social crisis, cultural indeterminacy and 125–6
social drama 98–9
social formation of aesthetic styles, principles of 65
social network theory 53
social ordering, intra-group rivalry and 14
social realm, football as supplanting 98
social science investigations, need for realist framework for 61
social simulations, potential for collective embarrassment in 11–12
social variables 18
sociality, civilisation and mechanisms of reciprocal concealment within 14–15
sociality, embedment of economy in 20
sociality, simulcra of 11–12
socio-cultural identities 9–10
socio-cultures of Brazil: hierarchies of 42–3; interpretative capacities of 11
sociology of absences 26
Sophist rhetorical skill 29
South America: cultural politics of 1–2; post-industrialisation in 4
space: kinaesthetic appropriation of 107; Merleau-Ponty's perceptions of 38; spatial-as-moral differentiations between home and street in 41
Spinoza, Baruch 27
Spivak, G. 11, 48, 55, 76, 120
sport sponsorship, business motives for 5
sportisation in Brazil 2–3
Squires, N. 120
Stasch, R. 69
Steele, Michael 112
Steinberg, P. 69
Stephens, T. 63
stereotyping, stereotypes and 14, 48, 51, 64, 67, 78, 109, 114, 116–17, 121, 122, 127; practical action, aesthetics and 22, 30–31, 32, 33–4
Stevenson, N. 119
Stiegler, B. 29, 53, 58, 82
Stocking, G. 11
Strain, E. 50
strategic planning for mega-events 5–6
Straw, W. 64
stylistics 21–7
subaltern agency, practices of 73–4
surveillance: cultural-moral economy and politics of 13–14; technologies of 7
sustainable development 24, 44
Swiss Laboratory for Doping Analysis 7
symmetrical inclusion 55
synaesthesia 42, 80; audiovisual technologies and 42
synaesthetic performativity 65–6
synchronisation: heritage, nationalism and 39–40; movement and 37
Szerszynski, B. and Urry, J. 18, 77

Tanner, J. 61
Tarde, G. 37, 78
Tate, S. 28, 119
Taylor, T. 60
technical being, definition of 29
technology: development of 39; status symbol of 8; *téchne* and 29–30; 'technique' and 'technicity' in 40, 82
technopoiesis 53–4, 55; ceremonial technopoiesis 55, 58
televisual innovation 7
Telles, E.E. 119
O Tempo 105–6
temporal lending, de Certeau's notion of 99
tempos mixtos (mixed epochs) 72, 77
thanatourism 10, 26, 28, 43, 69, 110, 123, 127
Thomas, N. 72
Thompson, D. 76
Thompson, J. 68
Thompson, P. 26
Thompson, R.F. 75
Thornton, T.M. 24
Thrift, N. 42, 45, 70, 126
Till, K.E. 107
time 39; Aristotelian division between *chrónos* and *kairós* 39; historical time

40; temporality, hermeneutic fixities of 39
Todd, K.E. 69
Tolia-Kelly, D.P. 42
Tomaselli, K.G. 12
Tomlinson, A. 2, 4, 73, 116
Tomlinson, A. and Young, C. 2
Tonkonoff, S. 37, 50
Tönnies, F. 97
topophilic rites 9–10
tourism: consumption and protest, interconnections of 10–11; economics of 7, 11; global sports tourism, mega-events and 62, 67, 73; host-guest reciprocities, tourist flows and 40–41; thanatourism 10, 26, 28, 43, 69, 110, 123, 127; tourism mobilities 9, 28, 62, 75; tourist sector, renewed significance of 7; World Cup (2014), tourist synaesthetes and 73
trans-modernity of Brazil 9–10; articulation of 47–52
transaction secrecy, neutralisation of 104
translation, tnterpretation and 60
transmogrification 79, 126
transnational capitalist pathways 6
transnational economy 5
transnational mobilities 52
transnational political movements 90
transnational spaces, norms and values of culture in 3
Tribe, J. 34, 43, 62
Tristes Tropiques (Lévi-Strauss, C.) 60–61, 73
Troelsen, Thomas 84
Trondman, M. 26, 45
tropicopolitan skies, clouds in 98–9
tropological traces, exhibition of 63
Tuan, Y.F. 9
Tudor, A. 63, 78, 118
Turner, B.S. 46
Turner, Tina 83
Turner, V. 87, 98
Turner, V. and Turner, E. 10, 11
Turner Bushnell, A. and Greene, J.P. 17, 19
Turton, A. 17
Tyers, A. 68, 70
Tzanelli, R. 4, 6, 9, 10, 11, 13, 16, 17, 18, 19, 126, 127; ceremonial scripts 68, 69, 73, 75, 76, 77, 79, 80, 82, 90, 92, 94; complementary articulations 49, 50, 52, 56, 57, 59, 61, 62, 63, 64, 65; defeat and loss 101, 103, 104, 110, 113, 116, 118; practical action, aesthetics and 22, 26, 31, 34, 37, 38, 39, 41, 42
Tzanelli, R. and Yar, M. 9

United Nations Educational, Scientific and Cultural Organization (UNESCO) 37–8
Universal Declaration of Human Rights (1948) 104
urban governance, strategic shift in 5
urban industrialisation, focus on 4
urbanisation 17
urbanism: splintering of 89–90
Urquìa, N. 80
Urry, J. and Larsen, J. 10, 42, 58, 65, 69, 115
Urry, John 2, 4, 5, 6, 14, 15, 18, 20, 44, 45, 52, 56, 58, 62, 65, 80, 102, 104, 111, 122
Uteng, T.P. and Cresswell, T. 55, 74, 77

Valente, F.L. 5
van der Westhuizen, J. 105
Van Gennep, A. and Douglas, M. 11
Van Gennep, Arnold 10
Vans, Los Van 94
Varela, F.J. 107
Vargas, Getúlio 23, 30, 35, 75, 77, 85, 89
Veblen, T. 35, 37
Veijola, S. 65
Veijola, S. and Jokinen, E. 65
Veijola, S. and Valtonen, A. 65
Veloso, C. 66, 88
venting 85
vertical ethics 100
victory and union, emotive elements of hosting World Cup 1
Vinod, T. 5
virtuality and virtualisation 71
visitor influx 57
Vovô, Antônio Carlos 83

Wacquant, Loïc 77
Waddington, D.P. 105
Wade, P. 115
Wagner-Pacifici, R. 99, 115
Walby, S. 119
Wallace, S. 106
Walter, Henry 84
Warnke, G. 12, 60
Watts, J. 106, 108
web searches 61–2

Weber, M. 29, 40
welfare underspending, accusations of 101–2
well-being in, ritual nature of 37–46
Wenning, M. 88
Wheeller, B. 73
Whitson, D. 3
Williams, R. 107
Willis, P. 110
Wiltz, T. 84
Witkin, R. 65
Wolff, J. 25
Worden, M. 4
'world cultures' 26
World Cup (2014) 1–2, 4, 5–9, 10, 11, 12–13, 14–15. 17–18; anthem 94–5; articulation of football 78; artwork of 77; artworld of, social world and 93; 'Brazilian character,' representations in ceremonial domains of 58–9; celebratory connections and 100–101; ceremonial art of 32; ceremonial technopoesis of 55; ceremonies of, presentation of 61–2, 63–4, 67–97, 116, 119; complementary articulations 48, 49, 50, 51, 52–7, 58–9, 60, 61–2, 63, 64, 65; consumerist ethos of 90–91; 'deferred action' of 63–4; delivery of, domestic disorder and 88; destiny and destination in 81; 'doubleness' in form of, recognition of 99, 115; embodied performances during 60; global communities of viewers 69; global modalities of visitors to 67; imports of foreign artistic and technical talent for 55–6; international market of 52; Internet and 61–2; legacies of 54, 101, 104–5; loss to Germany in, feelings as result of 98–9, 99–106, 109, 111–12, 113, 114–15; management of, debate about 122–3; neoliberal context of 66; paraplegic people and 81–2; political-moral economy 123–4; post-colonial desire, positives and negatives for 119, 120, 123, 125, 127; practical action, aesthetics and 24–5, 28, 31, 35–6, 40, 41–2, 44–5, 46; production of 57; promotion of values through 102; public 'style' of, emergence of 123; technological innovations 18–19; theme song 82–3; tourist synaesthetes and 73; transnational biomechanics of 49; transnational epistemic communities 126; transpersonal character of ceremonial of 59; World Cup cities 8; *see also* FIFA (Fédération Internationale de Football Association); mega-events
Wren-Lewis, J. and Clarke, A. 78

Yar, M. 7, 106
Young, R. 49
Yuval-Davis, N. and Webner, P. 119

Ziakas, V. and Costa, C.A. 5
Zukin, S. 104
Zweckrationalität ('instrumental/ goal rationality') 29

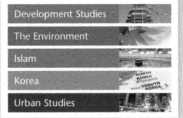